"Roland A. Carlstedt's impressive book creatively integrates research from multiple subdisciplines in psychology to arrive at a highly original and coherent theory of peak sport performance. Readers will benefit from Dr. Carlstedt's experience as a professional athlete and coach as well as his solid academic credentials and training in the areas of cognitive neuroscience, psychophysiology, behavioral medicine, and personality. His eclectic background brings new insights, methods, and findings to the field of sport psychology that will have an impact for years to come." — Roger Drake, Ph.D., Keck School of Medicine of the University of Southern California and Western State College of Colorado; cognitive neuroscientist

"Why do some professional athletes tend to 'deliver' in critical situations, while others are less dependable? Dr. Carlstedt's Mind–Body Model of Sport Performance focuses on this well-known and vexing performance difference between comparably talented professional athletes. He traces these differences to certain basic personality characteristics and their interplay. Depending on their strength and configuration, these general personal propensities may play either a facilitative or counterproductive (but potentially modifiable) role. Carlstedt's model is obviously of great relevance to sport psychologists. Because of its plausibility as well as its amenability to empirical scrutiny and continuing development, it also merits the attention of a wider readership. It has the potential for evolving into a general model for understanding consistent excellence in response to challenge." — Auke Tellegen, University of Minnesota; professor of psychology emeritus, personality psychologist, and behavioral geneticist

"Dr. Carlstedt brings a thoroughly innovative perspective to the field of sport psychology in this new book. His model of peak performance ambitiously and successfully integrates a wealth of physiological, psychological, and cognitive neuroscience data to forcefully make the case that athletic performance cannot only be studied in a controlled fashion, but can be improved systematically. Although scholarly in its methodologies, this book is highly readable, and will be of interest to a wide range of academics, coaches, athletes, and mental health and sport psychology professionals." — Sanjay Mathew, M.D., Columbia University College of Physicians and Surgeons, Department of Psychiatry; psychiatrist, neuroscientist, and former ranked tennis player

"This book provides a timely model for an evidence-based approach to assessment and retraining peak performance in athletes, particularly during critical moments of competition. Importantly, it points the way forward to bridge the gap between anecdote and testable brain science in this field." — Dr. Evian Gordon, founding director, Brain Dynamics Centre, Westmead Hospital, Sydney, Australia; CEO, The Brain Resource Company, developer of the world's first standardized International Database on the Human Brain; lead author and editor of Integrative Neuroscience

CRITICAL MOMENTS
DURING COMPETITION

A Mind–Body Model of
Sport Performance
When It Counts the Most

ROLAND A. CARLSTEDT

PSYCHOLOGY PRESS
NEW YORK • HOVE

Published in 2004 by
Psychology Press
270 Madison Avenue
New York, NY 10016
www.psypress.com

Published in Great Britain by
Psychology Press
27 Church Road
Hove, East Sussex
BN3 2FA
www.psypress.co.uk

Psychology Press is an imprint of the Taylor & Francis Group.
Printed in the United States of America on acid-free paper.

10 9 8 7 6 5 4 3 2 1

Library of Congress Cataloging-in-Publication Data

Carlstedt, Roland A.
    Critical moments during competition : a mind–body model of sport
performance when it counts the most / by Roland A. Carlstedt.
        p. cm.
    Includes bibliographical references and index.
    ISBN 1-84169-092-9 (hardback : alk. paper) — ISBN 1-84169-094-5
(pbk. : alk. paper)
    1. Sports—Psychological aspects. 2. Achievement motivation. I. Title.

    GV706.4.C364 2004
    796.01—dc22

                                                    2004009542

Contents

About the Author   vii

Foreword by Stanley Krippner, Ph.D.   ix

Acknowledgments   xiii

Section I. Theoretical Foundations

1   Introduction   3

2   The Theory of Critical Moments   7

3   The High-Risk Model of Threat Perception   19

4   Primary Higher Order Predictor Variables:
    Effects on Athletes and Performance   37

5   Neuropsychophysiological Concomitants
    of Primary Higher Order Factors   63

Section II. Emerging Evidence

6   Emerging Evidence: Introduction   71

7   Statistical and Empirical
    Implications   83

8   Psychophysiological Concomitants of
    Primary Higher Order Factors and the
    Athlete's Profile: Ambulatory
    Psychophysiology   115

Section III. Applied Sport Psychology: Assessing and Mastering
Critical Moments

9 Assessing Critical Moments   141

10 Toward a Global Physiological Marker of
Psychological Performance and Critical
Moments during Competition: Assessing
Zone or Flow States   169

11 Assessing and Predicting Psychological
Performance during Critical Moments on
the Basis of Psychophysiological
Stress Testing: A Case Study   179

12 Mastering Critical Moments:
The Carlstedt Protocol   189

13 Assessment and Intervention Using the
Carlstedt Protocol: A Case Study   199

14 Active-Alert Hypnosis: Description
and Case Study   207

15 A Design for Implementing and Testing the
Efficacy of a Biofeedback Protocol Created
for a Former Wimbledon Champion   217

16 An Internet-Based Athlete Assessment,
Analysis, Intervention, and Database Center:
Your Personal Sport Psychology Consultant   223

References   233

Index   255

About the Author

Licensed clinical psychologist and sport psychologist Dr. Roland A. Carlstedt is chairman of the American Board of Sport Psychology, a member of the Harold Abel School of Psychology of Capella University faculty, and director of Sport Psychology Research: Brain and Heart Processes with BioCom Technologies. He is also a research consultant to the Brain Resource Company's International Athlete Brain Database Project and Brainquiry, a developer of wireless EEG, HRV and biofeedback monitoring devices. A graduate of Saybrook Graduate School in San Francisco, Dr. Carlstedt was the recipient of the American Psychological Association Division 47 2001 Dissertation Award and was nominated for the Society for Neuroscience's 2001 Donald Lindsley Dissertation Award. He is a former professional tennis player and coach who followed the international professional tennis tours for more than ten years as a sport psychologist, researcher, and analyst for media worldwide. Dr. Carlstedt is clinical director of Integrative Psychological Services of New York City, an organization specializing in behavioral medicine, health and sport psychology, applied psychophysiology and biofeedback, behavioral nutrition, and general psychotherapy.

Foreword

I believe that the theory, hypotheses, models and applications presented in this book can be considered seminal, a watershed in the annals of research in sport psychology. I would not be surprised if Dr. Carlstedt's book became a classic in its field. It advances an original model of peak performance, the Theory of Critical Moments, in which knowledge from numerous subfields of psychology were elegantly synthesized to describe, explain, and predict psychological functioning in athletes.

Carlstedt's model implicates constellations of personality traits and behaviors as mediators of key elements of peak performance including physiological reactivity, attention, and certain cognitive processes. The model also identifies several neurophysiological concomitants of these measures and demonstrates how they interact to influence and sustain focus or allow disruptive negative thoughts to interfere with levels of attention required for peak performance. The model provides a long overdue lucid and highly plausible explanation for the dynamics of focus and effects of intrusive cognitions on sport performance.

It should be pointed out that it is one thing to formulate a theory, but it is another thing to find support for it. Carlstedt has done this in one of the largest studies of athletes to date. His model explained up to 44% of the variance in objective outcome measures, well exceeding previous attempts to account for performance on the basis of personality and behavioral measures. It should not surprise the reader to know that this study, in one form or another, has already won several honors including the American Psychological Association's Division of Exercise and Sport Psychology 2001 Dissertation Award.

This achievement did not occur by chance; it attests to Carlstedt's careful, scholarly analysis and selection of potent predictor variables, something that is demanded if regression models are to be revealing. The potency of his model in predicting performance outcome can be directly attributed to its multidimensional, integrative, and longitudinal approach as well as the selection of sensitive personality measures and outcome variables derived from microanalyses of objective performance statistics. Carlstedt persuasively demonstrates that isolating more sensitive predictor and criterion measures is crucial in order to explain more of the variance in the performance equation that can be attributed to psychological factors.

Readers of this book will be introduced to a novel and brilliant approach to the delineation and analysis of outcome measures that capture the essence of peak mental performance in sport, something previous research has failed to do. In an attempt to explain more of the variance in the performance equation and thus demonstrate empirically that peak performance may indeed be primarily mental, Carlstedt created customized sport psychological statistics to accurately quantify the impact of psychological factors on sport performance. His system for analyzing mental toughness during critical moments of competition is a milestone in psychological measurement in sport psychology.

Carlstedt's model also undertook the first attempt to quantify so-called zone or flow experiences on the basis of objective and longitudinally derived psychophysiological and performance outcome measures. These measures were obtained during actual official athletic competition, lending an unprecedented level of ecological validity to his model and data. For example, provocative findings on heart rate variability in athletes suggest that specific parameters of heart rate variability may mirror zone or flow states.

The methodologies and approaches Carlstedt has developed help bring Gallwey's popular Inner Game principles to life, in addition to advancing and illuminating aspects of other well-known theories of peak performance that have remained relatively nebulous. Carlstedt provides a scientific basis and empirical evidence that accounts for numerous anecdotal notions and platitudes in these theories and sport in general including "just do it," "ideal performance state," "mental toughness," sport is "90% mental," among others. Carlstedt has traveled where no researcher has ventured in quantifying these slogan statements, contentions, and myths, bringing new insights and data as to their meaning.

The emerging evidence presented in this book leads one to revisit the role of personality in the performance equation. Data showing that athletes exhibiting specific constellations of isolated Primary Higher Order personality traits will be more or less susceptible to experiencing negative intrusive cognitions and lapses in attention during critical moments of competition finally illustrate empirically the potency of select personality traits in mediating performance. This breakthrough helps rehabilitate personality in the context of performance and validates the intuitive notion that personality affects performance in a crucially important manner, something the field has failed to demonstrate despite hundreds of studies on the effects of personality on performance.

This book is also a valuable source for applied practitioners in sport psychology. It provides access to sophisticated methods, technologies, and advanced approaches to the evaluation and training of athletes. It presents an applied field-tested athlete assessment, intervention, and efficacy testing protocol that integrates research findings and methods from the previously mentioned subfields of psychology. The protocol was designed to assess the above Primary Higher Order (PHO) personality and behavioral measures. In addition to their direct link with the neuropsychophysiological processes associated with performance, research has demonstrated that constellations or combinations of these PHO factors play an important role in the ability to benefit from a particular intervention and should be routinely assessed. Thus, rather than recommend and teach mental imagery, hypnosis, or other procedures to athletes indiscriminately and en masse, Carlstedt advances an individualized approach to assessment on the basis of a constellation of PHO factors, a strategy that has been empirically validated in the clinical arena. His protocol also emphasizes in-the-field ambulatory monitoring of athletes using heart rate variability and heart rate deceleration analyses to evaluate psychological states and performance during competition. This protocol also serves to validate concurrently on-the-field and in-office findings on the basis of more ecologically valid indices of psychological performance, something that is rarely engaged in by sport psychology practitioners.

Athletes' on-the-field self-use of interventions is also discussed, including manipulation of cortical states and heart rate variability to achieve better levels of attention and self-regulation. Carlstedt's model also includes advanced assessment of cortical functioning using brain-scan methods, efficacy or outcome testing, critical moments analysis, and database management, all of which are sophisticated approaches to athlete evaluation that will soon be de rigueur.

The analysis, assessment, and intervention system that Carlstedt propagates and uses are on the cutting edge, yet accessible to every practitioner. The reader may doubt this assertion, considering the specialized training and equipment one would need to effectively apply these sophisticated methods. The answer lies in an Internet-based analysis center that both practitioners and athletes can access. Carlstedt and his trained associates are available to process and analyze test responses, neuropsychological tests, and heart rate variability data sent to the center via the Internet. Coaches, athletes, and sport psychology practitioners will have access to high technology methods and feedback from one of the preeminent applied practitioners and researchers in the field of sport psychology, along with a guided empirically validated protocol. Coaches, athletes, and practitioners also will have access to the Brain Resource Company and the Carlstedt-BioCom Technologies brain and heart rate variability databases for comparative and analytic purposes.

It should be no surprise that there are still major gaps in the literature of peak performance, just as one will find flaws even in the game of a star athlete. These fissures in knowledge result, in part, from the discrepancy between researchers and practitioners. How many neuroscientists were once professional athletes or coaches? How many athletes or coaches have a doctorate in psychology or a research background in the disciplines on which this book touches? How many applied sport psychology practitioners are coaches who have carried out neuropsychophysiological research projects? Very few indeed! Consequently, it took a multifaceted person like Carlstedt, who possesses solid academic credentials, experience as a professional athlete, coach and sport psychologist to put it all together and convincingly address and fill some of these gaps.

In conclusion, I consider this book to be a monumental work. Carlstedt's model, research, and data will generate much scrutiny, further study, and discussion for decades to come. It will substantially impact the field of sport psychology.

Stanley Krippner, Ph.D.
Saybrook Graduate School and Research Center

Acknowledgments

This book marks the culmination of a 30-year career as a professional athlete, coach, analyst, student, teacher, researcher, clinician and sport psychology practitioner. I do not believe that I could have generated the models, research and protocols that I present in this book without having experienced these roles and professions. These endeavors all resulted in knowledge that was integral to the advancement of my research and, indirectly, this book. My experience as an athlete who all too often wavered psychologically during critical moments of competition led me to wonder why, a question I could not remotely begin to answer until I became a graduate student and was exposed to Ian Wickramasekera's High Risk Model of Threat Perception, Stanley Krippner's ideas on consciousness, Tomarken and Davidson's neuro-physiological studies of repressive coping, as well as the investigations of EEG in athletes by Dan Landers and colleagues. Each of these and numerous other researchers provided pieces to the puzzle, pieces that in isolation provided illuminating, descriptive insight into emotions, personality, cognition and brain function both in clinical and athlete samples. I started to put these pieces together at Saybrook Graduate School in San Francisco in a quest to answer questions about the nature of peak performance including flow, zone, choking, critical moments, unconscious processes, intrusive thoughts and mental training.

At Saybrook I had the enormous good fortune to work with some incredible mentors including the aforementioned Drs. Wickramasekera and Krippner. My exposure to these and other great thinkers, researchers and practitioners at the school including Drs. Arne Collen (methodology), Eugene Taylor (history and theory of mind–body psychology, and expert on William James, at Harvard) and Jay Wagener (clinical and health psychology) helped me synthesize seemingly disparate research and start to advance an integrative psychology of peak performance.

By the time I was advanced to candidacy and reached the dissertation stage I had almost completed the puzzle. I formulated a theory and model that now needed to be tested. This task was made much easier thanks to my dissertation committee chairman, Dr. Auke Tellegen, the renowned personality psychologist, behavioral geneticist and methodologist at the University of Minnesota, who helped me articulate and conceptualize a study that would involve constructs from numerous subfields of psychology in an attempt to address questions I had about the nature of psychological performance in athletes. Special thanks also go to Dr. Roger Drake, a cognitive neuroscientist at Western State College of Colorado, who suggested that I incorporate a measure of relative cortical activation into my research. Following his advice I was able to make an actual discovery on brain functioning in athletes that has led to a publication in *Brain and Cognition*. This measure also went a long way toward reconciling the personality and behavioral constructs I chose to study with cortical functioning in athletes making my findings even more provocative.

All of these persons were in some way responsible for my research and this book. Without them I still would be wondering why I was not the most mentally tough athlete. Now, at least I have a plausible explanation and supportive data accounting for why some athletes excel under pressure while others fail.

A major goal of this book is to inspire practitioners, athletes and especially professional sport teams to participate in an Internet-based athlete brain and psychophysiological assessment and database project (see Chapter 16). This project was made possible because of the knowledge, talent and resources provided by Dr. Evian Gordon of the Brain Resource Company, Dr. Vadim Pougatchev and Mark Ferris of BioCom Technologies and Drs. Martijn Arns and Kamran Fallahpour of Brainquiry.

These professionals are committed to helping advance sport psychology to the next level.

A book is much more than an expression of a vision, theory or presentation of data. It involves much work, research and time. In order to complete this work an author needs support. I received plenty of support from numerous people including my fiancé Dr. Denise Fortino, a clinical psychologist with intimate knowledge of my model who is also a published author (three books to her credit) and professional editor. Her love and sacrifice helped make this book possible as we put our social life on hold for over a year.

I would also like to thank Dr. Robert Reiner of Behavioral Associates of New York City for giving me the opportunity to advance my career as a clinician. Under Dr. Reiner I learned to apply hypnosis, biofeedback, neurotherapy and cognitive-behavioral psychotherapy to a wide variety of patients, an experience that brought to life the constructs and methods I was theorizing about by allowing me to observe the effects of specific interventions on attention and physiological reactivity, key components of performance in real life as well as sport. Coincidently, I also met Dr. Robert Udewitz at Behavioral Associates, a psychologist and former elite long distance runner who gave me invaluable perspectives into the nature of absorption or focus in runners. His dissertation on the psychology of running is an important work that should be read by sport psychology practitioners.

I would also like to thank Jennifer Amran, who worked with me as a research assistant during her internship with the American Board of Sport Psychology, and Paul Dukes of Psychology Press, who supported this book project from its inception.

Last but not least, I would like to thank Dr. Roger Morgan, a clinician and researcher of ADD and its relationship to sport, for his support of the American Board of Sport Psychology.

Theoretical Foundations

Introduction

This book presents original research findings and empirically based perspectives, methods and applications in sport psychology emanating from an award-winning dissertation. It was conceptualized during the course of my graduate studies in response to thoughts and questions about the nature of sport performance that had I generated and encountered over the course of a 30-year career as a professional tennis player, coach, instructor, doctoral student, researcher, clinician and sport psychologist.

Data derived from one of the largest psychological studies ever conducted on athletes will be used to advance an original model of peak performance centering on a clearly emerging Athlete's Profile in which interactions among relative cerebral hemispheric activation, hypnotic ability/absorption, neuroticism and repressive coping are shown to play a critical role in the performance equation.

Repressive coping, a left-brain hemisphere localized behavioral tendency that has been shown to inhibit the interhemispheric transfer of negative affect from the right to the left half of the brain, plays a prominent role in this model. It functions to suppress or neutralize negative intrusive thoughts athletes often experience during competition. First-time data on this previously unexplored measure in athletes offers important insight into why certain athletes are more or less vulnerable to experiencing negative cognitions, especially during critical moments of competition. Repressive coping appears to be the critical psychological factor in the performance equation. It functions as the great moderator in facilitating zone or peak performance states.

Original data on absorption in athletes will also be presented. This bilaterally based behavioral measure and a correlate of hypnotic ability has been shown to interact with right-brain localized neuroticism and left-brain localized repressive coping to mediate attention, focus and cognition. Findings on absorption also suggest that imagery, or visualization, one of the most frequently used psychological interventions in sport, may not be ideally suited for most athletes without following a controlled neuropsychological assessment and imagery protocol.

Neuroticism, a trait associated with a tendency to fixate on catastrophizing thoughts and negative emotions that are often generated during periods of increased stress, reemerges in this model as the great disruptor of performance. Data extending on findings on this right-brain localized trait will illustrate how this measure can impact performance, especially when interacting with repressive coping, absorption and relative cerebral activation.

The emerging Athlete's Profile reveals that the most successful elite and highly skilled athletes are overwhelmingly relative left-brain hemisphere predominant and high in left-brain hemisphere-based repressive coping as well as low in bilaterally based absorption and right-brain hemisphere-based neuroticism. Such a profile will be shown to be linearly related to better performance on various longitudinal measures of success in a variety of sports. Athletes exhibiting a trait and state constellation of high absorption, high neuroticism and low repressive coping appear to be most susceptible to experiencing negative intrusive cognitions and lapses in attention during critical moments of competition. By contrast, athletes who are low or high in absorption, low in neuroticism and high in repressive coping appear to have greater protection from the potentially debilitating effects of high neuroticism on performance, especially during critical moments.

This book will also demonstrate that factors comprising the Athlete's Profile of cortical organization and functioning account for a significant portion of the statistical variance in the performance equation that can be attributed to psychological factors. In other words, components of the Athlete's Profile (factors that have been mostly overlooked in sport psychology) appear to be the most important psychological factors mediating performance. These so-called primary higher order (PHO) factors are fundamentally linked to key elements of athletic performance, including activation or physiological reactivity (intensity), attention and other cognitive processes.

The *Theory of Critical Moments* is also introduced in this book. It proposes that psychological factors and mental toughness are most crucial during specifically delineated periods of competition and explains when and why psychological measures influence performance. The theory maintains that to understand the impact of an athlete's psyche on performance it must be studied at the micro-level and in the context of potent and meaningful longitudinal dependent measures of performance, or critical moments, such as when a relief pitcher in baseball must get a batter out to win the game or when a gymnast must "hit" the dismount to achieve a top score.

A neuropsychophysiological assessment model for measuring the Athlete's Profile, zone and flow states and an individualized mental training protocol to enhance performance is presented in the Applied Psychology section of the book. The assessment model is interactive in nature. It encourages athletes and coaches to monitor, assess and analyze relative cerebral activation, emotions, attention and select outcome measures throughout the course of training and competition since knowledge of brain processes, psychophysiology, behavior and performance is crucial to the empirically based intervention protocol that accompanies this model. This new integrative performance enhancement system, the *Carlstedt Protocol*, centers on the application of intervention methods — both on and off the playing field — that can manipulate cortical states and physiology to facilitate positive emotions, attention and mind–body synchrony, or coherence.

For athletes who do not possess the ideal profile, the Carlstedt Protocol has been shown to induce positive change by providing them with self-help methods designed to manipulate brain, behavior and personality processes to enhance psychological performance. This protocol can also be used by athletes possessing an ideal profile who need to activate beneficial baseline or trait-like neuropsychological attributes that may remain dormant in certain situations, to achieve peak performance.

This protocol and assessment model are integrative and, importantly, interactive. The interactive nature of this comprehensive model allows for self- and coach monitoring of the Athlete's Profile as well as direct access to an Internet-based analysis center where data on athletes can be stored and analyzed longitudinally by qualified sport psychologists, including this book's author (see Chapter 16).

Outcome and efficacy studies are also central to this book's assessment model and intervention protocol. Consequently, athletes and coaches who utilize the methods presented in this book will know where they stand in terms of their psychological performance and mental training progress.

The book is divided into three major sections. Section I contains a review of the above constructs and elucidates the Theory of Critical Moments and the Athlete's Profile. Section II presents original research and data supporting the Theory of Critical Moments and the emerging Athlete's Profile. Section III is the applied portion of the book. This section presents assessment and intervention strategies for practitioners and includes the Carlstedt Protocol.

2

The Theory of Critical Moments

The Theory of Critical Moments (TCM) proposes that psychological factors are most crucial to performance during specifically delineated periods of competition and explains how select personality, behavioral, and psychophysiological measures influence sport performance when it counts the most. The theory maintains that performance must be studied at the microlevel to empirically assess and understand the effect of an athlete's psyche on competition and to explain more of the statistical variance in the performance equation that can be attributed to psychological factors. This means that performance must be viewed in the context of interactions between meaningful personality, behavioral, and psychophysiological variables and longitudinal microperformance outcome measures derived from analyses of critical moments of competition.

Although numerous psychological measures have been investigated in athletes, previous research has mostly been unifactorial in nature and has not attempted to link interactions or constellations of psychological factors with either important longitudinal microoperationalizations of performance or revealing objective performance outcome measures. To date, little is known about relationships between psychological factors and performance during critical moments of competition, with most research being unable to explain more than 10% of the variance in the performance equation that can be attributed to psychological factors, despite anecdotal notions that sport performance is mostly "mental" (Lufen 1995; review of PsychInfo entries from 1960–2003).

The inability of previous attempts to explain more of the variance in the performance equation can be attributed to the failure to isolate and investigate the specific psychological measures that are most essential to performance during critical moments of competition, when stress levels can be the greatest and attention, psychophysiology, and motor skills are most vulnerable to disruptive psychological influences.

Methodological Approaches and Tenets

The TCM emanates from a new theoretical and methodological approach to the study of relationships between psychological factors and performance (predictor-independent and dependent-criterion variables). This theory is based on the following methodological tenets: (1) the identification of Primary Higher Order psychological predictor or independent variables, (2) the study of psychological factors at the microlevel, and (3) the study of psychological factors longitudinally in the context of multiple objective outcome variables.

Identification of Specific Primary Higher Order Psychological Predictor or Independent Variables

Identification of specific primary higher order (PHO) psychological predictor or independent variables that have been shown to mediate performance and the effects of secondary lower order (SLO) psychological variables on performance and neuropsychophysiological concomitants of these PHO variables is one aspect of the TCM approach. PHO psychological variables should not to be confused with factor analytic order concepts. Instead, in the context of the TCM, they refer to the effects that specific psychological measures or constructs have in mediating or influencing behavior, psychophysiology, and ultimately, performance as reflected in variance explained.

Psychological measures that mediate the effects of other psychological measures and subsequent physiological responding and performance are considered PHO variables, whereas psychological measures that are affected by PHO variables are considered SLO variables. For example, although psychological measures such as anxiety and attention are considered central to theories of performance such as the Zone of Optimum Functioning (ZOF) (Hanin 1980) or the Catastrophe Theory (Hardy and Fazey 1987), the fact that these and numerous other psychological measures have not been able to explain much of the variance in the performance equation raises questions about their potency in affecting performance to any significant extent in the empirical sense. Although intuitively one might expect anxiety, attention, and various other psychological predictor variables to affect performance, it is difficult to determine precisely the empirical and practical, or "real," effects most psychological predictor variables exert on performance independently without analyzing the effect PHO variables have on SLO variables (e.g., anxiety and attention). This is especially the case in the context of critical moments of competition.

The inability of most psychological predictor variables to explain much of the variance in criterion or outcome measures forces one simultaneously to reconsider the real effect many psychological variables (SLO) have on performance and to consider the role other overlooked psychological factors (PHO) play in moderating, facilitating, or suppressing the effects of SLO psychological measures on performance.

The TCM contends that most psychological measures that have been investigated in relationship to performance are SLO measures that are subordinate to select PHO psychological processes in terms of their ability to affect performance. Thus, although it is widely accepted that measures such as attention and anxiety have an effect on performance, they can be disrupted or facilitated, especially during critical moments, by identified PHO measures.

According to the TCM, the low levels of variance explained on the basis of any given psychological measure can be attributed in part to the suppressive effects that PHO measures exert on psychological processes that can mediate or affect performance. Should the effects of PHO processes emerge during competition, an occurrence that is most likely to happen during critical moments, the potential positive or negative influences of SLO variables on performance may be attenuated or potentiated as a function of the level or strength of singular, constellation, or interaction of PHO measures. This dynamic will reveal itself in statistical analyses that are presented and discussed later, demonstrating that PHO psychological processes can act as suppressors or enhancers of the effects of SLO psychological processes on psychophysiology and performance.

In the case of anxiety or attention, the fact that even such obvious performance-relevant measures have been unable to explain much of the variance in the performance equation strongly indicates that other psychological factors are at work as well, or that criterion or dependent outcome measures are too global in nature to reflect psychological influences on performance.

Other constructs that have been the focus of research in sport performance, such as intensity, self-confidence, and determination, also lose their primacy (PHO status) in the performance equation when viewed in the context of variance explained, as research has shown that these and virtually every psychological variable investigated in relationship to objective outcome measures of performance have been minimally revealing at best.

Emerging evidence, including the findings presented in this book, demonstrates that sport performance research must be multifactorial or multidimensional in nature if revealing relationships between psychological factors and performance are to be discovered. Moreover, research must be cognizant of the potential effect that PHO psychological variables can have on virtually any SLO predictor and independent variable and psychophysiological response, especially when SLO predictor or independent variables explain little of the variance in the performance equation.

The TCM maintains that one can no longer view weak SLO predictors or independent variables as being central to sport performance unless such measures can be shown empirically to play a primary role in mediating and predicting performance as reflected in objective outcome measures. Potent PHO psychological variables that have been shown to affect constructs considered central to performance, including attention, anxiety, and cognition, must be integrated into future research to demonstrate the "real" effects psychological factors have on performance, which appear to have been underestimated in most research to date.

The TCM hypothesizes that PHO predictor variables are intrinsically involved in mediating mind–body processes associated with peak performance, zone, or flow states. PHO measures are hypothesized to be centrally located in specific regions of the brain and are most likely to manifest themselves in response to the perception of threat during critical moments of competition. The activation of PHO measures can independently or interactively facilitate or hinder performance by directly affecting physiological reactivity and motor ability. The TCM maintains that during critical moments of competition, an athlete's profile of cortical and psychophysiological functioning underlies successful psychological performance and is marked by specific shifts in brain hemispheric activation, heart rate variability, and muscle tension.

Study of Psychological Factors and Performance at the Microlevel

Another aspect of the TCM approach is the study of psychological factors and performance at the microlevel by isolating and investigating criterion or dependent outcome measures in the context of critical moments of competition.

Analyzing performance outcome measures (criterion/dependent variables) at the microlevel during critical moments of competition is crucial for determining the effect that psychological factors have on performance.

Past and recent attempts to associate psychological factors with performance have not sufficiently reduced performance outcome measures to the microlevel or differentiated critical moments from routine phases of competition. As a result, potential relationships between and among psychological and performance outcome measures may have gone unnoticed. In previous research, most outcome performance measures usually have been global in nature, contrived indices of performance, or comparisons of one psychological construct with another. Global measures have included basic performance statistics of specific sports, including won–loss percentage and shooting percentage. Contrived measures have included distance to hole when putting or other practice tasks and post hoc self-rating of performance. Comparisons of the effect of one psychological construct on another, using self-report, have included comparing the effects of precompetitive anxiety with those of postcompetition anxiety. The comparison of psychological measures derived from self-reports with others of this kind is an especially weak predictor of "real" and objective performance outcomes, as rarely have attempts been made to link associations between psychological constructs with objective microlevel performance outcome measures. For example, even though the level of self-reported precompetition anxiety may be associated with the recall of competitive anxiety, such a relationship has not been linked to objective performance outcome measures, rendering such an expected finding trivial and wanting in terms of what such an association means to actual performance.

Unfortunately, researchers have come to rely on contrived macro or global criterion and independent outcome measures as being the "best" reflectors of psychological influences on performance, even though virtually no psychological factor or combination of factors has been able to explain much of the variance in the performance equation.

Considering that the practice of applied sport psychology is predicated on being able to identify psychological influences on performance, the failure to make significant headway in isolating the effects of psychological measures on objective measures of performance is troubling and calls for a new approach to the analysis of predictor–criterion variable relationships. An analysis of microlevel moments of competition, similar to what is presented in this book, will better illuminate the roles that select psychological and behavioral factors have in differentially facilitating or hindering performance, especially during critical competitive situations, which are most likely to elicit psychophysiological stress, resultant hyperreactivity, and motor dysfunction.

Study of Psychological Factors Longitudinally and in the Context of Multiple Objective Performance Outcome Measures

The final aspect of the TCM approach that we will explore here is the study of psychological factors longitudinally and in the context of multiple objective performance outcome measures.

A longitudinal and multiple-criterion measure approach to the study of performance is designed to increase the probability of discovering meaningful relationships between psychological predictor and performance outcome (criterion) variables. Such relationships are not likely to be revealed in one-shot attempts to study the effects that personality and behavioral and psychophysiological measures may have on performance. The discovery of new relationships between and among psychological factors and performance is contingent on the selection of potent psychological predictor variables and reliable performance outcome measures. Reliable predictor and criterion measures are crucial to the predictive capability of any regression model. In studying the influence that psychological factors have on performance, one must be especially certain that a performance outcome measure is capable of reflecting the influences of psychological processes on a sport-specific task. This is more likely to occur at the microlevel of performance, with longitudinal analyses of critical moments over the course of many competitions expected to be the most revealing objective microperformance outcome measures.

Potent and Meaningful Objective Microoperationalizations of Performance Outcome

Psychological predictor measures including those the TCM identifies as most important to performance ultimately become more potent and revealing in the context of objective longitudinal microoperationalizations of performance outcomes, or critical moments of competition. This becomes apparent when one attempts to associate psychological predictor measures with macro or global measures of performance. PHO psychological measures are most likely to demonstrate their effects on performance when outcome measures are sensitive to psychological influences. This will most likely occur at the microlevel or critical moment when attention, physiological reactivity, and thought processes are most vulnerable to disruption by psychological processes.

What Are Critical Moments?

Critical moments can be defined as instances or situations that are pivotal to the successful outcome of a competition. These moments test athletes' ability to perform their best when it counts the most, demanding extraordinary control over mind–body processes. In a tennis match on a grass court, a critical moment might be a break point opportunity against a good server. In golf, a critical moment might involve having to reach the green with an approach shot to have a chance at making a birdie. In basketball, a critical moment might be a free throw with the game on the line. In football, a less obvious critical moment might occur when a lineman has to block a rusher to prevent pressure from being put on the quarterback at a key juncture of a game.

The TCM hypothesizes that athletes will be more or less vulnerable to psychological influences on performance during critical moments as a function of their constellation of PHO factors. The "mentally toughest" athletes are predicted to be those who are capable of suppressing negative psychological influences when it counts the most, a capability that is facilitated by an "ideal" Athlete's Profile of TCM isolated PHO factors. These factors will be elaborated later.

Critical moments can be operationalized quantitatively, whereby microlevel outcome measures are identified and analyzed using a hierarchical system that rates the psychological effect that critical moments are expected to exert on an athlete's psyche, or to what extent certain psychological factors either facilitate or hinder performance. The Carlstedt Critical Moment Psychological Performance Index (CCMPP-I) uses expert raters consisting of coaches and highly skilled athletes to establish criteria for defining what constitutes a critical moment in particular sports. This involves selecting specific instances or events during competition that are defined and numerically weighted in terms of their criticality. The CCMPP-I assigns a criticality weight (1–5, with 5 being the most critical) to each point, event, or play during competition. Applied to tennis, the first point of a match might have a criticality weight of 1, whereas a 15–30 point against a powerful and efficient server could receive a criticality weight of 5. An example of a hierarchy of microlevel events or critical moments in baseball might include the following instances (numbered in order of psychological significance from 1 [less critical or global macroevent] to 5 [extremely critical microevent]): 1) batting average for season, 2) batting average with player in scoring position, 3) batting average with player in scoring position with game outcome on the line, 4) batting average with player in scoring position with two outs and game outcome on the line, 5) batting average with player in scoring position with outcome of playoff game on the line.

The criticality level of a competitive moment is not necessarily constant. It can fluctuate dynamically as a function of constantly changing conditions. For example, using the above illustration from tennis, the criticality level of 5 attributed to a break-point opportunity against a good server on a grass court might receive only a level 3 rating during the same situation on a slower surface such as clay. The dynamics of the CCMPP-I will be elaborated on in Chapter 9.

The magnitude of a microlevel critical moment can be used as a predictor variable or as a criterion (outcome) variable depending on the design of a study. For example, one could investigate the effect of encountering a magnitude 5 critical moment on heart rate variability or determine whether athletes with more pronounced slow-macro brain potentials (see Andreassi 1995) perform better when encountering magnitude 5 critical moments (e.g., higher batting or shooting average during such moments). Essentially, an analysis of performance outcome at the microlevel is designed to distinguish more routine moments (macromoments) of competition that elicit "normal" or baseline levels of psychophysiological responses from microlevel critical moments that demand utmost psychophysiological control or self-regulation. Making such distinctions is necessary to better discern which athletes are the "toughest" mentally. For example, a baseball batter with a .350 batting average, a golfer who reaches the green in regulation 85% of the time, or even a tennis player ranked in the top 10 in the world may not necessarily be mentally tougher than an athlete having weaker macrolevel statistical indices, because macro performance statistics reflect global performance proficiency without adequately considering performance during microlevel critical moments—the most stressful times of competition. Without analyzing performance at the microlevel, it is difficult to determine whether the 60% field goal shooter in basketball is really mentally tougher than the 40% shooter or is merely a great technician. An analysis of performance during critical moments might reveal a drop in shooting to 35% in the 60% shooter, whereas the 40% shooter might hit at a rate of 80% during critical moments.

The study of psychological factors and performance at the microlevel involves isolating and investigating competitive moments that are critical to performance outcome or winning. Analyzing microlevel critical moments helps to partition out physical, technical, and motor-ability (talent) variables that drive global performance during routine phases of competition, while isolating and analyzing the effect select psychological factors have on physical, technical, and motor talent variables during critical moments. An analysis of microlevel critical moments is expected to better illuminate the role of select psychological factors in differentially facilitating or hindering performance during competitive situations that are most likely to elicit psychophysiological stress and hyperreactivity.

The failure to analyze performance outcome measures at the microlevel, or critical moment, can lead to faulty evaluations of an athlete's psychological proficiency by overemphasizing and not controlling for confounding physical and technical factors—processes that are most likely to be disrupted by psychological factors during critical moments.

It should be noted that one of the reasons for the failure to investigate psychological factors and performance relationships in the context of microlevel outcome measures is that conventional statistics used in most sports are often simply too global in nature. With the exception of baseball, few sports analyze performance statistically at the microlevel, although even from this sport statistics do not extend to the most microlevels of criticality. As a consequence, unfortunately, researchers attempting to associate psychological factors with performance have had to rely on available outcome statistics that may not be sensitive enough to reflect the influence of most psychological measures on performance. This problem was acknowledged by Piedmont, Hill, and Blanco (1999), who, in the only identified study that attempted to associate personality factors with objective performance outcome measures, had trouble finding meaningful statistics kept on soccer players that reflect psychological performance.

Future attempts to study relationships between psychological factors and performance outcome statistics will require that researchers keep "psychological" or microlevel critical moment statistics to gain better insight into psychological performance and to increase the probability of explaining more of the statistical variance in the performance equation that can be attributed to psychological factors.

Central to how critical moments are dealt with or mastered by an athlete are conscious or unconscious thought processes that differentially facilitate or hinder performance. The TCM has isolated select PHO personality and behavioral measures that have been shown to mediate thought processes and subsequent physiological and motor responses in clinical situations. Interactions or constellations of PHO measures are hypothesized to affect performance by differentially influencing both the cognitions and the psychophysiology of athletes during critical moments of competition. These PHO factors cause susceptible athletes to fixate on or ignore intrusive and negative thoughts that occur during a game's most critical moments. Fixation on negative intrusive thoughts leading to undesirable shifts in relative brain hemispheric activation, physiological functioning, and motor responses are more likely to occur in athletes exhibiting negative constellations of PHO factors. By contrast, athletes who possess the most positive constellations of these measures are more likely to focus on preparatory thoughts dealing with carrying out effective motor and tactical responses while suppressing negative intrusive thoughts. This latter response tendency facilitates shifts in cerebral laterality associated with optimal cardiovascular and motor responding and performance.

Potential negative manifestations of certain constellations of PHO factors are expected to remain relatively dormant until critical moments during competition, when the conscious or unconscious perception of threat leads to the disruption of attention and motor skills. Conversely, ideal constellations of PHO factors that also lie relatively dormant during routine phases of competition will insulate athletes from conscious or unconscious perception of threat during critical moments to facilitate peak physical, tactical, and technical performance. Athletes who have the most negative PHO constellations are more likely to perceive threat during critical moments and to experience autonomically mediated disruptions of attention and motor skills. Moreover, they will be less likely to recover and overcome episodic decrements in performance compared with athletes who have an ideal Athlete's Profile of PHO personality and behavioral measures.

Counterintuitively, the TCM suggests that many successful athletes are not necessarily the most mentally tough ones, because technically proficient and physically superior athletes are often capable of dominating competition to the extent that they may rarely encounter critical psychological moments. By contrast, technically and physically weaker athletes who possess the ideal athlete's profile of PHO traits and behaviors can compensate psychologically for technical and physical deficiencies during critical moments. For example, a highly ranked or rated athlete who is not in possession of an ideal PHO constellation might still routinely defeat less skilled opponents who possess an ideal PHO constellation, but remain vulnerable to defeat or to being outplayed during critical moments of competition and eventually lose to lesser opponents who are mentally tougher when it counts.

However, this does not preclude the possibility that successful athletes can excel both technically and mentally and exhibit an ideal Athlete's Profile; it is just that there is not a linear relationship between success as an athlete as measured in conventional terms (e.g., won–loss record) and mental toughness. The evidence that will be presented in this book that is based on microoperationalizations of what constitutes a critical moment indicates that athletes possessing specific constellations of PHO traits and behaviors are more likely to master critical moments successfully regardless of their relative level of technical or physical skill (see Section II).

Potent and Meaningful PHO Psychological Predictor Variables: Toward a Mind–Body Model of Sport Performance

The TCM has identified constellations of personality traits and behaviors that have been shown to be potent mediators of attention, cognitive processes, and physiological reactivity—key components of sport performance. These measures are considered PHO variables capable of affecting other (SLO) psychological processes to drive psychophysiology and symptomology in clinical patients—and motor ability and performance in athletes. Specific findings on these measures that are relevant to athletes emanate from research in the fields of behavioral medicine, psychophysiology, and neuroscience. Emerging evidence from these fields suggests that similar traits and behavioral mechanisms that have been shown to mediate physiological reactivity/ anxiety/intensity, attention, motivation, cognitive processes, and resulting somatic complaints in clinical patients, including differential levels and interactions of hypnotic ability/absorption, neuroticism, and repressive coping, can also affect the performance of athletes.

Although athletes may be insulated from the negative health consequences associated with undesirable interactions or constellations of these measures, their performance may be adversely affected by the physiological concomitants of faulty cognitions and unconscious processes that have been shown to underlie specific interactions or combinations of these measures (Wickramasekera 1988). Conversely, desirable constellations of these traits and mechanisms that have been shown to exert a protective effect on health can facilitate sport performance.

Hypnotic ability/absorption, neuroticism, and repressive coping have mostly been overlooked in sport psychology despite the fact that research in behavioral medicine, especially studies of the High-Risk Model of Threat Perception (HRMTP), has established clear links between these measures and physiological reactivity, attention, and unconscious processes. The HRMTP addresses the effects that mind–body interactions have on physiology and health (Wickramasekera 1988). Central to this model is the hypothesis that hypnotic ability/ absorption, neuroticism, and repressive coping interact in the presence of the perception of threat, leading to changes in physiological reactivity and immune function as well as increases in a person's susceptibility to experiencing somatic symptoms and illness. Because this model addresses personality traits and behavioral mechanisms that have been shown to mediate physiology, attention, and cognitive processes—important aspects of sport performance—it is well-suited for the study of athletes and performance. This model has also generated findings indicating that unconscious processes play an important role in mediating physiological reactions to stress. As a consequence, the empirically supported HRMTP may also help elucidate the role of consciousness in athletes, a topic that has been neglected in the literature of sport psychology.

Although this is a book on sport performance, it is important that readers understand the rationale for applying constructs and elements from an essentially behavioral medicine model to the study and analysis of athletes and sport performance. Thus, before addressing constructs from the HRMTP in a more sport-specific context, I will present an overview of the model.

3

The High-Risk Model of Threat Perception

The High-Risk Model of Threat Perception (HRMTP) is a theoretical and applied model that attempts to assess and predict the risks specific mind–body interactions pose for the development of psychological and physical symptoms and illness. It has isolated a set of primary higher order (PHO) behavioral and personality risk factors (predictor variables) that have been shown to increase stress, drive physical symptoms, and contribute to illness, including three measures that are relevant to sport performance: high or low hypnotic ability or absorption, high neuroticism/negative affect (NA), and high or low repressive coping (RC).

The HRMTP also advances an eclectic multifaceted approach to intervention consisting of psychophysiological psychotherapy (PPT), hypnosis, biofeedback, and cognitive–behavioral therapy (Wickramasekera 1998). The application of these interventions is highly individualized and based on a person's constellation of risk factors. The model has shown that persons possessing certain constellations of these risk factors are more or less amenable to specific interventions. For example, a patient who is high in hypnotic ability and neuroticism and low in RC would not be given the same intervention as a patient exhibiting the opposite profile. Applied to sport, the HRMTP approach to intervention could be used, for example, to assess an athlete's ability to benefit from an intervention (e.g., mental imagery) on the basis of their constellation of these risk factors.

The HRMTP approach does not assume that everyone will necessarily benefit from the same intervention and has demonstrated that a discriminating and individual differences-based approach to treatment is more effective than the application of interventions en masse. Because there is a tendency in sport psychology to apply interventions indiscriminately under the faulty assumption that most athletes are capable of benefiting from the same intervention, a more individualized approach as advocated by the HRMTP may be advantageous to athletes and coaches.

A major goal of the HRMTP approach to intervention is to illuminate and document incongruence between verbal reports of distress and the actual physiology that patients exhibit during episodes of dysfunctional behavior, somatic complaints, and illness. Depending on a patient's constellation of risk factors, his or her verbal report of pain or distress is correspondingly more or less likely to be consistent with actual medical tests or physiological data. For example, somaticizers and hypochondriacs, most of whom are high in hypnotic ability and neuroticism and low in RC, often report acute pain and distress that cannot be substantiated or validated on the basis of objective clinical tests. In contrast, many patients who are low in hypnotic ability and neuroticism and high in RC fail to report symptoms or psychological distress, yet tests reveal that they have an underlying disease or psychological problem of which they were not consciously aware. Exposing such mind–body incongruence is accomplished by continuously monitoring the physiology of patients during psychotherapy or by comparing self-report with objective medical tests. Ultimately, physiological and medical data are used to validate or refute a patient's self-report to arrive at a more accurate diagnosis and to intervene appropriately to alleviate symptoms and maladaptive behavior.

The ability to expose mind–body incongruence in athletes is also very important because there is a tendency on the part of coaches and sport psychologists to readily believe that "what you see is what you get" when it comes to the body language, verbalizations, and self-report of athletes, despite the strong possibility that there may be inconsistencies between external behavior and behavioral cues and internal (subliminal) psychophysiological reactivity. Inaccurate interpretations of the meaning of athletes' body language, verbalizations, and self-report can lead to faulty decisions on the part of coaches as well as to inappropriate applications of mental training interventions. For example, just because an athlete exhibits "poor" body language does not necessarily mean that he or she is not motivated or lacking in some other mental quality. Body language often is a temporally isolated (post facto) reaction to a preceding event—a response that is often fleeting. Similarly, athletes who verbally express anger will not necessarily mentally be out of control beyond the inciting incident. Thus, it is presumptuous to assume that body language, verbalizations, or self-report will reveal the same thing in all athletes, as though a facial expression, style of walk, posture, or verbal emoting in one athlete will result in the same physiological response and performance consequences in all athletes.

The belief that body language accurately tells us something profound about an athlete's mental state is tenuous and more myth than reality. As a consequence, training athletes to alter their body language or verbalizations to suit a coach or sport psychologist's notion of how an athlete should act or behave will not necessarily facilitate performance. On the contrary, indiscriminant attempts to manipulate behavior and apply interventions that fail to consider individual differences in psychophysiological reactivity are more likely to foster mind–body incongruence that will disrupt rather than facilitate performance. Just as in clinical patients, it is important to continuously monitor and analyze the physiology of athletes during practice and competition before attaching performance-relevant meaning to body language, verbalizations, and self-report. Unfortunately, physiological monitoring of athletes is rarely done, especially during practice or competition, making it difficult to concurrently validate analyses of athletes' behavior or self-report. However, without knowing the underlying physiology of an athlete, it is speculative to assume that congruence exists between what an athlete's external behavior is and what a coach or sport psychologist believes it to mean.

The HRMTP approach to interventions has shown that in addition to revealing mind–body incongruence, shifts in physiological reactivity that are elicited during psychotherapy reflect the movement of the perception of threat from unconscious to conscious memory, an event that is thought to occur when conflict is brought to the consciousness (Wickramasekera 1988, 1994). The concept of perception of threat is central to the HRMTP, with levels of hypnotic ability/absorption, neuroticism, and RC and manifestations of their interactions on health (or performance) expected to be the greatest under conditions of high stress, when one's perceived well-being (or ability to compete free from worry and pressure) is threatened. Dramatic change in physiological reactivity in response to stimuli that are presented during psychotherapy (or when monitoring an athlete) is thought to reflect unconscious conflict or perception of threat reaching conscious awareness. Such an occurrence is associated with an increase in psychological distress, but it also frequently leads to an attenuation of maladaptive physiological reactivity, behavior, and symptoms (Wickramasekera 1988). For example, a person being monitored during psychotherapy may exhibit a highly reactive physiological profile (e.g., high heart rate at baseline, excessive sweat activity) yet admit to no psychological distress before suddenly, on acknowledging previously repressed trauma or conflict, exhibit sudden reduced physiological reactivity. A person who finally reveals a previously unacknowledged emotion (e.g., being unhappy about a relationship) often experiences an immediate reduction in baseline and longitudinally present levels of sympathetic arousal and the accompanying physical complaints (e.g., excessive muscle tension, fatigue) as suppressed feelings and thoughts come to consciousness. Immediately thereafter, the person may feel conscious psychological distress associated with a new awareness of an issue they did not want to confront, but are nevertheless pleasantly surprised when their chronic symptoms attenuate. Once this occurs, patients are on their way to achieving or restoring mind–body harmony.

The following case study illustrates the dynamics of unconscious processes associated with the perception of threat reaching consciousness in an athlete. A tennis player with whom I have worked perceived himself to be mentally tough despite the fact that he frequently "choked" on big points (during critical moments). To demonstrate his mind–body incongruence, his physiology was monitored both off and on the court and during actual competition. First, off the court, he was monitored while he watched a video recording of himself playing a match. Initially he exhibited a relaxed physiological profile (nonreactive baseline values for heart rate variability, respiration, etc.) until he saw himself encounter a "big point." At that moment he suddenly exhibited excessive physiological arousal (tachycardia, rapid breathing, strong galvanic skin response). His sudden and excessive physiological responses were thought to reflect manifestations of the unconscious perception of threat to an emotional stimulus (seeing himself play a big point). The observed increased physiological reactivity associated with watching a big point also occurred in vivo during an actual tennis match, when unconscious intrusive thoughts about facing a critical point led to excessive physiological reactivity (heart rate acceleration) and consequent poor performance. The player's excessive physiological responses revealed his unconscious fear of facing the most critical moments in tennis—the big points. In this case, the therapeutic or mental training goal was to bring to consciousness the fact that the player was afraid of playing big points, a task that can be difficult depending on what constellation of risk factors a particular athlete may possess. This player was high in hypnotic ability/absorption, high in neuroticism/NA, and low in RC, making him very vulnerable to unconscious intrusive thoughts in stressful situations. After undergoing intensive cognitive restructuring and concurrent physiological monitoring, this player finally admitted that he was indeed afraid of the big points, and although he was no longer able to fool himself about his mental toughness, eventually he was better able to self-regulate his psychophysiological processes and improve his performance during these critical moments.

According to Wickramasekera (1988), these dynamic psychophysiological processes reflect secrets that are kept from the mind, but not the body. In other words, you can try to fool yourself, but you cannot fool your body. The HRMTP predicts that specific interactions or constellations of risk factors (hypnotic ability, neuroticism, and RC) are sufficient to account for somatic complaints, or positive physical findings. In the case of athletes, these psychophysiological risk factors are expected to differentially hinder or facilitate important processes associated with performance, including attention, physiological reactivity, and cognition, to affect performance and outcome (e.g., winning or losing and success or error on a task; physiological monitoring of athletes and new approaches to interventions in sport psychology will be elaborated in Section III).

The Theory of Critical Moments (TCM) predicts that hypnotic ability/absorption, neuroticism, and RC can independently, in concert, or as a function of specific combinations or constellations of these factors affect the influence of virtually any psychological, behavioral, or psychophysiological measure, especially during critical moments of competition. As previously mentioned, these measures are considered PHO predictor or independent variables and should be assessed and investigated in all studies on the psychological aspects of sport performance.

Specific interventions that are customized to individual constellations of HRMTP factors are presented later in this section.

Primary Higher Order Mind–Body Predictor Variables

Hypnotic Ability

Hypnotic ability is the measure of a person's ability to enter a hypnotic state or to become hypnotized. It is also considered to be a longitudinally stable psychophysiological trait independent of formal hypnosis, as cognitive and perceptual processes associated with hypnotic ability have been found to be ongoing outside the realm of actually being hypnotized. In other words, a person's hypnotic ability manifests itself throughout the day in response to internal and external stimuli and even during sleep. For example, while driving, a person who is high in hypnotic ability may become so immersed in looking into "nothingness" that he or she dissociates and becomes deeply focused on some other internal or external stimuli instead of on operating the car. This sort of experience has been reported in athletes, especially distance runners, or during "flow" and "zone-like" experiences (Udewitz 1993). Although no formal hypnosis has taken place in these instances, persons who are high in hypnotic ability are more prone to frequently entering altered states—if only for a moment—during their daily activities. These unconscious lapses or episodes of intense absorption have obvious consequences for performance, both in the positive and negative sense depending on the situation in which they occur and on their duration.

Hypnotic ability plays an important role in mediating to what extent a person focuses on external or internal stimuli. According to Crawford, persons who are high in hypnotic ability

have a greater disposition for more focused and sustained attention, deeper absorptive involvement in experiences be they positive or negative in nature, and a greater cognitive flexibility, that is, the ability to shift from one strategy to another or from one alternative state of consciousness to another and show superior performance on certain attentional tasks and faster reaction times to complex decision-making tasks (INBABIS 1998)

It has been demonstrated that about 20 to 30% of the population can either readily access the hypnotic mode of information processing or are incapable of doing so (Hilgard 1965; Wickramasekera 1988). The style of information and perceptual processing associated with persons high or low in hypnotic ability has been linked to symptoms and illness in clinical settings. For example, Wickramasekera (1983) found that 85% of a sample of 103 patients who presented with psychophysiological symptoms were either very high or low in hypnotic ability.

Individuals who are high in hypnotic ability (highs) have a tendency to attend too much to themselves, especially if they are also high in neuroticism. They are found to often exaggerate minor physical sensations to a level of self-perceived major significance, whereas those who are low in hypnotic ability (lows) attend too little and generally ignore physical symptoms (Wickramasekera 1988). Three components of both high hypnotic ability (highs) and low hypnotic ability (lows) are thought to place these people at high risk for developing somatic symptoms

1. *Highs have the capacity to hallucinate voluntarily.* Their ability to generate realistic images of seeing, hearing, feeling, and smelling what is being talked about and their engaging in fantasy activity during up to 50% of waking time has physiological consequences that are likely to lead to somatic conditions in highs who are also high in neuroticism (Wickramasekera 1988). Wilson and Barber (1982) reported that 86% of subjects having illnesses or physical symptoms directly related their problems to thoughts, fantasies, or memories. Wickramasekera (1988) hypothesizes that the vivid and convincing perceptual and cognitive experiences of highs—in the presence of the perception of threat and in conjunction with the physiological consequences of these experiences—provides a basis for developing chronic symptoms. For example, persons high in hypnotic ability may interpret minor pain as the signal of an oncoming illness. This in turn may cause them to constantly focus on their pain and the resultant negative cognitions, which eventually leads to excessive physiological reactivity, symptoms, and illness. In contrast, highs who are high in positive affect can readily experience euphoria or mania. This state may facilitate healing and have implications for achieving "flow-like" states in sports (Csikszentmihalyi 1990).

2. *Highs are hypersensitive to psychological and physiological change.* Hypersensitivity is thought to be a process of symptom induction that is partly genetic and partly learned, whereby highs appear to exhibit a superior sensory memory or ability to transfer information from sensory memory to short-term memory (Ingram et al. 1979; Saccuzzo et al. 1982). Wickramasekera (1988) hypothesizes that highs learn, remember, and incubate the experience of acute pain all too effectively, allowing it to become a chronic pain disorder. An additional learning mechanism of symptom induction in highs may be their hypersensitivity to sensory stimuli and their superior ability to discriminate between visceral sensations. For example, without analgesic suggestions, highs are less tolerant of pain than are people of low hypnotic ability (Barabasz 1982). Highs also have an unusual capacity for attention to and absorption in subjective events such as pain and fear (Tellegen and Atkinson 1974). This ability may be used to magnify their response to even minimal sensory and visceral stimuli (Wickramasekera 1988). This latter ability can also have an adaptive function when interacting with high positive affect.

3. *Highs have the ability to voluntarily alter states of consciousness and memory functions* (Evans 1977; Kihlstrom 1985). This ability may be a protective reflex for dealing with biological hypersensitivity (Wickramasekera 1988). For example, highs can easily induce sleep at different times in diverse locations, can wake up at preselected times without an alarm, and are capable of learning during sleep without waking up. Retention of simple information from such state-dependent learning has been demonstrated up to 6 months (Evans 1977). It appears that maladaptive or aversive physiological responses can be learned in states of hyperarousal or hypoarousal (such as sleep). Wickramasekera (1988) suggests that negative-aversive expectations may alter the content of rapid eye movement dreams and establish maladaptive patterns of muscular and vascular response in sleep. Furthermore, highs can readily learn fear and pain responses but are unaware of what was learned and where it was learned. Thus, the phenomena of incidental learning, source amnesia, or state-dependent learning in highs may be the foundation for the strong resistance to extinction of over-learned and incubated maladaptive responses associated with the development of somatic illness (Wickramasekera 1988).

Wickramasekera (1988) hypothesizes that the ability to enter states of altered consciousness (e.g., hypnosis) that highs demonstrate may facilitate the use of CNS processes like suggestion to reset dysfunctional peripheral (ANS) feedback systems. For example, the neurogenic regulation of blood pressure through the resetting of baroreceptors restoring homeostasis after a stress incident illustrates such regulation (Cannon 1932).

Individuals who are low in hypnotic ability (lows) also display three traits that place them at increased risk for developing somatic symptoms or illness (Wickramasekera 1988):

1. Hyposensitivity to psychological and physiological changes
2. A tendency to deny any psychological causation of behavior
3. Delay in seeking medical investigation

Lows are relatively insensitive to or deficient in attention to interrelationships between psychological (verbal–emotional) and physiological (proprioceptive–interoceptive) states (Wickramasekera 1988). Lows tend to engage a skeptical, critical, and analytic mode of information processing and typically deny or attenuate minimal sensory cues from their bodies. They also tend to lack or do not want to use verbal fantasy and imagination and prefer to think in specific and distinct terms. Low hypnotic ability overlaps with the concept of alexithymia, a disorder in which a person lacks words to describe and communicate moods, first identified in people with psychosomatic disorders. Frankel, Apfel-Savitz, Nemiah, and Sifneos (1977) found that 73% of subjects who were lows were alexithymic, whereas 92% of highs were classified as nonalexithymic. Alexithymics tend to attribute psychological changes to external physical causes and are likely to verbally inhibit or deny their feelings; Pennebaker (1985) reports that such verbal inhibition of trauma is associated with higher levels of physiological arousal. Thus, in lows, somatic complaints may be the physical manifestation of inhibited and nonverbalized psychological conflicts (Wickramasekera 1988). Lows may be inhibited in resetting dysfunctional neurogenic (hypothalmic-pituitary-adrenal) feedback systems after stress-related incidents (i.e., arousal levels only slowly return to baseline states). They are also less aware of stress factors and deny the role psychological factors play in the etiology of physical dysfunctions and are more susceptible to psychophysiological disorders as a result (Wickramasekera 1988).

Absorption

Absorption is a measure of personality marked by episodes of total attention and engagement of perceptual, imaginative, and ideational capacities (Tellegen and Atkinson 1974). Most widely assessed by the Tellegen Absorption Scale (Tellegen and Atkinson 1974), absorption is moderately correlated with a lower order factor of hypnotic ability. For purposes of the TCM, absorption is used interchangeably with hypnotic ability unless otherwise noted. Studies on the HRMTP using absorption in place of hypnotic ability have resulted in findings similar to those that would have been expected had a measure of hypnotic ability been used. Because absorption is much easier to assess and shares many of the descriptive and empirically established characteristics of hypnotic ability, much that has been written and hypothesized about hypnotic ability could be applied to absorption. As a consequence, absorption was used to test hypotheses regarding the nature of hypnotic ability in the context of the TCM. Ultimately, the merit of using absorption to test hypotheses that were originally based on hypnotic ability will lie in the resulting findings.

Tellegen (1992) defines absorption as "a disposition to enter under conducive circumstances psychological states that are characterized by marked restructuring of the phenomenal self and world." He states further that, "these more or less transient states may have a dissociated or an integrative and peak experience-like quality" and that,

27

"they may have a sentient external focus, or may reflect an inner focus on reminiscences, images, and imaginings." Moreover, Tellegen notes that the trait of absorption "subsumes these diverse possibilities in a remarkable cohesive correlational structure" (1992, p. 2). Absorption has further been characterized as a trait marked by intense focus and unawareness of distracting stimuli (Kihlstrom et al. 1989).

Neuropsychophysiological studies indicate that absorption involves bilateral processing, with the right hemisphere playing more of a role in the visual and imaginative components of absorption and the left hemisphere appearing to be more involved with the verbal and narrative aspects of these imaginative components (Taylor et al. 1997). Highs may also exhibit greater cortical specificity than lows, with Davidson et al. (1976) reporting that highs could readily inhibit cortical activity in regions of the brain (i.e., the occipital region) that were considered irrelevant to a kinesthetic counting exercise, whereas lows showed more activity in this region. This finding was interpreted to suggest that lows may have a lower threshold for distracting stimuli, especially when facing increased demands on their attention (Davidson et al. 1976). Some interpretations of studies on absorption and on the manipulation of physiological measures indicate that external demands on attention interfere with the cognitive and psychophysiological performance (e.g., relaxation response) of highs and facilitate the performance of lows, especially when biofeedback is used to facilitate relaxation (Qualls and Sheenan 1979, 1981; Roche and McConkey 1990). However, Tellegen (1981) takes issue with this point of view, arguing that successful relaxation requires different mental "sets" for highs and lows. That is, contrary to what Qualls and Sheenan (1981) report, a person's level of absorption interacts with how absorption is to be achieved irrespective of whether the attentional demands are internal or external.

According to Tellegen (1981), highs will more readily experience relaxation (or any desired state) when a so-called experiential set is used or achieved, whereas lows require an instrumental set to attain reduced levels of arousal. The experiential set facilitates openness to experiencing sensory or imaginal stimuli and events as they occur—or involuntariness—whereas the instrumental set is a state of readiness to engage in "active, realistic, voluntary, and relatively effortful planning, decision making, and goal-directed behavior" (Tellegen 1981, p. 222). Shea's (1985) study showing that highs reduced their heart rate more when they used imagery in contrast to lows, who were more successful slowing their hearts under hypnosis, illustrates the role "sets" appear to play in mediating relationships between absorption and attention. In Shea's study, instructions to use imagery functioned as an experiential set to facilitate performance in highs, whereas the hypnotic condition, an instrumental set, helped lows achieve better control over heart rate.

Neuroticism or Negative Affect

Another risk factor for developing somatic illness or symptomology is high NA or neuroticism. High NA is characterized by a tendency to recognize and recall predominantly aversive past memories (Watson and Clark 1984; Wickramasekera 1988). It is assessed using various self-report test instruments, including the Eysenck Personality Inventory (Eysenck and Eysenck 1968).

High NA is considered a longitudinally stable trait independent of objective stress. In clinical samples, there is nearly always a large incongruence between self-report of distress (i.e., NA) and direct psychophysiological measures of stress (Wickramasekera 1988). NA is based on autonomic lability or degree of reactivity of the sympathetic nervous system and appears to have a genetic basis (Eysenck 1960; Shields 1962). Self-report of NA has been linked to the limbic system by Eysenck (1983) and is manifested psychophysiologically by elevated baselines of muscle tension, skin conductance, heart rate, blood pressure, and delays in returning to baseline after episodes of stress (Eysenck 1983). High NA appears to be an amplification of physical concerns as opposed to a sign of physical disease per se (Wickramasekera 1988).

The tendency to display a stable profile of sympathetic response (autonomic response specificity) appears to have clinical implications. For example, people showing maximum reactivity in the cardiovascular system may be at high risk for developing myocardial infarction or stroke (Krantz and Manuck 1984), whereas those revealing the strongest response on a measure of elevated baselines of muscle tension may be at greatest risk for back pain or tension headache (Phillips 1977; Flor, Turk, and Birbaumer, 1985). Wickramasekera (1988, p. 17) views the most physiological reactive system as a person's "window of maximum vulnerability" for developing clinical symptoms when under stress; high NA can frequently lead to catastrophizing. In earlier conceptualizations of the HRMTP, catastrophizing was presented in its own right as an independent risk factor (Wickramasekera 1988). However, catastrophizing, which is marked by a person's tendency to expect the worst to happen when looking at the future, has been viewed more as a consequence of interactions between high hypnotic ability and high NA (Wickramasekera 1994).

Catastrophizing is defined by Wickramasekera (1988) as becoming intensely and frequently absorbed in a negative psychological or sensory event and potentiating aversive properties of such an event with negative self-talk or autosuggestion. Catastrophizing has at least two response components. First, attentional focus is kept on the sensory or visceral events that are consequences of symptoms, and second, a wide variety of negative physical and psychosocial consequences and antecedents of the aversive or symptomatic event are remembered or anticipated (Wickramasekera 1988). It is hypothesized that many internal or external cues that trigger catastrophizing are outside of conscious awareness (Dixon 1981). Numerous studies have linked catastrophizing to somatic complaints. For example, Chaves and Brown (1978) found that the majority of chronic pain patients are catastrophizers as rated by interjudge/expert raters and ad hoc self-report scales. The catastrophizers also had higher pain ratings than copers did. In addition, 86% of these catastrophizers were prescribed anti-anxiety or antidepressant medication, whereas only 12% of copers required drug intervention for dealing with pain (Chaves and Brown 1978). Wickramasekera (1988) also proposes that the psychophysiological predisposition to experience spontaneous panic attacks that is central to the formation of phobias is mediated by catastrophizing cognitions that subjectively reduce pain tolerance, spiral anxiety, and generate self-report of hopelessness. Moreover, it appears that chronic pain, panic, fear disorders, and depression may have common biological bases involving serotonin and norepinephrine metabolism (Sternbach et al. 1976).

Repressive Coping

RC is another risk factor. It is characterized by implicit (unconscious) defensiveness and the tendency to inhibit affect. The Marlowe-Crowne Scale (MC) is frequently used to measure this capacity for blocking negative perceptions, memories, and moods from consciousness, a style of coping that appears to promote inattention to aversive situations and the amplification of positive situations (Crowne and Marlowe 1960).

Persons scoring high on the MC are characterized by an RC style. They frequently exhibit incongruence between subjective positive self-report and physiological and behavioral indicators of distress, and they tend to have a poor memory for negative emotional experiences (Weinberger et al. 1979; Lane et al. 1990; Wickramasekera et al. 1996b). The self-deception associated with RC appears to make individuals high in this trait susceptible to developing somatic or behavioral symptoms (Lane et al. 1990). In contrast, lows, who are considered less adept at self-deception, appear more likely to experience psychological symptoms such as depression and anxiety but appear less likely to experience psychophysiological symptoms (Lane et al. 1990; Wickramasekera 1998).

RC is also viewed as a "self-enhancing cognitive style" that promotes the rapid dampening of negative affective responses to stressors, maintenance or enhancement of self-esteem, and a lowered risk for psychopathology (Tomarken and Davidson 1994, p. 339). Neurophysiological studies of RC have led some researchers to characterize RC as a "functional disconnection syndrome" between the left hemisphere and other cortical or subcortical regions that mediate autonomic and neuroendrocine components of affective responsivity (Davidson 1984; Schwartz 1990). For example, Davidson (1984) demonstrated relative deficits in interhemispheric transfer of NA from the right to the left hemisphere. This deficit in reduced cross-callosal transfer of aversive information is thought to account for reduced psychopathology in highs (Tomarken and Davidson 1994).

Heightened autonomic and endocrine activation in high repressors is thought to reflect the mobilization of processes that inhibit distress, facilitate goal-oriented behavior, or both (Tomarken and Davidson 1994).

Predictions from the HRMTP

Emerging research on the HRMTP has led to the following predictions:

1. *Development of somatic symptomology and illness is always a function of multidimensional interactions among psychological risk factors and genetics.* This first prediction forms the basis of the TCM PHO tenet. It implies that specific constellations of HRMTP identified risk factors are potent enough to mediate differential physiological responses to stress and that these factors have primacy over other psychological factors (secondary lower order factors) in driving physiological reactivity. The primacy of HRMTP-identified constellations of personality traits and behaviors is expected to emerge in the context of sports and critical moments, where they will take on the status of PHO factors.

2. *Trait neuroticism and state of NA are essential but not sufficient for development of psychosomatic symptoms and illness.* This prediction implies that neuroticism and NA play central roles in the etiology of symptoms and illness. Similarly, in sports and athletes,

it is expected that neuroticism and NA will drive the negative intrusive thoughts that have been associated with disruption of performance.

3. *Individuals who are high in hypnotic ability and low in RC are more likely to develop both psychological and somatic symptoms.* Athletes who are high in hypnotic ability/absorption and low in RC can be expected to experience psychologically mediated problems during critical moments of competition, especially in the presence of high neuroticism, leading to performance-specific somatic symptoms in the form of disruption of motor ability. However, those athletes who are low in hypnotic ability and high in RC will develop primarily somatic symptoms; high RC will exert a protective effect in preventing negative intrusive thoughts from disrupting performance, regardless of the level of hypnotic ability/absorption.

4. *Individuals who are high in hypnotic ability with somatic symptoms are more likely to seek help for their problem in the mental health sector.* Individuals who are high in hypnotic ability with somatic symptoms are more likely to seek help for their problem in the mental health sector as opposed to the medical sector, as they are more likely to recognize the involvement of mind–body interactions in the disease process. This prediction has indirect relevance to sports and athletes, as athletes who are high in hypnotic ability/absorption are more likely to seek help from sport psychology practitioners than are athletes who are low in this trait, as highs are inherently more aware of or open to the suggestion that psychologically mediated performance problems have a mind–body etiology.

5. *The majority of patients in primary medical care settings will be low in hypnotic ability and high in RC and are more likely to avoid referral to mental health settings.* In contrast to the preceding prediction, athletes who are low in hypnotic ability/absorption are inherently less likely to seek assistance from sport psychology practitioners because the athletes tend to be skeptical or unaware of mind–body interactions that influence performance. These athletes can benefit from biofeedback as a mental training intervention because it is an intervention modality that provides objective information about psychophysiological processes that are important to performance. However, because athletes possessing these levels of hypnotic ability/absorption and RC can be difficult to motivate to engage in mental training, the HRMTP "Trojan horse" approach should be considered as a method for covertly and subtly introducing potentially beneficial performance-enhancement

modalities (the Trojan horse method is briefly discussed below and in the section on Applied Sport Psychology).

HRMTP and Individualized Interventions: Psychophysiological Psychotherapy

The HRMTP approach to interventions relies heavily on physiological monitoring and subsequent PPT. PPT is a complex clinical investigative tool designed to analyze and reveal mind–body interactions involving a six-phased method of psychotherapy that includes continuous physiological monitoring (Wickramasekera 1994).

The goal of PPT is to reduce autonomic measures of threat perception and expand cognitive flexibility and adaptability in order to reduce or eliminate somatic symptoms (Wickramasekera 1994). The inhibition or disruption of dysfunctional cognitions or cognitive style and resultant perception of threat is achieved using hypnosis, self-hypnosis, other cognitive-behavioral methods, or biofeedback in an attempt to reduce autonomic nervous system correlates of threat perception, including hypertension and cardiac hyperreactivity (Wickramasekera 1994). It is hoped that PPT will disinhibit long-term unconsciously and consciously entrenched dysfunctional memories, images, and emotions, thereby facilitating new creative and adaptive cognitive responses to the perception of threat (Wickramasekera 1988).

PPT is indicated when patients presenting physical complaints without underlying disease cannot be effectively treated medically. It attempts to challenge previous notions and myths regarding the etiology of a patient's somatic complaints by illuminating the extent to which a person's thoughts can mediate the development of symptoms (Wickramasekera 1988).

PPT has been shown to be effective in treating a wide variety of somatic afflictions including vasovagal syncopy, headaches, clinical pain, Raynaud's disease, fecal and urinary incontinence, and hypertension (Wickramasekera et al. 1996a; Wickramasekera 1994, 1988). Individualized applications of PPT and hypnosis are applied on the basis of the following HRMTP risk factor profiles (Wickramasekera 1993).

High Hypnotizability/Absorption, Low Neuroticism, and High Repressive Coping

Although these types of patients tend to score in or below the normal range on widely used psychological tests (e.g., MMPI-2), they are at risk for "transducing" the perception of threat into somatic symptoms, yet they are often unaware of clinical pain and anxiety (Wickramasekera 1993, p. 602). Patients exhibiting this profile are thought to have at least two mechanisms that suppress pain or fear and avoid their conscious perception: high hypnotic ability and high RC. Nevertheless, despite not being aware of pain or fear, perception of threat is thought to occur implicitly or unconsciously in these patients, as is reflected in increases in various measures of autonomic function including blood pressure, heart rate, or electrodermal response.

These types of patients are considered vulnerable to serious medical disorders including cancer and heart disease, especially during middle age, when unhealthy lifestyle factors can override whatever protective genetic attributes the athletes may possess (Wickramasekera 1993, p. 603). According to Zillmer and Wickramasekera (1987), the high hypnotizability/absorption, low neuroticism, and high RC patient will benefit the most from hypnotherapy with a psychodynamic or Gestalt orientation and from delayed biofeedback.

Low Hypnotizability/Absorption, Low Neuroticism, and High Repressive Coping

This type of patient should be involved in a treatment modality that allows a rapid and reliable shift into a state of low physiological arousal that facilitates the subjective perception of muscular and vascular changes (e.g., reduction of muscle tension, peripheral temperature manipulation). As a consequence, immediate biofeedback is indicated. Often this can only be successfully implemented using the Trojan horse role-induction method (a covert method of assisting lows in recognizing the effects emotions and cognitions can exert on physiology) to help these patients verbalize and feel shifts in perception, a necessary requisite in preparation for conventional psychotherapy (Wickramasekera 1988). Failure to prepare the skeptical lows and to make them aware that alterations in physiological arousal and somatic sensations can be cognitively induced often results in their terminating therapy (Zillmer and Wickramasekera 1987).

High Hypnotizability/Absorption, High Neuroticism, and High Repressive Coping

Because high neuroticism and RC are characteristics of "explicit defensiveness" (i.e., repression), this type of patient requires a gradual approach to psychotherapy. Initially these patients should receive cognitive-behavioral therapy that focuses on somatic symptoms and the reduction of catastrophizing cognitions (Wickramasekera 1993, p. 603). Once a trusting therapeutic relationship has developed, hypnotherapy can be introduced (which obviously is amenable to highs). Hypnotic suggestions that selectively focus on and retain positive memories and emotions should be used to restructure this patient's propensity to attend to threatening stimuli. After a time, when defensive barriers are reduced, hypnoanalysis can be introduced to access unconscious resistance to greater levels of social intimacy, social support, and interpersonal vulnerability (Wickramasekera 1993). Essentially, psycho- and hypnotherapy with these patients strive to "boost psychological immunity" by increasing cognitive and behavioral adaptive coping skills and reducing "acting out" (Wickramasekera 1993, p. 603).

Summary

The HRMTP is a multidimensional model composed of quantifiable components that separately may be weak predictors of clinical outcome but that in concert are strong predictors of the complex mind–body interactions observed in clinical situations (Wickramasekera 1988). Persons at greatest risk are those who are positive for all predisposing features, who are deficient in support systems and coping skills, and who have experienced a massing of multiple major life changes or hassles. The persons at lowest risk are those who have none of the personality features mentioned above and who have effective multiple support systems and coping skills (Wickramasekera 1988).

4

Primary Higher Order Predictor Variables: Effects on Athletes and Performance

I hypothesize that similar mind–body mechanisms thought to drive physiological hyperreactivity and the resulting clinical complaints in patients can disrupt performance, and athletes who can control attentional focus, cognitive activity, and intensity are more likely to perform to their peak potential (Hanin 1980; Wickramasekera 1988; Carlstedt 1998; Taylor 1996). Although athletes are not necessarily expected to incur the negative health consequences that are associated with undesirable constellations of hypnotic ability/absorption, neuroticism, and repressive coping (RC), their ability to perform to peak potential may be affected by the negative physiological concomitants of dysfunctional cognitions and unconscious processes that have been shown to underlie these measures. In contrast, positive constellations of these traits and the mechanisms that protect and promote health may facilitate sport performance.

Because specific constellations of hypnotic ability/absorption, neuroticism, and RC have been empirically linked to differential physiological reactivity in clinical and laboratory settings, it is predicted that they can also affect attention, cognition, and physiological reactivity in athletes and that they should be routinely assessed. The presence of specific interactions of these risk factors in athletes may lead to "motor complaints," or the disruption of fast coordinated responses to specific tasks in sports. It is also thought that certain combinations of these risk factors may facilitate performance.

The detrimental and facilitative effects of these primary higher-order (PHO) personality traits and behavioral mechanisms are also capable of singularly influencing performance; that is, they are independent of one another. Although the constellations of hypnotic ability/absorption, neuroticism, and RC are expected to be most potent in the context of critical moments, they can affect performance independently during baseline or routine phases of competition, when the perception of threat is not present or substantially reduced. For example, when looking at sport-relevant characteristics associated with hypnotic ability, we see the descriptor "superior concentration." Normally this would be considered a good thing, which it is at baseline or across the course of more routine moments of competition. Superior concentration also is crucial to developmental processes associated with becoming an elite athlete; after all, if you cannot concentrate for long periods of time, you probably will not train enough to consolidate the complex motor skills necessary for high-level performance in procedural memory. However, once critical moments are encountered during competition, singular traits and behavioral mechanisms can lose their individual facilitative baseline function and work against peak performance. For example, a potentially beneficial trait like high hypnotic ability or absorption, when interacting with high neuroticism and low RC during stressful critical moments, can suddenly turn superior concentration away from important external stimuli such as the flight of the ball toward internal (conscious or unconscious) stimuli (negative intrusive thoughts), causing performance to be disrupted.

In addressing hypnotic ability/absorption, neuroticism, and RC in the context of athletes and performance, keep in mind that each of these factors can affect an athlete positively or negatively—and independently—during baseline conditions, but that they are likely to be most potent in concert (when interacting) during critical moments of competition, when the perception of threat is the greatest. During these moments, neuropsychophysiological processes that may remain relatively stable and task-oriented at baseline can become hyperactivated in response to the perceived criticality of a competitive moment.

Hypnotic Ability in Athletes

Hypnotic ability can be considered the "zone" trait when it comes to sport performance because a high level of this trait is associated with effortlessly achieved intense states of attention, focus, or absorption characteristic of being in "zone" or "flow" states. Anecdotal descriptions and reports of being in these high-performance states are replete with adjectives that similarly characterize the cognitive and perceptual experiences of persons who are also high in hypnotic ability, including descriptors such as intense focus, effortlessness, and involuntariness. As such, high hypnotic ability or absorption is hypothesized to mediate "flow" and "in the zone" experiences reported by athletes.

Although "flow" or "zone" states result from and require the effortless focus that is associated with high hypnotic ability, one might think that high hypnotic ability is a more favorable or desirable trait in athletes than low hypnotic ability. The intuitive tendency to associate high hypnotic ability with better performance may be faulty, however, because although hypnotic ability is associated with intense but effortless focus, like flow and zone states, it can also be short-lived and clusive. Indeed, these are states that can be easily disrupted, especially in athletes characterized as "highs." As a consequence, high hypnotic ability can be a double-edged sword, as attending to or focusing on the wrong thing at the wrong time can disrupt performance and obviate sustaining any desirable flow or zone states. Whereas high hypnotic ability, when focused on the task at hand and free from negative intrusive thoughts, may drive the feeling of dissociation athletes have reported when experiencing being in the zone, the flow feeling appears only to remain active as long as intrusive negative thoughts remain dormant. Keeping such thoughts at bay during critical moments may not be that easy, especially in athletes who are concurrently high in neuroticism and low in RC. As a consequence, although hypnotic ability can help an athlete who is high in this trait reach the zone or flow state more easily, in the presence of high neuroticism—and especially during critical moments—the facilitative aspect of hypnotic ability can quickly be disrupted, turning a potentially beneficial trait into a detrimental one.

To date there has been very little research on hypnotic ability in athletes. One of the few notable exceptions was the work of Josephine Hilgard (1968), whose data and insights involving a sample of 45 athletes and nonathletes provided clues about the nature and prevalence of hypnotic ability in athletes. Hilgard (1968) studied both competitive athletes who had no other interests that would lead them into hypnosis and who, as such, were found "quite unsusceptible," and those athletes who had other interests that are associated with hypnotic ability (Hilgard 1968, p. 289). Of the 45 subjects she tested, 25 were rated as high in athletic interests, and of these 25, 13 had one or more interests related to hypnotic ability (e.g., reading, art, music) and 12 did not. The other 23 subjects did not have great interest in athletics. Of these subjects, 13 had one or more interests relating to hypnotic susceptibility, and 7 did not.

Hilgard (1968) identified intense involvement (in an activity) as one characteristic of the hypnotic experience, and because interests reflecting involvement, such as an interest in sports (as a participant/athlete in this context here) tend to be associated with hypnosis, she asserted there is a myth that all "involvements" are related to hypnosis (or hypnotic ability; 1968, p.288). According to Hilgard (1968), three types of involvement or interests, although often fully absorbing in nature, when found alone (i.e., existing as the only interest or involvement of a person) are associated with hypnotic "insusceptibility" (1968, p. 288). These include scientific curiosity, recreation taking the form of work, and competitive athletics. Hilgard (1968, p. 288) maintained that, "when interest in athletic competition is found to be high, in the absence of other kinds of involvement, hypnotic susceptibility tends to be minimal.... Such people, generally nonhypnotizable, provide an illustration or capacity for deep involvement, but the kind unrelated to the involvement within hypnosis."

Hilgard's successful and involved athletes (low hypnotic ability) who lacked other interests exhibited the following characteristics. First, they were sensitive to exact information from the environment. For these athletes, the demands of reality were constantly in the forefront. Stimuli from the environment were used for exact information about that reality and were interpreted according to their precise meanings. Information that was to be used for accomplishment of a particular task was evaluated according to its relevance to that task. Second, they tended to focus on those aspects that lead to decision and control. The goals of these athletes included a desire for greater skill and for better performance against an opponent. As such, their bodily responses were primed for coordinated and automatic responses in the service of that decision and control. Athletes who have long trained to know precisely what body movements they are making speak of difficulty in attempting hypnosis when the hypnotist tells them the body is doing something that they know immediately it is not doing. They have well-learned decision signals connected with the "body in space" (Hilgard 1968, p. 291). Third, the athletes stressed activity: Achievement and competition require constant activity, vigilance, and striving. Mental alertness to precise meanings of incoming stimuli or signals becomes heightened, and the "metered" appropriate response is ready and well-learned. Both detection and response require an active alertness (Hilgard 1968, p. 291).

Moreover, Hilgard's successful athletes (those without other interests) were not able to experience a wide range of imagination and feeling, tended to find less enjoyment in the moment than in anticipation of the outcome ("the final victory"), and were uncomfortable with passive or receptive experiences in light of their action orientation. They also were not prone to contemplation and relaxation (which might indicate higher levels of negative affect or propensity to have elevated levels of SNS activity; i.e., a tendency to be hyperreactive; Hilgard 1968, p. 291). Overall, the involvements of these athletes contrasted markedly with the hypnotizable athletes who were readers (i.e., highs having an interest in reading [a correlate of hypnotizability]) and with hypnotizable adventurers (Hilgard 1968).

Self-report from a Hilgard subject (a low) underscores differences between highs and lows engaged in focused attention:

> You have complete control of yourself in most situations...you lose yourself in the game, but the game has an object, to put the ball in the basket... you are completely concentrated on something in the real world (Hilgard 1968, p. 290; compare this account with that of the high below and note the similarities).

In contrast to losing control during hypnosis (a subsidence of the planning function; Hilgard 1965), this subject stressed "controlled attention" in describing his focus or concentration during sports; a level of attention that is possibly achievable both by highs and lows, outside of hypnosis.

Although most of Hilgard's (1968) sample scored low for hypnotizability regardless of their level of involvement within and outside of sports, there were athletes who were highly susceptible by virtue of other interests. In accounting for these exceptions Hilgard asked the question, "Why do not these other interests (fantasy, free imagination, etc.) interfere with their athletic prowess?" (Hilgard 1968). She concluded that, first, some competitive athletes are able to dissociate the athletic activity from other types of absorption, keeping these spheres of attention entirely separate. Thus, the hypnotic ability, evident in other activities, does not disrupt the reality orientation of competition in these athletes. Second, other competitive athletes have ways of making use of their hypnotic abilities in competition through the kinds of athletic roles they play (e.g., a pitcher in baseball may have different attention demands than a right fielder). Finally, many of these athletes were possibly not primarily competitors at all and, as such, their interests merged with those called "physical space travelers" (Hilgard 1968, p. 292).

The following self-report of an athlete who was high in hypnotic ability is consistent with the first and second points:

> Before a ball game, I set myself emotionally in a particular mood through concentration on making my senses more keen, and my mind more alert. It's a state of mind that's carried me through a ball game. It supports itself, once I set myself.... It's a feeling of complete confidence that I am going to do well, that I'm going to play to the peak of my ability (Hilgard 1968, p. 293).

Interestingly, Hilgard's explanation for why athletes who are highs can focus during competition stresses their ability to prevent the "non-reality" type of absorption or fantasy proneness they tend to engage during other activities (such as reading or viewing art) from manifesting itself during competition and their ability to mobilize information-processing resources more conducive to athletic performance (such as reality-oriented focused attention). Paradoxically, Hilgard maintains that these abilities are more observable in athletes who are lows.

The focused attention athletes who are highs and lows experience outside of hypnosis may demand similar kinds of self-control. Hence, lows and highs who are successful athletes may possibly experience a similar kind or level of attention during competition. Moreover, if attention is one of the most important factors affecting performance, as many contend, then it stands to reason that not only highs are capable of initiating and sustaining intense levels of focused attention, especially because most of Hilgard's athletes were low in hypnotic ability. Otherwise, one is forced to reconsider the role attention plays in successful performance. Thus, if lows are not capable of sustained heightened attention, then some other factor or factors must account for the possibility that successful athletes are not exclusively highs or lows.

In addressing attention during hypnosis, Hilgard (1968) describes the attention highs experience during hypnosis more of in terms of a state of "selective inattention" (in contrast to recent neurophysiological findings that emphasize the ability of highs to enter focused states of attention both in and out hypnosis). She cites evidence showing that hypnotized subjects learn poorly during hypnosis and that the more sustained attention paid to a task is, the less hypnotizable subjects are. This evidence questions the prevalent notion of heightened attention during hypnosis (Das, as cited in Hilgard 1965). Thus, in the context of Hilgard's "selective inattention," the results from her study may not be as paradoxical as they seem (1965, p. 7). However, these differences in attention (heightened vs. selective inattention) may be state dependent. That is, the superlative (attentive) attributes used to describe highs may only be at work at baseline or outside of hypnosis (operating as an omnipresent psychophysiological trait and mode of information processing), but once hypnotized, highs exhibit the selective inattention to which Hilgard refers. This sort of attention may, in fact, not be the kind that is conducive to peak performance and may undermine performance during critical moments, especially when an athlete is concurrently high in neuroticism. Ironically, if this is true, then highs may be better off not using hypnosis in attempting to improve performance and should instead rely on their natural, traitlike propensity for entering focused attention (a type of spontaneously occurring self-hypnosis) in preparation for and in response to salient stimuli, independent of hypnosis.

Accordingly, attention may manifest itself differentially depending on what state an athlete is in (at baseline vs. during induction or hypnotic state or critical moments) and as a function of the estimated level of hypnotic susceptibility a person possesses (Holyroyd 1992).

The Theory of Critical Moments (TCM) hypothesizes that lows may be capable of the same levels of attention that are intrinsically attributed to and experienced by highs during salient tasks and when motivated and as a function of influences of neuroticism and RC on hypnotic ability and absorption, especially during critical moments. Indeed, just because differences in attention have only been documented neurophysiologically at baseline or during hypnosis (in laboratories) does not mean that lows will not exhibit a neurophysiological profile similar to highs during motivated performance. Crawford (1999) agrees that this may be possible because these differences have never been investigated in an ecologically valid setting (e.g., before athletic competition).

Although Hilgard's and the TCM's explanations for the effects of differential levels of hypnotizability on performance may appear divergent, they converge when accounting for the possibility that both highs and lows have the ability to access the highest levels of attention during competition. For example, Hilgard suggests that lows may not be at a disadvantage when it comes to sports, and she does not equate high susceptibility in athletes (regardless of having involvement or noninvolvement in other interests related to hypnotizability) with being necessary for successful performance. On the contrary, her data indicate that low hypnotizability may be more prevalent in competitive athletes. She even proposes that highs who are successful athletes tend to dissociate and revert to styles of information processing and attention more characteristic of lows. For example, before or during competition, athletes who are highs shift to modes of attention that are reality oriented and that focus on the real perceptual and cognitive demands of a sport. In essence, according to this interpretation, successful highs appear to "turn into" lows when competing in sports (at baseline, but not necessarily during critical moments).

In contrast, the TCM proposes that highs may indeed have an intrinsic advantage over lows when it comes to athletic performance at baseline and in the absence of high neuroticism or in the presence of high RC, but TCM stresses that successful lows are capable of accessing a similar mode of information processing and of attaining levels of attention that are characteristic of highs as a function of motivation and of the salience of tasks during competition. Moreover, athletes who are low in hypnotic ability and absorption and who are also low in neuroticism and high in RC will be less burdened with intrusive thoughts than are athletes who are high in hypnotic ability and neuroticism during critical moments. Essentially, in this latter scenario, lows "turn into" highs but are not as susceptible to the downside associated with hypnotic ability and absorption that certain highs will experience under stress. The TCM also predicts that lows will exhibit similar EEG or HRV profiles before or during competition, as highs before and during hypnosis during noncritical routine phases of competition (Harris et al. 1993; Graffin et al. 1995). This latter prediction will be elaborated in the chapter on emerging evidence, in which an Athlete's Profile of neurophysiological functioning will be presented.

Both of the above proposals, although perhaps counterintuitive, strongly indicate that lows have the capacity (or even have an advantage) to enter and sustain states of focused attention during athletic performance, which is consistent with data that will be presented later.

It should again be noted that Hilgard's (1968) findings and hypotheses from the TCM regarding the nature of hypnotic ability in athletes must consider the potential mitigating effects of neuroticism and RC on hypnotic ability. Hypnotic ability can only be viewed singularly or as an independent factor and a potential mediator of attention in the context of baseline and more routine phases of competition. Once stressful critical moments of competition emerge, specific interactions of hypnotic ability/absorption, neuroticism, and RC are expected to differentially influence performance more than any singular TCM-identified PHO factor.

A Case Study: John McEnroe vs. Ivan Lendl

The following case study illustrates how hypnotic ability might exert its influence on performance at baseline and during routine periods of competition. Two former tennis champions—seemingly opposites in terms of personality—are used to show how differential levels of hypnotic ability might influence performance. Although these players were not assessed for hypnotic ability, observable features of their competitive behavior are consistent with the theoretical and empirical nature of this trait.

John McEnroe, considered to be one of the most talented tennis players in history, had an uncanny ability to go into matches with very little practice and still win. This ability indicates that his motor skills were well consolidated in implicit or procedural memory and primed for action. By contrast, Ivan Lendl, another great player, needed long practice sessions before he felt comfortable enough to play a match. He appeared to have more difficulty priming his implicitly stored motor skills for action. These disparities could reflect differences in hypnotic ability, with McEnroe exhibiting tendencies in motor responding more consistent with what one would expect of an athlete who is high in hypnotic ability, whereas Lendl's motor performance propensities are more consistent with persons low in hypnotic ability.

McEnroe was also known for playing at very high levels of technical and tactical proficiency, or in a manner consistent with being in the zone or flow. His ability to effortlessly play up to peak potential is legendary. However, he frequently lost his concentration, at which time he would readily leave the zone and display a major drop in performance. His apparent hypersensitivity to sensory stimuli (e.g., a line-person's decision) may have caused the frequent emotional outbursts he exhibited, with consequent excessive psychophysiological reactivity disrupting his tremendous motor ability and flow states. However, McEnroe's adeptness at quickly altering his stream of consciousness after such outbursts and returning to an attentive and zone state often saved him from certain losses. These tendencies would be expected in an athlete who is high in hypnotic ability.

On the other hand, the reality orientation, stubbornness, and rigidity for which Ivan Lendl was known reflect qualities associated with low hypnotic ability. Lendl's penchant for practicing for hours on end and his ability to ignore pain and injuries are also consistent with the hyposensitivity to psychological and physiological changes that characterizes persons low in hypnotic ability. His realistic and analytic approach to tennis also corresponds with the cognitive style and mode of information processing most frequently accessed by persons who are low in hypnotic ability. For example, Lendl, who never won

Wimbledon (the premier tournament in tennis), undertook one of the most systematic attempts in the history of tennis to win the event late in his career (it turned out to be a failed attempt that was marked by elaborate and even obsessive preparation and planning).

It would have been interesting to assess these two champions for neuroticism and RC (assuming they were accurately appraised regarding hypnotic ability) and to apply criticality statistics to their matches to determine which athlete performed better during critical moments. I suspect that McEnroe was high in neuroticism and Lendl low to midrange in this trait, with both being high in RC, making McEnroe slightly more vulnerable to negative psychological influences during critical moments than Lendl. Both were known as being "clutch" players; however, such anecdotal evidence is often rendered meaningless when subjected to a criticality analysis of objective, longitudinal critical moments of competition.

Characteristics that are associated with hypnotic ability in athletes are summarized in Table 1.

High Hypnotic Ability

- *#1 and #2 Trait Characteristics and Clinical Manifestations:* Attends too much to physical symptoms/exaggerates physical symptoms
- *Sport Performance Analogy:* Excessive attention to technique and physical sensations/vulnerable to motor complaints

Just as the clinical patient often focuses on and exaggerates physical symptoms and their meaning, athletes who are high in hypnotic ability can be perfectionists regarding technical aspects of their game. Highs are expected to be more concerned with how their game or technique looks than with actual performance or outcome. They are often more interested in style than results. Conversely, highs are often very aware of physical sensations and exact body positions associated with technique. They know what their technique looks like, feel when it has gone awry, and are capable of making and feeling corrections. At lower levels, aspiring athletes who are high in hypnotic ability quickly learn technique because of their ability to feel and see technique internally and externally.

A major downside for highs, however, is a tendency to see and feel their technique and physical experience associated with their game more than achieving the goal of the game. "Motor complaints" can be frequent, leading to dissatisfaction with technique that does not correspond with an internal image of what one's technique should look

Table 1 High and Low Hypnotic Ability

	High Hypnotic Ability		Low Hypnotic Ability	
	Clinical Relevance	**Performance Relevance**	**Clinical Relevance**	**Performance Relevance**
1.	Attends too much to physical symptoms	Excessive concern with technical aspects	Ignores physical symptoms	Less concern about technical aspects
2.	Exaggerates significance of physical symptoms	Motor complaints and breakdown in technique	Underestimates significance of symptoms	Less concern about technique and technical problems
3.	Rich images of seeing, hearing, and feeling	Surplus pattern recognition, excess awareness of crowd, noise, opponent and other distractions or superior imagery ability	Skeptical, critical, and analytic mode of information processing	More focused in the here and now, less distractable, reality oriented
4.	Hypersensitivity to psychological and physical change	Need for ideal conditions to perform at best	Deny sensory cues from their bodies	Not as sensitive to psychological and physical changes
5.	Less pain tolerance, heightened awareness of fear (more likely to perceive threat)	Problems when encountering pain, fear of critical moments	Greater pain tolerance	Plays through pain, less likely to fear critical moments
6.	Superior sensory memory and transfer from short- to long-term memory	Heightened motor learning ability, rapid learning consolidation, talent	Less efficient transfer from short- to long-term memory	Longer learning process to integrate physical aspects of game
7.	Deep absorption and focus	Superior concentration, vulnerable to selective inattention	Reality oriented focus	Incremental goal oriented focus
8. / 3.	Cognitive flexibility	Ability to alter mental states to suit the situation	More rigid cognitive style	Less ability to shift focus in accord with changing demands

like. Satisfaction is not so much attained by winning as when perfect technique has been engaged in.

- *#3 Trait Characteristics and Clinical Manifestations:* Rich images of seeing, hearing, and smelling, especially with regard to threatening perceptions
- *Sport Performance Analogy:* Surplus pattern recognition; excess awareness of crowd, noise, opponent, and other distractions; superior imagery ability is involved.

Whereas the clinical patient often uses his rich ability to imagine, see, hear, and smell to focus on threatening perceptions including symptoms and fears, athletes who are high in hypnotic ability can become exceedingly aware of the crowd, noise, their opponent, and other distractions, to the detriment of performance. Their tendency toward surplus pattern recognition, if not channeled into focusing on the task at hand, can undermine their natural propensity or ability to enter zone or flow states. If properly harnessed, surplus pattern recognition allows athletes to see the "big picture," or the whole playing field, the movements of their opponent or opponents, where the players have to move, and whom they need to avoid. This recognition quality facilitates strategic planning and tactical execution. The best way to harness surplus pattern recognition is to use their associated superior imagery ability.

- *#4 Trait Characteristics and Clinical Manifestations:* Hypersensitivity to physical and psychological change
- *Sport Performance Analogy:* Hypersensitivity to changes in playing conditions, progression of competition and personal performance

Clinical patients (highs) are overly aware of change; in fact, they are constantly on "red alert" for change as they monitor symptoms and pain that affect their ability to maintain the equilibrium they so desire. Athletes who are high in hypnotic ability thrive when conditions remain constant. They have a great ability to focus and concentrate on maintaining a high level of technical and tactical performance. They also tend to monitor their progress. If all goes well, they can dominate and stay in the zone, but if things go wrong with their technique, conditions change (e.g., weather, critical moments), or temporal patterns are disrupted, they can readily experience a major drop in performance.

- *#5 Trait Characteristics and Clinical Manifestations:* Less tolerance for pain, heightened awareness of fear (more likely to perceive threat)
- *Sport Performance Analogy:* Less tolerance for pain, greater fear of critical moments.

Persons who are high in hypnotic ability are very aware of bodily sensations and frequently experience minimal discomfort as major pain. They are also more likely to attach meaning to pain, often fearing that even minor pain is a precursor of catastrophic consequences. Athletes who are high in hypnotic ability may have less tolerance for pain occurring during the course of intense competition, as well as a heightened fear of critical moments. These tendencies can lead to psychosomatic reactions such as sudden stomach problems and vomiting, muscle cramps, and other symptoms of pain and subsequent defaulting or being taken out of the game.

- *#6 Trait Characteristics and Clinical Manifestations:* Superior sensory memory and transfer from short to long-term memory
- *Sport Performance Analogy:* Heightened motor learning ability, rapid learning consolidation, talent

Although the superior sensory memory and memory consolidation clinical patients exhibit can lead to learning maladaptive behaviors, in athletes this quality may facilitate motor learning and underlie talent. Athletes who are high in hypnotic ability may require less practice to maintain motor skills once a high level of proficiency has been reached.

- *#7 Trait Characteristics and Clinical Manifestations:* Deep absorption and focus capability
- *Sport Performance Analogy:* Superior concentration, vulnerable to selective inattention

Athletes who are high in hypnotic ability can become deeply absorbed in the task at hand. Applied to the demands of performance, high hypnotic ability can greatly facilitate focus and performance. However, highs can also lose task-specific focus if they become interested in competing stimuli whether it be internal (e.g., an intrusive thought) or external (e.g., noise of the crowd). Selective inattention can inexplicably occur in an apparently highly focused athlete who is high in hypnotic ability.

- *#8 Trait Characteristics and Clinical Manifestations:* Cognitive flexibility
- *Sport Performance Analogy:* Ability to readily alter mental states

Athletes who are high in hypnotic ability often shift their focus or attention from one stimulus to the other. Although this characteristic can have an adaptive function in nonthreatening situations (at base line/routine moments), it can lead to cognitive chaos during stress-laden periods of competition, especially if an athlete is high in neuroticism.

Highs who get angry during noncritical moments of competition usually can quickly regain their composure by shifting attention back to the task at hand, even if they are high in neuroticism. However, during critical moments, shifts in mental states can occur so rapidly that focus on the task at hand is virtually impossible, especially in the presence of high neuroticism.

Low Hypnotic Ability

- *#1 and #2 Trait Characteristics and Clinical Manifestations:* Ignores physical symptoms/underestimates their significance
- *Sport Performance Analogy:* Less concerned with technique and technical problems

Athletes who are low in hypnotic ability tend to be less concerned about the technical aspects of their game during actual competition. Lows are usually more concerned with the results rather than the process and are often more interested in substance than style. However, this does not necessarily mean that lows cannot have excellent technique, it is just that they are not as aware of their technique or how it looks. Lows tend to be unaware of physical sensations and the exact body positions associated with their technique. As a result, they are less capable of making and feeling corrections without intense practice. Aspiring athletes who are low in hypnotic ability need time and patience to learn technique because of their lessened ability to feel and see technique internally and externally. An advantage lows have over highs in this area is that they have a tendency to just play the game, as opposed to being hyperaware of the process. Lows obtain more satisfaction from winning than from performing well or exhibiting good technique. They have nothing against "winning ugly" or getting "dirty," so long as they win. Lows usually need to work harder to become talented, maintain their skills, and be prepared to compete.

- *#3 Trait Characteristics and Clinical Manifestations:* Skeptical, critical, and analytic mode of information processing
- *Sport Performance Analogy:* More focused in the here and now, less distractable, reality oriented

Although athletes who are low in hypnotic ability cannot usually achieve the effortless intense levels of focus that highs can, with effort and practice, lows are capable of maintaining focus on the task at hand and are less burdened with the high's tendency to shift focus from one stimulus to the next. Thus, even though highs at baseline are more likely to achieve "flow," lows are less vulnerable to being distracted over the course of competition. In other words, although highs can focus more intensely without trying, they are more likely than lows to experience a dropoff in concentration as competing internal or external stimuli are encountered during more stressful critical moments of competition. Lows need to practice and train and to increase what I call "concentration intervals," using reality-oriented methods. The reality orientation of lows makes them poor candidates for imagery- or hypnosis-based mental interventions. Lows need to train in real-time, simulating impending competition, to improve their ability to focus. Behavioral techniques should be used to boost the concentration of lows.

- *#4 Trait Characteristics and Clinical Manifestations:* Deny sensory cues from their bodies
- *Sport Performance Analogy:* Not as sensitive to psychological and physical changes

The clinical patient who is low in hypnotic ability is generally unaware of physical and psychological change, often failing to recognize potentially serious symptoms that need medical attention. Athletes who are low in hypnotic ability tend to be unaware of psychological and technical issues associated with performance. Lows have a difficult time recognizing the causes of technical problems and correcting them during competition. They also are less capable of recognizing or admitting that psychological factors may be affecting their performance. For example, athletes who are low in hypnotic ability would not readily admit they lack confidence or that constant outbursts of anger cause them to make excessive errors. The tendency to deny mind–body–performance interactions can also situationally have an adaptive function. Rather than focusing on the mental and physical aspects of carrying out technical and tactical requirements, lows tend to go into competition with more of a "just do it" attitude.

- *#5 Trait Characteristics and Clinical Manifestations:* Greater tolerance for pain
- *Sport Performance Analogy:* Plays through pain, less likely to fear critical moments

Clinical patients who are low in hypnotic ability are generally less aware of bodily sensations. They are also more likely to ignore bodily feelings and pain or to report psychological distress and are less likely to seek medical or psychological attention. Athletes who are low in hypnotic ability have a greater tolerance for pain and are likely to play through bouts of minor injuries and fatigue, and they rarely admit that they are psychologically distressed. Their tendency to ignore physical and psychological stress, although considered admirable by coaches, can lead to excessive physiological reactivity even in the face of no apparent psychological stress. Lows frequently exhibit the previously described incongruence between body language and verbalizations and underlying physiology, which can disrupt motor performance.

- *#6 Trait Characteristics and Clinical Manifestations:* Less efficient transfer from short to long-term memory
- *Sport Performance Analogy:* Longer learning process for integration of physical aspects of game into procedural memory

Athletes who are low in hypnotic ability may require more practice to achieve and maintain motor skills at all levels of technical proficiency. They are generally less adept than highs at using tactile feedback and sensory cues to better consolidate motor learning in long-term procedural memory.

- *#7 Trait Characteristics and Clinical Manifestations:* Reality-oriented focus
- *Sport Performance Analogy:* Incremental goal-oriented focus/reality-based focus

Athletes who are low in hypnotic ability have a more reality-based form of focus or attentional style. Although highs achieve intense focus more effortlessly than lows, lows are less affected by surplus pattern recognition (e.g., noise of the crowd, changes in the environment) that can shift the focus of highs from the task at hand. Lows tend to have a more consistent level of focus but have more difficulty entering the flow or zone states associated with intense, but effortlessly achieved, focus.

- *#8 Trait Characteristics and Clinical Manifestations:* More rigid cognitive style
- *Sport Performance Analogy:* Less able to shift focus in accord with changing demands

In contrast to highs, athletes who are low in hypnotic ability shift their focus or attention from one stimulus to the other less frequently. However, although lows may be less distractable, they are also less capable of changing focus when it might be desirable; for example, during a phase of poor play. Their tendency to rigidly adhere to familiar routines, behavior, and thought patterns can get in the way of creative problem solving in a crisis situation or critical moments. Lows are more adept at practicing and perfecting technique and fixed patterns of play than changing an entrenched pattern of play when it is not working. They are less likely to engage in creative problem solving in the course of competition than highs, preferring instead to rely on efficient preparation and planning.

Absorption in Athletes

As was previously mentioned, absorption is moderately correlated with hypnotic ability (Fromm and Nash 1992) and is considered a lower order factor or component of hypnotic ability and the hypnotic experience. It is also much easier to reliably assess than hypnotic ability, which can be quite time consuming. As a consequence, absorption has often been used in research as an approximate measure of hypnotic ability. Such a practice appears justifiable in that much of the research on the High-Risk Model of Threat Perception that has substituted absorption for hypnotic ability has reported findings on the relationships between absorption and diverse outcome measures consistent with what one would have expected had hypnotic ability been used.

As with hypnotic ability, it is expected that both highs and lows will be equally capable or incapable of experiencing the levels of absorption necessary for optimum performance, situationally. Research addressing what conditions facilitate the deep absorption necessary for relaxation has identified the concept of sets to explain how highs and lows best achieve absorption. An experiential set was found to facilitate absorption in highs, and an instrumental set helped lows better become absorbed (see earlier section on absorption). As a consequence, an important issue relative to absorption and athletes is what sports intrinsically involve experiential or instrumental sets. Assuming that this question can be answered, one might expect highs and lows to perform differentially (when physical and technical factors are equal) depending on the nature of a sport's "set." For example, it is possible that individual sports like tennis, where action and match progress are continuous and incremental, with success being contingent on constant attention and goal orientation, will favor athletes who are low in absorption, whereas such sports as long-distance running, which have minimal external demands on attention, may favor highs. Relative to "peak-like" experiences, although highs may be able to enter a flow-like state more readily than lows, the hypothesized instrumental nature of most sports may render highs incapable of sustaining the experiential set they need to maintain peak or flow-like experiences. Because most competitive sports require planning, decision making, and goal orientation, one might expect most athletes to be low in absorption. The very nature of most sports appears to require an instrumental set to succeed. Thus, for highs to succeed, it may be necessary to suspend their preferred set and to access another one. It is conceivable that successful highs, in contrast to less successful highs, may be more capable of dissociating from their experiential style in favor of an instrumental one during competition, an interpretation that Hilgard (1968) appears to endorse.

The ability of highs and lows to excel at a sport may also be a function of coaching, with the most successful athletes being those who are guided toward their ideal "set" by a coach who is sensitive to high–low differences. As Tellegen suggests (1981, p. 225),

> Using one's knowledge of the trait (absorption), one could contrive conditions under which even for low-absorption subjects the probability of absorbed experiencing would be increased substantially. This might be accomplished through a combination of optimally suggestive instructions (coaching) and the use of highly engaging or even inductive stimuli.

Neuroticism in Athletes

If hypnotic ability/absorption can be viewed as the flow or zone trait, then neuroticism can be seen as the flow or zone "buster," as it is associated with the negative intrusive thoughts and resulting hyperreactivity that are thought to undermine peak performance.

Neuroticism plays an important role in mediating physiological reactivity and thought processes in athletes. High neuroticism is associated with a slow return to baseline after excessive activation of heart rate, blood pressure, EMG, skin conductance, peripheral temperature, or respiration. Thus, one might expect that athletes who are high in neuroticism (highs) to be more susceptible to falling out of their ZOF (Hanin 1980; Wickramasekera 1988). Such athletes (highs) may experience delays in returning to baseline levels of reactivity after stressful situations and during critical moments. For example, an athlete who is high in neuroticism may take longer to recover from an emotional incident like making an easy mistake or getting a bad call from a referee, and they might have difficulty regaining control over his or her motor skills.

A concomitant of high neuroticism (especially in the presence of high hypnotic ability) is the tendency to catastrophize or anticipate the worst possible outcomes when thinking about the future (Wickramasekera 1988). Catastrophizing is a cognitive style of becoming intensely and frequently absorbed in negative psychological or sensory events and talking or thinking about them in ways that increase their aversive properties.

Catastrophizing has indirectly been associated with the disruption of attention in the anecdotal literature and research of sports. Gallwey (1974), in his classic work, *The Inner Game of Tennis*, warns that negative thoughts can interfere with performance. Waller (1988) reported that a lack of thinking and absence of negative intrusive thoughts characterized episodes of peak performance in the athletes she studied.

The catastrophizing athlete can often be heard engaging in negative self-talk during competition. Statements such as "I'm no good," or "I can't hit a ball today" often precipitate spiraling feelings of losing control. One of the most dramatic examples of the effects of catastrophizing involved Miroslav Mecir, a former top-ranked tennis player, who in a match against Jimmy Connors was incapable of getting his serve in. His situation became so extreme that he was forced to serve underhanded. Conceivably, anxiety resulting from his dismal serving that day coupled with his previous reputation as a poor server induced catastrophizing cognitions, negative self-statements, and faulty self-perceptions, which led to a breakdown in his ability to serve.

Mecir's focus of attention may have been on sensory or visceral events that were antecedents or consequences of symptoms, or memories and anticipation of negative physical and psychological consequences as well as antecedents of an aversive event during performance (e.g., serving badly in the past). Such a thought process is believed to precipitate phobias and panic attacks in clinical settings and may have accounted for Mecir's "performance panic attack." Although almost every athlete has experienced a performance panic attack, marked by a breakdown of motor skills during competition, athletes who are higher in neuroticism may be more vulnerable to experiencing such incidents, which are thought to involve a dysfunction in serotonin and norepinephrine metabolism (Sternbach et al. 1976; Wickramasekera 1988).

Although high neuroticism may appear quite detrimental to performance, like hypnotic ability/absorption, at baseline, in the context of more routine phases of competition, it may not manifest its potential negative effects, and it may possibly even be beneficial to certain athletes. Conceivably, high neuroticism could facilitate physiological activation or intensity in athletes who are situationally underactivated. In such instances, athletes who are high in neuroticism, by using certain cognitive strategies (e.g., visualizing aggressive behavior during a match), may be capable of generating emotions that increase activation to levels associated with one's ZOF. Athletes who are high in neuroticism may also benefit from random events occurring during competition that incite them, thereby raising a state of situational sympathetic underactivation to a level necessary for good performance. John McEnroe, the volatile tennis player, was known for performing better after getting a bad call from an umpire or making an easy error—match events that incited or "fired" him up. He may have benefited from a high level of neuroticism at times.

Athletes who are low in neuroticism (lows) are not necessarily better off than highs, as they may have a tendency toward situational underactivation, leading to slow starts (i.e., take longer to reach their ZOF). Such athletes may at times exhibit levels of sympathetic activation that are too low (hypoactivation) for optimum performance. Hence, lows, similar to highs, may benefit from cognitive strategies to generate higher state levels of negative affect (a component/correlate of neuroticism) in an attempt to raise levels of activation (i.e., intensity). For example, lows may resort to thinking of his or her opponent as someone they do not like (a cognition that may be easier to generate by highs).

Neuroticism has two distinct components: one is more cognitive in nature, whereas the second involves psychophysiological responding that occurs as a function of thought processes, with persons high in neuroticism being more likely to become hyperreactive to stressful or negative cognitions. At baseline and during more routine phases of competition, neuroticism-mediated physiological reactivity can benefit the underactivated low- or high-neuroticism athlete. However, once stressful and critical moments of competition are encountered, highs are much more likely to experience the detrimental effects of negative cognitions associated with this trait on psychophysiology and, ultimately, motor ability and performance. The negative effects of high neuroticism will be exacerbated in athletes who are concurrently high in hypnotic ability and low in RC. By contrast, during critical moments, athletes who are low in neuroticism are less likely to experience the same negative intrusive thoughts that highs are apt to encounter.

Although there are references to neuroticism in the literature of sport psychology, most research has failed or has not attempted to link this trait with specific outcome or operationalizations of performance during actual competition. In essence, these studies merely describe mean values for neuroticism in certain populations of athletes but do not demonstrate how this trait may affect performance. For example, Daino (1984) reported that adolescent male and female tennis players were less neurotic than teenagers who did not participate in sports, but the authors did not show or suggest how this finding might be relevant to performance. Geron, Furst, and Rotstein (1986) investigated manifest anxiety (a lower order factor of neuroticism; Watson and Clark 1984) among other traits in heterogeneous groups of athletes participating in various sports. Again, although differences in levels of this trait were found between and within groups, neuroticism was not investigated in the context of specific objective performance outcome criteria (e.g., won–loss record, ranking, etc.).

In general, research indicates that athletes may be lower in neuroticism than nonathletes, although this finding is far from being unequivocal (Eysenck et al. 1982; Becker 1986; Egloff and Gruhn 1996). Although these studies are descriptive and have established limited norms for neuroticism in certain populations of athletes, they appear to have minimal predictive validity.

Neurophysiological studies have located neuroticism in the right brain hemisphere (Davidson 1992a, 1992b; Tomarken et al. 1992a). Interestingly, a recent study of neuroticism extending on previous right hemisphere findings reported not only that neuroticism and depression appear to be linked to right frontal activation but that right activation may also be associated with reduced thresholds for pain in depressive neurotics (Pauli et al. 1999). This finding would be consistent with the anecdotal notion that athletes have a higher threshold for pain and findings that athletes are less prone to depressive psychopathology and high neuroticism.

As with all TCM-identified PHO factors, neuroticism is most likely to exert its effects in the context of critical moments of competition and in interaction with hypnotic ability/absorption and RC.

Repressive Coping in Athletes

RC can be viewed as the "great moderator" of thought processes and the facilitator of self-confidence in athletes. It has important implications for athletes, especially in light of recent research indicating that persons who are high in RC (highs) have an implicit "ability" to prevent negative cognitions, memories, and affect from reaching awareness (Tomarken and Davidson 1994). The ability to "focus" away from aversive situations and memories and the propensity to amplify positive thoughts and self-perception that characterizes highs may have a positive effect on performance. Because negative intrusive cognitions have been associated with right-brain hemisphere activity, the ability of highs to functionally "disconnect" the right from the left hemisphere and other cortical or subcortical regions that are implicated in mediating autonomic and neuroendocrine components of affective responsivity may insulate them from the potential disruptive consequences of such thoughts (Davidson 1984; Fox and Davidson 1984). Moreover, the tendency of highs to have poor memory for negative emotional experiences may help them maintain a positive outlook even after episodes of poor performance during competition (Weinberger et al. 1979; Lane et al. 1990; Wickramasekera et al. 1996b). For example, rather than catastrophize about an easy error, highs may more readily forget such an incident and move on to the next task.

Although the self-deception and concurrent increases in physiological reactivity associated with RC are thought to make highs more susceptible to developing somatic or behavioral symptoms in clinical contexts, increased activation in the absence of high neuroticism may be beneficial to performance. Indeed, heightened autonomic activation in highs is thought to reflect the mobilization of processes that inhibit distress, facilitate goal-oriented behavior, or both—factors that are thought to have an adaptive and positive function in athletes (Bonanno et al. 1991; Tomarken and Davidson 1994; Taylor 1996).

By contrast, lows, who are considered less adept at self-deception, appear more likely to experience psychological symptoms such as depression and anxiety, but less likely to experience psychophysiological symptoms (Lane et al. 1990; Wickramasekera 1998). The implication here is that lows may experience more negative intrusive thoughts and the resulting susceptibility to mental lapses or breakdowns during competition. On the other hand, because lows are less likely to experience physiological hyperreactivity, it is possible that they may be more stable physiologically (i.e., they may be less likely to experience levels of activation that may be detrimental to performance) during baseline and more routine phases of competition.

Because RC is also viewed as a "self-enhancing cognitive style" that promotes the maintenance or enhancement of self-esteem, it may be a trait common to most elite athletes, who are known for having high levels of self-confidence and ego-strength (Carlstedt 1995; Tomarken and Davidson 1994, p. 339). Self-serving and preserving perceptions such as "I am better than my opponent" appear to be important for reaching the upper echelons of a sport (Carlstedt 1995).

Although RC appears to have an adaptive function and benefits for elite athletes, the self-deception component of this trait may also have adverse developmental consequences. For example, highly skilled athletes can be difficult to coach at times (Carlstedt 1995): There is a tendency among some elite athletes to "know it all," with those who get to top of their sport liking to portray themselves as persons who are perfect in the physical and technical sense and wanting to be thought of as "mentally tough" and free of psychological weaknesses (Carlstedt 1995). As such, certain elite athletes often fail to recognize or admit their frailties and have a tendency to reject constructive criticism from coaches (Carlstedt 1995). This may arrest or limit the progress and advancement of certain athletes, especially those who need to develop better skills or who are trying to break out of a slump (i.e., an extended period of performance decrement; Carlstedt 1995; Lufen 1995). RC has not previously been studied in athletes.

Predictions: Constellations of PHO Factors and Performance

Consistent with predictions from the High-Risk Model of Threat Perception in clinical settings, it is expected that specific constellations of hypnotic ability/absorption, neuroticism, and RC in athletes will be more powerful predictors of performance than these individual measures alone, especially during critical moments of competition. The TCM predicts the following:

1. Hypnotic ability/absorption is the PHO factor most directly associated with attention and cognitive/perceptual processes in athletes. Athletes who are high in hypnotic ability/absorption, in the presence of high neuroticism and low RC, will be most vulnerable to negative intrusive thoughts during competition compared with other constellations.
2. High RC will protect athletes who are high hypnotic ability/ absorption from intrusive thoughts that are associated with neuroticism, thereby facilitating the high-hypnotizable's capacity for sustained focused attention.

3. High RC will modulate negative cognitive activity that is associated with neuroticism by preventing aversive intrusive thoughts from reaching consciousness during critical moments of competition regardless of level of hypnotic ability/absorption and neuroticism.

4. High RC mediates intensity levels, or the ideal level of physiological reactivity necessary for optimum performance. High RC will help stabilize physiological reactivity in athletes who are high in neuroticism by preventing negative intrusive thoughts from raising physiological reactivity to levels outside an athlete's ZOF. Conversely, high RC will raise levels of physiological reactivity in athletes who are low in neuroticism that tend to be underactivated.

5. The most mentally tough athletes will be high or low in hypnotic ability/absorption, low in neuroticism, and high in RC. Athletes possessing this constellation of PHO factors will have a distinct implicit advantage during critical moments of competition.

6. The worst possible PHO constellation is high hypnotic ability, high neuroticism, and low RC. Athletes possessing this PHO constellation will be at a distinct and implicit disadvantage during critical moments of competition.

7. Specific neuropsychophysiological responding will occur as a function of an athlete's constellation of PHO factors during critical moments of competition, including shifts from left to right relative cerebral hemispheric activation, increased heart rate deceleration, and decreased muscle tension in secondary (nontask essential) muscles, including the frontalis, in athletes possessing the ideal constellation of PHO measures or Athlete's Profile during critical moments.

Rationale

As previously noted, high hypnotic ability is associated with the capacity for sustained focused attention, an absolute requisite for optimum performance. High hypnotic ability has also been linked to high cardiac vagal tone, a potentially important factor relating to heart rate deceleration that is mediated by the parasympathetic nervous system (i.e., vagally mediated; Carlstedt 1998; Harris et al. 1993). Because HRD is an important marker of attention, cognition, and physiological reactivity and occurs most frequently during episodes of intense focus on a salient, external stimulus (such as a ball during competition), a state more readily accessible by high hypnotizables, athletes who are high in hypnotic ability may have an implicit advantage when it comes to performance at baseline, and in the presence of low neuroticism and high RC during critical moments. High hypnotic ability in the presence of optimum levels of neuroticism and RC may also facilitate attaining flow or zone states associated with effortless peak performance.

High hypnotizables appear to have an inherently enhanced ability to focus on salient tasks, especially in the absence of internal distractions such as intrusive thoughts associated with high neuroticism, especially in the presence of high RC.

Although low hypnotizables may not have an inherent advantage when it comes to focus or readily be able to attain flow or zone states, these athletes may be inherently less vulnerable to internal and external distractions. Athletes who are low in hypnotic ability and neuroticism and high in RC are as likely to benefit from the positive effects of these PHO measures as highs. The type of focus associated with low hypnotic ability is more of an instrumental or reality- and goal-oriented focus that differs from that of highs, which is more esoteric and imagery laden or mediated. In essence, the lower distractibility associated with lows parallels the high-hypnotizables' enhanced ability to rapidly enter states of intense focus situationally.

The only research to date on hypnotic ability in athletes found low hypnotic ability to be more prevalent than high hypnotic ability (Hilgard 1968). This suggests that low hypnotic ability may be at least as beneficial, if not more, than high hypnotic ability in the absence of high neuroticism and the presence of high RC. The fact that low hypnotic ability is associated with an imperviousness to psychological distress (e.g., intrusive thoughts) and physiological signals (e.g., pain), and that low hypnotizables are not introspective or prone to dwell on emotional or interpersonal conflicts, may enhance lows' ability to "just do it," as opposed to thinking about doing it. In general, their realistic and critically oriented cognitive style may enhance their ability to attend, especially when focusing on a salient task during critical moments.

The presence of high RC in an athlete's PHO constellation serves not only to suppress the interhemispheric transfer of negative intrusive thoughts but also to regulate intensity as a function of an athlete's level of neuroticism. In athletes who are low in neuroticism, at baseline, RC can exert its influence to drive motivation and goal orientation, thereby facilitating levels of physiological reactivity necessary for peak performance.

Just as it is predicted that there are ideal constellations of PHO measures, certain constellations will put athletes at an implicit disadvantage during critical moments. The PHO constellation that is expected to be the most detrimental to performance during critical moments consists of PHO factors high hypnotic ability, high neuroticism, and low RC. Athletes exhibiting this profile are hypothesized to be at a distinct and implicit disadvantage compared with athletes exhibiting a more favorable constellation of PHO factors during critical moments.

High hypnotic ability in the presence of high neuroticism and in the absence of high RC may lead to a preponderance of intrusive and catastrophizing thoughts that the high-hypnotizable athlete will tend to focus on obsessively, especially during critical moments of competition. The tendency on the part of high hypnotizables who are concurrently high in negative affect to generate and attend too much on negative intrusive cognitions and visceral sensations (e.g., the subjective sensation that something does not feel right), is hypothesized to interfere with shifts in cerebral laterality and heart rate variability, as focusing on cognitive activity (i.e., internal thoughts) has been linked to heart rate acceleration, a physiological response considered undesirable immediately before action in most competitive situations, as well as to continued relative left-brain hemispheric activity when a shift to right hemisphere activity should be occurring.

Without high RC to suppress the transfer of negative cognitions from being from the right to the left cerebral hemisphere (suppression of relative left-brain hemispheric activity and shift to right-brain hemispheric activity is associated with increases in HRD), athletes having this profile may fall victim to the catastrophizing thoughts associated with high neuroticism and will experience levels of arousal (excessive hyperreactivity) that are not conducive to ideal performance.

5

Neuropsychophysiological Concomitants of Primary Higher Order Factors

In addition to its criticality and primary higher order (PHO) tenets, the Theory of Critical Moments (TCM) advances a multidimensional mind–body model of sport performance. This neuropsychophysiological model of performance identifies key tendencies in neuro- and psychophysiological responding that are thought to underlie peak performance during critical moments of competition. This model consists of an Athlete's Profile of relative brain hemispheric activation at baseline (neuro-developmental trait component) and before critical moments of competition (PHO-state component), a heart rate variability profile marked by psychologically mediated heart rate deceleration during critical moments of competition, and a psychologically mediated muscle tension (EMG) control profile marked by reductions in tension in muscles nonessential to specific sport performance tasks during critical moments.

Ultimately, it is expected that neuropsychophysiological response propensities will help to concurrently validate the PHO tenet and thereby also increase the predictive validity of the TCM. An ancillary goal of this component of the TCM is to more specifically delineate vagaries surrounding the nature of optimum arousal advanced by peak performance models such as the ZOF and Catastrophe theories. My performance models challenge researchers to define parameters of neuropsychophysiological response during competition.

Relative Brain Hemispheric Activation: The Athlete's Profile of Cortical Functioning

The TCM–Athlete's Profile proposes that specific constellations of hypnotic ability/absorption, neuroticism, and repressive coping will induce shifts in relative brain hemispheric activation that can facilitate or undermine performance during critical moments of competition. It was conceptualized in an attempt to integrate previously observed tendencies in neurophysiological (EEG) responding in athletes with brain localization studies of TCM-identified PHO and secondary lower order measures.

Although cortical functioning has been investigated in athletes using EEG, most such research has not considered the role personality traits and behavioral measures play in mediating observed trends in relative hemispheric activation. For example, although it has been shown that just before shooting, the EEG of highly skilled marksmen exhibits reductions in left and increases in right hemispheric activation, it has not been determined whether specific PHO and secondary lower order factors or constellations facilitate or disrupt this profile of situational cortical activity (Rossi and Zani 1986; Hatfield et al. 1987; Salazar et al. 1990).

Cortical Organization and Functioning: Predictions

The TCM predicts that left-brain hemisphere-based repressive coping functions to suppress negative intrusive thoughts associated with right-brain hemisphere-based neuroticism from reaching the left-brain hemisphere.

This helps facilitate the left-brain to right-brain hemispheric shift observed in select EEG studies of athletes immediately before action. This shift in relative cortical activation is most likely to occur in athletes possessing the ideal Athlete's Profile of PHO constellation of high or low hypnotic ability/absorption, low neuroticism, and high repressive coping.

In the absence of high repressive coping, it is predicted that negative intrusive cognitions associated with high neuroticism will be more likely to reach the left hemisphere and disrupt performance. In such instances, the ideal Athlete's Profile will not manifest itself;

instead, relative left hemispheric activation would not shift or give way to right activation immediately before action, indicative of continued relative activation of the verbal, dominant left hemisphere when it should be suppressed (reflective of rumination on negative intrusive thoughts).

It is also predicted that the level of hypnotic ability/absorption will have a differential effect on performance as a function of level of neuroticism. Athletes who are high in hypnotic ability/absorption and neuroticism will tend to ruminate on negative intrusive cognitions associated with high neuroticism, especially during heightened episodes of stress and during critical moments. The presence of high neuroticism in the presence of high hypnotic ability/absorption will disrupt the experiential set that high–hypnotic ability/absorption athletes need to attend well. In this case, the left-to-right shift in EEG that is associated with focus and attention will be disrupted.

Conversely, athletes who are low in hypnotic ability/absorption are expected to be more impervious to negative cognitions associated with neuroticism and will be capable of sustaining the instrumental set they need for optimum performance regardless of the level of neuroticism.

It is also predicted that high repressive coping will modulate the potential negative consequences of high neuroticism on persons high in hypnotic ability/absorption to help maintain their experiential set, thereby allowing highs to attend as well as lows, situationally. In these cases, left-to-right shifts in EEG are less likely to be disrupted.

The dynamics formulated in the above framework are predicted to occur as a function of critical moments. That is, the more critical an instance of competition is, the more likely hypnotic ability/absorption, neuroticism, and repressive coping are expected to exert their effects on neuro- and psychophysiological responding and, ultimately, technical and physical performance (Figures 1–3).

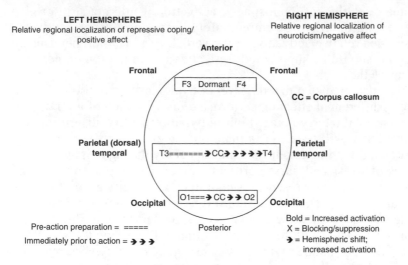

LEFT HEMISPHERE
Relative regional localization of repressive coping/
positive affect

RIGHT HEMISPHERE
Relative regional localization of
neuroticism/negative affect

Anterior

Frontal

Frontal

F3   Dormant   F4

CC = Corpus callosum

Parietal (dorsal)
temporal

Parietal
temporal

T3=======➔CC➔ ➔ ➔ ➔T4

O1===➔ CC➔ ➔ O2

Occipital

Occipital

Pre-action preparation = =====

Posterior

Immediately prior to action = ➔ ➔ ➔

Bold = Increased activation
X = Blocking/suppression
➔ = Hemispheric shift;
     increased activation

Neurophysiological dynamics during routine moments of competition

1. In the absence of critical moments constellations of or individual PHO factors (hypnotic ability/absorption, neuroticism and repressive coping) will remain dormant to contribute positively to technical performance.

2. Pre-action mental preparation will be marked by greater relative activation of the left hemisphere, especially in the region spanning T3 to O1.

3. Immediately prior to action a relative left-to-right hemisphere shift will occur marked by decreasing activation in the general T3 and O1 regions. Increased activation will occur in the general T4 region and especially in the O2 region.

4. A brief period of internal focus gives way seamlessly to right-brain hemisphere external stimulus-oriented focus.

Heart rate deceleration pattern during routine moments of competition

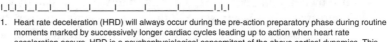

1. Heart rate deceleration (HRD) will always occur during the pre-action preparatory phase during routine moments marked by successively longer cardiac cycles leading up to action when heart rate acceleration occurs. HRD is a psychophysiological concomitant of the above cortical dynamics. This neurocardiologic dynamic can be facilitated or disrupted as a function of constellation of PHO factors, especially during critical moments.

Figure 1. Hypothesized relative brain hemispheric activation as a function of a sport-specific task during routine moments of competition.

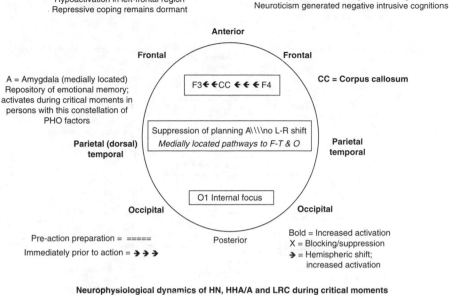

LEFT HEMISPHERE
Hypoactivation in left-frontal region
Repressive coping remains dormant

RIGHT HEMISPHERE
Hyperactivation in right-frontal region
Neuroticism generated negative intrusive cognitions

Anterior

Frontal

Frontal

A = Amygdala (medially located)
Repository of emotional memory;
activates during critical moments in
persons with this constellation of
PHO factors

CC = Corpus callosum

F3 ◄◄ CC ◄ ◄ ◄ F4

Suppression of planning A\\\\no L-R shift
Medially located pathways to F-T & O

**Parietal (dorsal)
temporal**

Parietal
temporal

O1 Internal focus

Occipital

Occipital

Pre-action preparation = =====
Immediately prior to action = ➔ ➔ ➔

Posterior

Bold = Increased activation
X = Blocking/suppression
➔ = Hemispheric shift;
increased activation

Neurophysiological dynamics of HN, HHA/A and LRC during critical moments

1. Amygdala-mediated emotional response activates F4 general region.
2. Resulting negative intrusive thoughts infiltrate F3 general region.
3. Leads to suppression of pre-planning stage prior to action (left hypoactivation).
4. Increases rumination on negative cognitions.
5. Bi-laterally localized hypnotic ability/absorption affects occipital region O1-O2, leading to a disruption of external focus on stimulus (e.g., ball) immediately prior to action as reflected in reduced rCBF, MRI and/or EEG activity in this region when more of such activity should be occurring.
6. Results in loss of focus, motor control and performance.

Concurrent heart rate deceleration pattern associated HN/HHA/A-LRC-CMs

__ l__ l__ l__ l__ l_ l_ll_l_l_ _l_l_l
(depiction of heart rate acceleration–shorter cardiac cycle)

1. Heart rate deceleration will be lacking due to less baroreceptor control over cortical blood flow to the above brain regions, contributing to excessive neuropsychophysiological activation.

Figure 2. Hypothesized effects of high neuroticism, high hypnotic ability/absorption and low repressive coping during critical moments of competition on cortical functioning.

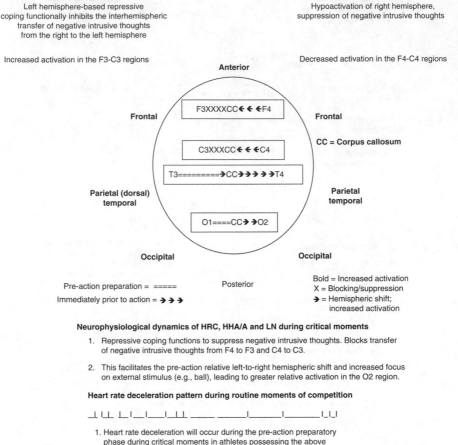

LEFT HEMISPHERE
Left hemisphere-based repressive
coping functionally inhibits the interhemispheric
transfer of negative intrusive thoughts
from the right to the left hemisphere

RIGHT HEMISPHERE
Hypoactivation of right hemisphere,
suppression of negative intrusive thoughts

Increased activation in the F3-C3 regions

Decreased activation in the F4-C4 regions

Anterior

Frontal

F3XXXXCC◄ ◄ ◄F4

C3XXXCC◄ ◄ ◄C4

T3=========➔CC➔➔➔ ➔ ➔T4

O1====CC➔ ➔O2

Frontal

CC = Corpus callosum

Parietal (dorsal)
temporal

Parietal
temporal

Occipital

Posterior

Occipital

Pre-action preparation = =====
Immediately prior to action = ➔ ➔ ➔

Bold = Increased activation
X = Blocking/suppression
➔ = Hemispheric shift;
increased activation

Neurophysiological dynamics of HRC, HHA/A and LN during critical moments

1. Repressive coping functions to suppress negative intrusive thoughts. Blocks transfer
of negative intrusive thoughts from F4 to F3 and C4 to C3.

2. This facilitates the pre-action relative left-to-right hemispheric shift and increased focus
on external stimulus (e.g., ball), leading to greater relative activation in the O2 region.

Heart rate deceleration pattern during routine moments of competition

_I I_I_ I_I__I__I____I_I_I _____ _____I_____I_____I_I_I

1. Heart rate deceleration will occur during the pre-action preparatory
phase during critical moments in athletes possessing the above
constellation of PHO factors.

Figure 3. Hypothesized cortical dynamics of the ideal athlete's profile of PHO factors (high repressive coping, high or low hypnotic ability/absorption and low neuroticism) during critical moments.

II

Emerging Evidence

6

Emerging Evidence: Introduction

The Theory of Critical Moments (TCM) and Athlete's Profile were conceptualized in response to provocative data emanating from my doctoral dissertation research. In addition to establishing a clear profile of relative brain hemispheric activation in athletes, or an Athlete's Profile of cortical functioning, this research, encompassing a large sample of athletes from various sports, provides new insight into how relationships between psychological predictor and performance outcome criterion measures vary significantly as a function of the selected performance statistic. The results also support the TCM proposition that hypnotic ability/absorption, neuroticism, and repressive coping function as primary higher order (PHO) psychological factors in mediating performance.

Several hypotheses were tested. They were designed to determine whether relationships between select predictor variables and objective performance outcome measures would be established, determine whether these relationships would vary as a function of the level of criticality of multiple criterion variables, and determine whether the selected predictor variables would emerge as PHO factors.

Hypotheses

Hypothesis 1: Testing the PHO and the Criticality Tenets

Hypothesis 1 predicted that relationships between and among the selected predictor variables (e.g., PHO factors) and performance outcome measures (e.g., critical moments) would vary from zero to a ceiling level of variance explained as a function of the microlevel of a criterion measure. This hypothesis forms the theoretical basis of the TCM's PHO predictor and criticality tenets (see Figure 4).

This tenet can be supported or rejected on the basis of establishing relationships between TCM-identified PHO psychological predictor variables and select performance outcome measures of varying levels of criticality. The more relationships that emerge between or among the selected predictor variables and the objective statistical indices of performance outcome, the greater the probability that these predictor variables can be considered PHO psychological factors that are capable of influencing the effects secondary lower order psychological variables have on performance, and of performance itself.

Hypothesis 2

Hypothesis 2 predicted that neuroticism and repressive coping interact to affect performance. At lower levels of repressive coping, neuroticism will be negatively correlated with performance. At higher levels of repressive coping, neuroticism will be less negatively correlated with performance.

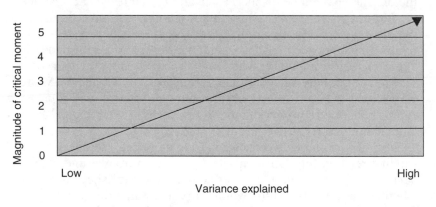

Figure 4. Theoretical relationship between criticality weight and variance explained.

Hypothesis 3

Hypothesis 3 predicted that neuroticism and absorption interact to affect performance. At higher levels of absorption, neuroticism will be negatively correlated with performance. At lower levels of absorption, neuroticism will be less negatively correlated with performance.

Hypothesis 4

Hypothesis 4 predicted that the interaction of neuroticism and absorption in affecting performance varies with level of repressive coping. At lower levels of repressive coping, the neuroticism–absorption interaction will be stronger. At higher levels of repressive coping, the neuroticism–absorption interaction will be weaker.

Hypothesis 5

Hypothesis 5 predicted that rightward errors on the Line-Bisecting Test would be associated with better performance statistics.

Hypothesis 6

Hypothesis 6 predicted that athletes would make more and greater-magnitude rightward errors on the Line-Bisecting Test than nonathletes.

Hypothesis 7

Hypothesis 7 predicted that independent of interactions among absorption, neuroticism, and repressive coping and select criterion measures, singular relationships (correlations) between these measures and performance would emerge at greater microlevels of criticality.

Hypothesis 8

Hypothesis 8 predicted that the most frequent constellation of PHO measures in highly skilled athletes would be low hypnotic ability/absorption, low neuroticism, and high repressive coping.

Participants and Sampling

Participants in this study consisted of college baseball (male), softball (female), basketball (male and female), tennis (male and female), golf (male and female), and soccer (male and female) players who competed in divisions I, II, or III of the National Collegiate Athletic Association, with 699 athletes from approximately 40 colleges and universities volunteering to take part in this study. In addition, control groups totaling 2000 students from previous research were obtained for comparative purposes (Eysenck 1968; Tellegen 1992; Drake and Myers 2000; Nordstrom, unpublished data; Wickramasekera, unpublished data).

In the original design of the study, it was expected that the criterion or dependent variable would be about equally sensitive to the psychological influences associated with the predictor variables (e.g., repressive coping would exert the same effect on performance regardless of sport and criterion/dependent variable). As such, this study planned to use the entire pool of participants (from all sports). However, on scrutinizing the data (especially the criterion/dependent variable) of participants from various subsets of the total sample, it was determined that the wide variability (both qualitative and quantitative) observed in this measure across sports precluded analyzing the data according to the original plan.

Although this discovery was initially disturbing and was thought to be a threat to the external validity of the study, further examination of subsets of data across sports and multiple-criterion variables revealed some very interesting findings and essentially led to the conceptualization of the TCM.

These findings strongly indicate that psychological factors may affect performance uniquely or not at all as a function of a sport-specific baseline conditions during competition and, most important, during critical moments.

Predictor Variable Measures: Test Instruments

Several instruments were used to measure the predictor variables used in the study.

Marlowe-Crowne Scale (MC)

The Marlowe-Crowne Scale (MC) was originally designed to measure social desirability. However, the MC has come to be considered a measure of self-deception and repressive coping (Crowne and Marlowe 1960; Lane et al. 1990). High scores are thought to indicate unconscious psychological defensiveness, as opposed to conscious attempts to deceive others (Lane et al. 1990). The MC consists of 33 items. Eighteen of the items represent highly unlikely positive behaviors (an individual giving a psychologically defensive/repressive response would answer "true" to each of these). Fifteen of the items represent highly likely negative behaviors (the defensive/repressive response would be "false" for each item; Crowne and Marlow 1960, appendix E). Internal consistency (split-half reliability) as high as 0.88 and test–retest reliability as high as 0.89 have been reported (Crowne and Marlowe 1960). Scores on the MC range from 0 to 33 and are based on true–false responses.

Eysenck Personality Inventory

The Eysenck Personality Inventory (EPI) is considered a valid and reliable measure of extraversion–introversion and neuroticism (Eysenck and Eysenck 1968). Test–retest reliability in the range of 0.84–0.94, and split half-reliabilities of 0.80–0.89 in normals and 0.87–0.93 in neurotics have been reported (Eysenck and Eysenck 1968). Scores on the EPI range from 0 to 36 and are based on true–false responses. Although there are numerous valid and reliable instruments that measure neuroticism, the EPI was selected because of its empirical association with physiological reactivity.

Tellegen Absorption Scale

The Tellegen Absorption Scale (TAS) is considered a reliable and valid measure of absorption (Tellegen 1992). It consists of 34 dichotomous (true–false) items involving 9 factors, or content clusters, relating to the trait of absorption, including responsiveness to engaging stimuli, responsiveness to inductive stimuli, ability to often think in images, ability to summon vivid and suggestive images, having "cross-modal" experiences, ability to become absorbed in one's own thoughts and imaginings, ability to vividly reexperience the past, experiencing of episodes of expanded awareness, and ability to experience altered states of consciousness (Tellegen and Atkinson 1974; Roche and McConkey 1990). The score range is from 0 to 34. The (TAS) is reported to have an internal consistency of 0.88 and a 30-day test–retest reliability of 0.91 (Tellegen 1982).

Line-Bisecting Test

The Line-Bisecting Test is considered a valid and reliable measure of relative brain hemispheric activation (Drake and Ulrich 1992). This study used the Drake Paradigm, in which eight lines of varying length (4, 5, and 6 inches) are placed on an A4-size piece of paper from the top to the bottom of the page horizontally in an alternating and offset manner. The direction of errors when neurologically intact persons bisect a series of lines indicates a predominance of cerebral activation in the hemisphere opposite the direction of the error in line bisection (Drake and Myers 2000).

Errors are calculated on the basis of 1/16th-inch increments that deviate to the left or right of true center of a series of eight horizontal lines. Each increment is then multiplied by two to arrive at the error score for each line. Error scores for the eight lines are added to obtain the net error score. Errors to the left receive a negative valance, whereas errors to the right receive a positive valance (Drake paradigm; Drake and Ulrich 1992; Drake and Myers 2000). For example, six lines totaling +30 and two lines totaling 10 would result in a net error score of +20 for the eight lines, indicative of relative left-hemispheric predominance.

The internal consistency of the Line-Bisecting Test was found to range from 0.70 to 0.80. These reliabilities were derived from subsets of athletes from this study, a control group of nonathlete students, and an unpublished investigation of substance abusers (Fortino 2002).

Edinburgh Handedness Inventory

The Edinburgh Handedness Inventory is considered a reliable and valid measure of handedness (Oldfield 1971). This test is the most widely used inventory to assess which hand a person prefers to use the most when engaging in routine activities such as writing, drawing, throwing, brushing one's teeth, or using a spoon. An algebraic formula is used to arrive at a handedness score that ranges between 0 and 100. Only those persons scoring above +60 (persons who are strongly right handed) were studied relative to the Line-Bisecting Test.

Criterion Variables

Several criterion variables were investigated. They were selected on the basis of team-provided statistics. Criterion variables are listed in the order of their hypothesized macro-micro/criticality level in this study, with 5 being the most micro and 1 the least microlevel/most macrolevel:

5. Basketball: Three seasons of player free-throw shooting percentages (most critical)
4. Baseball/softball: Three seasons of player batting average
3. Basketball: Three seasons of player field-goal shooting percentage
2. Soccer: Two seasons of player field-goal shot percentage
1. Tennis: Player won–loss record over three seasons
1. Golf: Player average score per round three seasons (least critical)

The rationale for determining the above levels of criticality is as follows:

1. It was decided that of all the available statistics, free-throw shooting in basketball is the most psychologically mediated because it is a self-paced task dependent on cognitive preparation, free from the direct external interference or influence of an opponent, and thus, possibly more vulnerable to potentially disruptive cognitive processes the TCM has identified (PHO mediated).
2. The baseball and softball outcome measure of batting average was rated slightly lower than basketball free-throw shooting in terms of criticality level, with the pitcher being the extraneous variable in influencing batting performance. Although batting can be self-paced to a certain extent and requires considerable psychological preparation, eventually the pitcher has a significant influence on the batter and batting average, mitigating psychological influences at more macrolevels of criticality. This is reflected in low success rates related to batting, with batting averages in the 30 to 35% range considered to be very good.
3. Although field-goal shooting in basketball is a self-initiated task, it differs from the free-throw in that it is a highly variable task, with shots being taken from varying distances, often with a defender or defenders attempting to disrupt the shot. It is a more spontaneous act, but it can be less deliberate in terms of psychological preparation and involves many physical and extraneous variables. Thus, it was hypothesized that more routine field-goal shots that occur outside the context of critical moments are likely to be less psychologically mediated. Psychological influences on field-goal shooting are more likely to occur at microlevels of competition during critical moments. Compared with free-throw shooting where success rates lower than 70 to 75% are considered average to poor, success rates between 45 and 60% are considered good to very good for field-goal shooting.
4. Soccer shots on goal are even more variable and are affected by more extraneous factors than basketball field goal shooting, with

psychological influences being the greatest during critical moments when the game is on the line. Because such occurrences are not that frequent in soccer, it is difficult deriving enough statistics to adequately test psychological influences on performance in soccer based on shots on goal (nonpenalty shots).

5. The provided tennis (won–loss percentage) and golf statistics (scoring average) were the most global and as a consequence were thought to be the least potent in terms of measuring psychological influences.

In accord with hypothesis 1, it was expected that the greatest amount of variance explained would occur in relationship to micro- or criticality level 5 (most critical), with the least variance explained predicted to occur at level 1 (least critical). It should be again noted that the above criterion measures were rated in terms of criticality in the context of the statistics teams provided for this study. These statistics do not necessarily capture the essence of "true" critical moments that extend much further into microlevels of competition. However, as the results will show, the available statistical outcome measures were sensitive enough to reflect singular/independent relationships between select PHO factors and performance outcome, which attests to the potency of these measures in establishing associations even with more global measures of competition.

Results

The following findings provide support for the TCM criticality and for the PHO tenets and Athlete's Profile. It should be noted that certain nonrevealing relationships between predictor and criterion variables are still considered meaningful and consistent with the TCM criticality tenet—that significant relationships between predictor and criterion variables are most likely to manifest themselves as a function of the potency of the criterion variable, with longitudinal microlevel criterion variables or measures of critical moments (level 5 in this study) being the most potent. For example, although certain multiple regression models as well as simple correlations between a PHO predictor or set of predictor (constellation) variables and specific outcome measures were not revealing, nonfindings are supportive of the TCM if they occur at lower levels of criticality (more macroless microlevels of the criterion measure).

Although this study used objective longitudinal multiple outcome measures that were rated in terms of their microlevel or criticality, these measures were derived from team-provided statistics. They do not reflect specific operationalizations of critical moments that future research must use to test the TCM. It is expected that the deeper one delves into microlevels of performance outcome measures, or the more critical the critical moment, the greater relationships will be between constellations of TCM PHO factors and performance outcome.

Hypothesis 1

Hypothesis 1 was supported on the basis of findings from tests of hypotheses 2 through 5 on basketball, baseball/softball, soccer, and tennis players and golfers, where correlations and variance explained fluctuated widely as a function of the micro- or criticality level of a criterion measure (see Figure 5).

The strongest relationships among PHO predictor variables and performance outcome occurred at levels 4 and 5 on the criticality scale used in this study, as predicted. Conversely, non- or weak relationships occurred at levels 3, 2, or 1.

The fact that the identified PHO variables emerged independently or interactively to influence criterion measures of varying levels of criticality provides support for the hypothesis that the selected PHO factors will affect performance across sports and across athletes. Because no previous studies could be found in which secondary lower order factors predicted performance on the basis of one or more objective statistical performance outcome measures (in single or multiple sports), the findings of this study are especially noteworthy.

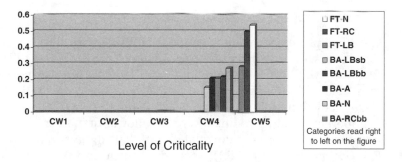

Figure 5. Correlations (*r*) between singular PHO factors and performance. FT = free throw; BA = batting average; N = neuroticism; RC = repressive coping; LB = line-bisecting; A = absorption; sb = softball; bb = basketball.

Hypotheses 2 through 7

Basketball Players: Male and Female

In basketball players, line bisecting was significantly negatively correlated with free-throw percentage ($r = 0.28$, $P = .07$; effect size [d] $=.26$; variance explained [r^2] $= 0.08$). Neuroticism was significantly correlated with free-throw percentage ($r = 0.54$; $P = 0.001$; $d = 0.53$; $r^2 = 0.29$), and repressive coping was significantly negatively correlated with free-throw percentage ($r = 0.50$; $P = .001$; $d = 0.50$; $r^2 = 0.25$), consistent with hypotheses 7.

Interesting and supportive of the TCM hypotheses 1 and 7 is the fact that multiple regression analyses revealed that repressive coping and neuroticism accounted for 44% of the variance in free-throw percentage (level 5 criticality) but did not affect field-goal percentage (level 3 criticality). This is the highest amount of variance explained in an objective longitudinal performance outcome/criterion measure on the basis of psychological predictor variables in any published study to date.

Baseball Players: Male

In baseball players (males), line-bisecting performance was significantly correlated with batting average (performance statistic; $r = 0.22$, $P = .025$; $d = 0.22$; $r^2 = 0.05$). In addition, repressive coping was significantly correlated with batting average ($r = 0.21$, $P = .011$; $d = 0.22$; $r^2 = 0.04$) consistent with hypothesis 7.

Softball Players: Female

In softball players (females), neuroticism was significantly negatively correlated with line-bisecting performance ($r = 0.27$, $P = .003$; $d = .26$; $r^2 = 0.07$). Repressive coping ($r = 0.14$, $P = .08$) was positively correlated with line-bisecting performance consistent with the directional prediction of this hypothesis.

Important general findings were as follows: first, neuroticism was significantly negatively correlated with batting average ($r = 0.15$, $P = .03$; $d = .15$; $r^2 = 0.02$); second, absorption was significantly negatively correlated with both batting average ($r = 0.21$, $d = 0.20$; $r^2 = 0.04$) and line-bisecting performance ($r = 0.17$, $P = 0.04$; $d = .17$; $r^2 = 0.03$). These findings are consistent with hypothesis 7.

Baseball and Softball Players: Combined

In the combined sample of baseball and softball players, neuroticism was significantly negatively correlated with line-bisecting performance ($r = 0.13$, $P = .04$; $d = 0.13$; $r^2 = 0.02$). Important general findings were as follows: first, repressive coping was significantly correlated with batting average ($r = 0.15$, $P = .005$; $d = 0.15$; $r = 0.02$); second, absorption was significantly negatively correlated with batting average ($r = 0.14$, $P = 0.009$; $d = 0.14$; $r^2 = 0.02$). These findings are consistent with hypothesis 7.

Multiple regression analyses in baseball and softball players revealed significant analysis of variance results, indicating that interactions among line-bisecting performance (cerebral laterality), absorption, neuroticism, and repressive coping predicted performance (batting average) to a degree greater than what could be expected by chance alone. Although the variance explained peaked at 0.08 in these regression analyses, this can be considered consistent with predictions from the TCM because the analyses occurred at lower levels of criticality.

Hypothesis 6

Hypothesis 6 (athletes will make more and greater magnitude rightward line-bisecting errors than will nonathletes) was supported in the entire sample of eligible athletes ($N = 250/485$; Edinburgh Handedness Score of 60 or above) from all sports. The robust t statistic ($t = 8.7$, $P < .001$; $d = 1.28$) revealed a large effect size relative to differences in line-bisecting performance between athletes (college students) and nonathletes.

Hypothesis 8

The combination of low absorption, low neuroticism, and high repressive coping was the constellation of personality and behavioral measures exhibited by most athletes, consistent with hypothesis 8 (92 athletes filled the cell associated with this constellation, 26 would have been expected by chance; $P < .001$).

Predictor Variables: Athletes vs. Age-Matched Nonathletes

The entire sample of eligible athletes from all sports revealed that athletes ($N = 485$) were significantly lower in absorption ($M = 16$, SD = 7 vs. 20 [$N = 800$ nonathletes], SD = 7.1; t statistic > 1.96, $P < 0.001$; $d = 0.57$). Athletes and nonathletes did not differ significantly in repressive coping ($M = 14.9$, SD $= 4.9$ [$N = 387$] vs. nonathletes, $M = 14.7$, SD $= 5.1$) and neuroticism ($M = 10.7$, SD $= 4.8$ vs. $M = 10.9$ [$N = 1003$ nonathletes], SD $= 4.7$).

7

Statistical and Empirical Implications

Hypothesis 1

The driving hypothesis of the Theory of Critical Moments (TCM) was supported, with the highest amounts of variance explained on the basis of Primary Higher Order (PHO) factors occurring at criticality levels 5 and 4. No significant amounts of variance explained occurred at criticality levels 3 to 1 (see Figure 6).

Forty-four percent of the variance in basketball free-throw percentage (criticality level 5) was explained on the basis of the PHO factors neuroticism and repressive coping. This is a remarkable finding considering the inability of previous research to explain more than about 10% of the variance in the performance equation on the basis of any combination of psychological factors. This finding is both paradoxical and intriguing in that it runs counter to the hypothesized role the constructs of neuroticism and repressive coping are expected to play in mediating performance. However, at the same time, if interpreted in the context of the presented caveats to the TCM PHO tenet, the results are plausible and explainable. One is reminded that the TCM-identified constructs and their singular, interactive, or combined effects are expected to be the greatest during the most critical moments of

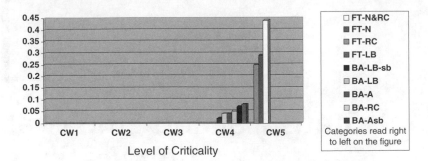

Figure 6. Variance explained on the basis of PHO factor(s). FT = free throw; BA = batting average; N = neuroticism; RC = repressive coping; LB = line bisecting; A = absorption; sb = softball.

competition. Because the free-throw shooting percentage statistics that were available for this study encompassed three seasons worth of free-throw performance and did not specifically isolate critical moments, this statistic, although the highest microlevel category in this study, overall, in relationship to a "perfect" global hierarchy of micro- or critical moments, is in fact still a macrolevel performance outcome measure. In other words, even though global macrolevel free-throw-shooting performance was influenced by neuroticism and repressive coping in a manner running contradictory to what would be predicted regarding their effects during critical moments, the influence of these and other PHO measures on performance can vary from what would be expected during baseline or routine macromoments of competition (noncritical moments).

Despite this finding, it is still predicted that neuroticism and repressive coping will affect performance to an even greater extent in the expected direction during the most real critical moments of competition (exceeding r^2 of 0.44). Thus, findings based on statistics that primarily reflect more routine phases of competition rather than real critical moments per se, and that run contrary to the predicted influences of TCM PHO-identified factors on performance, are considered baseline or noncritical moment findings. Such findings do not necessarily call the primary TCM PHO predictions into question. These primary predictions involving complex two- and three-way interactions of PHO factors are expected to hold up during critical moments of competition.

As a consequence, findings deviating from the main predictions that reflect what occurs during routine macromoments of competition, although not supporting the criticality tenet, do support the PHO tenet that TCM-identified psychological and behavioral factors will affect performance, as shown in a wide array of criterion outcome measures. The more associations that can be established between and among PHO factors/constellations and diverse outcome measures, the more confident one can be in deeming TCM-identified psychological predictor variables as PHO factors that will affect secondary lower-order factors and other processes involved in sport performance (e.g., attention).

The findings on free-throw shooting can also be reconciled in the context of the TCM Athlete's Profile. Although the negative correlation between line bisecting and field-goal shooting percentage runs contrary to the prediction that rightward errors (relative left-brain hemispheric activation) in line bisecting would be associated with better performance, this finding is consistent with brain localization studies of neuroticism and repressive coping. It provides support for the Athlete's Profile, because one would expect that lesser magnitude of rightward error (indicative of a shift to relative right brain hemispheric activation) would be associated with a greater influence of neuroticism and a lesser influence of repressive coping on performance, as was found to be the case relative to free-throw shooting.

Hypotheses 2, 3, 4, and 7

Although the complex multiple regression models proposed in hypotheses 2, 3, and 4 were only partially supported (two- and three-way interactions), variations of these models emerged as supportive of the TCM. Consistent with the TCM, it was expected that widely varying results would occur as a function of the macro-micro level of a criterion variable (i.e., criticality level/critical moment), rendering nonsignificant findings meaningful when viewed in relationship to significant findings. Regarding the failure to fully support hypotheses 2, 3, and 4, these findings can also be explained on the basis of the TCM criticality tenet, with the criterion measures used to test these hypotheses being too macro in nature and, thus, incapable of reflecting PHO influences on performance as proposed in the regression model of hypotheses 1, 2, and 3. Accordingly, complex psychological influences on performance as expressed in multiple regression models containing predictions involving two- and three-way interaction of PHO factors are expected to be the most sensitive and revealing in the context of the most microlevel outcome measure or level of criticality of a critical moment—something future research should consider.

Nevertheless, it should be noted that certain predicted complex interactions held up at the level of the analysis of variance in various multiple regression analyses and, most important, that variations on the initial predictions involving combinations of specific TCM PHO variables were highly revealing, approaching 0.44 of the variance explained.

Independently, individual PHO factors were significantly associated with line bisecting and task-specific sport performance, supportive of hypotheses 5 and 7. In addition, hypothesis 6 was fully supported. Hypothesis 8, which compared personality measures in athletes with those of nonathletes independent of any performance measure, was also partially supported.

Hypothesis 8

As predicted, the most frequent constellation of PHO factors was low absorption and neuroticism and high repressive coping. This finding is consistent with what one would expect on the basis of tendencies in relative cerebral hemispheric activation in athletes. Both cerebral activation and trait/behavior constellations have developmental implications, indicating that the process of becoming a highly skilled athlete is associated with unique cortical organization and behavioral responding. This finding will be elaborated shortly.

The above results were primarily discussed in the context of the TCM PHO and criticality tenets. In the next section, I will discuss the practical and theoretical implications of the above findings and their relevance to applied sport psychological assessment and interventions, starting with the robust findings on relative cerebral activation in athletes and the TCM Athlete's Profile.

Relative Brain Hemispheric Predominance/Activation: Cortical Organization in Athletes

Clearly, the most robust finding was that athletes made significantly more rightward errors on the Line-Bisecting Test than did nonathletes. In addition to a large effect size ($t = 8.7$, $d = 1.28$), reflecting differences in the direction and magnitude of error, it was remarkable that approximately 90% of all eligible athletes erred to the right of center, compared with only 49% of nonathletes. Moreover, when comparing the athlete population of this study with samples from other research, differences in line bisecting became even more pronounced, with only 16 to 45% of participants making rightward errors (Drake and Myers 2000; Jewell and McCourt 2000). This study demonstrated for the first time that highly skilled athletes exhibited marked neglect (rightward errors) when bisecting a line, indicating relative predominance of relative left-brain activation in this population.

Although it was predicted that highly skilled athletes would make more rightward errors on the Line-Bisecting Test, it was not expected that such a high preponderance of athletes sampled would demonstrate relative left-brain hemispheric activation. The robustness of this finding strongly indicates that highly skilled athletes have a cortical organization (trait) or neurophysiological response system (state/trait) that is different, and as Etnier et al. (1996) maintain, more efficient than novices or less skilled athletes. Evidence supporting these contentions include Etnier et al.'s (1996) and Landers et al.'s (1994) studies showing that highly skilled athletes learned new motor skills faster than nonathletes, a process that was associated with relative left-hemispheric predominance. In addition, Fattapposta et al. (1996) demonstrated that elite athletes allocated cortical resources more efficiently when attempting to learn a motor skill they had never engaged in than did nonathletes.

Although learning was not investigated in this dissertation, the fact that relative left-hemisphere predominance stood out to such a great degree is consistent with Etnier et al.'s (1996) and Landers et al.'s (1994) research and tends to support their contentions that the constant repetition associated with achieving a high level of skill may lead to permanent changes in the brain. These changes appear to occur most in the left hemisphere, helping explain why the vast majority of athletes in this study made rightward errors in line bisecting.

Rightward errors in line bisecting may reflect the unique cortical organization of highly skilled athletes, and on the basis of a behavioral measure of cerebral laterality, the line-bisecting results appear to concurrently validate EEG findings, indicating that learning motor tasks is associated with greater changes in the left-brain hemisphere (Landers et al. 1994; Etnier et al. 1996).

One question raised by this apparent discovery is how one can distinguish successful from unsuccessful performance on the basis of indices of cerebral laterality if virtually all athletes exhibit the same basic neurophysiological profile.

Salazar et al.'s (1990) study of elite archers, in which it was found that the left hemisphere not only played a predominant role in the preparation phase of shooting but also was related to better shooting performance, may help answer this question. These researchers demonstrated that the distinguishing marker of success, compared with failure on an athletic task—although still associated with the left hemisphere—appears more specific and is temporally linked to the final phase of carrying out a task (releasing the bow), with subtle alterations in EEG in this last phase (changes in alpha power) accompanying differential outcome (shots on target vs. shots missed). Hence, even though the left hemisphere remains predominant through most phases of action, EEG changes at the microlevel appear to differentiate good from poor performance or outcome (Salazar et al. 1990).

The finding on line bisecting and baseball players (males) in which greater magnitude of error was associated with higher batting averages appears consistent with Salazar et al.'s (1990) study. It also indicates that rightward error on the Line-Bisecting Test may be a longitudinal (trait) behavioral correlate of the predominantly left hemisphere EEG profile that athletes appear to develop as a function of learning and that they exhibit in preparing to engage in a sport-specific task, a profile that has also been associated with better performance.

The fact that line-bisecting error was not related to better performance in females is explained on the basis of the previously advanced thesis that high neuroticism and absorption mediated a negative state-induced response to the line-bisecting task (e.g., heightened emotional reactivity), marked by right hemispheric predominance and leading to poorer performance. Essentially, it is hypothesized that high neuroticism and absorption prevented the Athlete's Profile from manifesting itself; instead a predominantly right-brain hemispheric state disrupted the attentional set that is thought to be necessary for athletes high in absorption to perform successfully. This interpretation finds support in Davidson et.al.'s (1976) study reporting that females demonstrated greater right-hemispheric specificity in response to emotional stimuli.

Because the previously cited research on EEG activity in athletes did not control for PHO factors or emotional reactivity, it is also conceivable and predictable, consistent with the data from this study and the TCM, that the stable relative "left" profile exhibited by fairly homogeneous groups of athletes in a structured laboratory setting may not hold up in the presence of PHO factors/constellations having the potential to disrupt the Athlete's Profile or in the context of more ecologically valid situations involving "real world" stressors (Fahrenberg and Myrtek 1996).

The fact that repressive coping (a protective factor) was related to better performance in males and neuroticism and absorption (disruptive factors) were negatively correlated with performance in females appears to support the above contention and may further help explain why the Athlete's Profile was apparent in men but not women.

Athlete's Profile: State and Trait Issues

The findings on relative cerebral activation in athletes can be attributed to trait, state, or combined state–trait influences on relative brain hemispheric predominance. Hypothesized mediators of line-bisecting tendencies and relative cerebral activation in highly skilled athletes include PHO personality and behavioral measures, situational variables (trait and state), and perceptual, visual (state), and developmental factors (trait) related to cortical organization and neurophysiological functioning (Drake and Ulrich 1992; Drake and Myers 2000; Jewell and McCourt 2000).

In this study, an attempt was made to associate line-bisecting performance and relative cerebral activation with athletic performance and PHO factors. Associations between these variables would tend to support the trait perspective that tendencies in line bisecting reflect stable relationships between cortical organization and personality measures that have been linked to specific regions of the brain. Thus, it might be expected that athletes who made greater rightward errors in bisecting (a marker of left-activation) would be higher in repressive coping and lower in neuroticism than athletes who made less rightward errors, as the former measure or measures are left hemisphere and the latter right hemisphere based. Relative linear relationships between these variables as described would help support the trait view. In addition, a positive correlation between line bisecting and performance would also help advance the trait view, because criticality level 3, 4, and 5 performance statistics in this study are longitudinal markers of sport performance.

Although an analysis of the data revealed significant correlations between certain PHO factors and line bisecting, they did not hold up across gender. For example, even though neuroticism was significantly negatively correlated with line bisecting in females (softball players), no such association was found in males (baseball players). Furthermore, the overall linear trend in females, whereby higher repressive coping approached being significantly correlated with line bisecting (in support of the trait perspective) failed to be replicated in males. Similarly, the significant negative correlation between absorption and line bisecting in females was not evident in males.

Because traits are considered longitudinally stable measures or attributes (Costa and McRae 1997), and because no studies could be found reporting that the personality measures of this study vary significantly as a function of gender, certain data also support a state view of line bisecting. This conclusion was based on the finding that line bisecting was significantly correlated with performance in males but not females. This could be expected, as a driving premise of the TCM criticality tenet is that PHO factors will emerge to affect cerebral activation and performance as a function of the perception of threat during critical moments of competition. As a consequence, gender differences could be seen as noncritical moment findings supportive of the PHO and criticality tenets. It is expected that gender differences will not exist in the context of real critical moments, where constellations of PHO factors are predicted to exert their effects on performance as conceptualized in the TCM criticality tenet, irrespective of gender.

The line-bisecting task can be viewed as a performance task (e.g., a task similar to batting in baseball) or as a state-specific task that may elicit a competitive response. In this study, such a response varied as a function of gender, with all PHO measures being correlated with line-bisecting performance in females (softball players) but not males (baseball players). In particular, neuroticism and absorption stood out as being negatively related to line bisecting in females.

From the state perspective, these findings can be interpreted to indicate that females may be more psychologically reactive to the task of line bisecting compared to males, in whom no significant personality mediated responses were elicited (i.e., no personality measures were remotely associated with line bisecting). High neuroticism in combination with high absorption has been associated with heightened psychophysiological reactivity to laboratory stressors (Wickramasekera and Price 1997). It is possible that most female athletes viewed even an innocuous task such as line bisecting as a competitive challenge, whereas male athletes simply viewed this task as a nonspecific exercise having no real implications in the personal or competitive sense. Indeed, anecdotal evidence including the accounts of some coaches indicates that female athletes may be more reactive to seemingly insignificant moments and situations before and during competition than are men (Pilic 1989). In other words, females may take a seemingly mundane task (such as line bisecting) or noncritical situations in competition more seriously than do males.

There is also empirical support for the contention that females may be more reactive to impending competitive situations than males. For example, Jones and Cale (1989), Gill (1988), and Martens et al. (1990) found that females scored higher on sport-specific trait anxiety, especially immediately before competition, a finding that was replicated by Jones, Swain, and Cale (1991).

If females did, in fact, view line bisecting as a competitive challenge, precompetitive anxiety could have been mediated by catastrophizing cognitions associated with high neuroticism and the propensity of persons high in absorption to focus on their own cognitions, consistent with the TCM tenet that PHO factors will emerge to affect secondary lower-order measures such as competitive anxiety (Wickramasekera and Price 1997). This would help explain the negative correlation between neuroticism and absorption and line bisecting, where it was found that athletes (female) who were high in these traits erred more to the left than athletes who were low in these measures, in support of the state view of relative cerebral activation.

However, one could also argue that gender-specific responses to line bisecting or any task perceived to be competitive in nature represents a differential trait-like propensity, with females being more apt to respond emotionally to most competitive stimuli, regardless of the level of stress that is conventionally associated with such stimuli (or task). By contrast, males may be more (unconsciously) selective as to when they will respond psychologically to specific tasks and less reactive to stimuli that are considered less threatening or neutral (relative to their arousing properties), a tendency that may be mediated by repressive coping.

Certain data of this study lend support to this argument. For example, the fact that neuroticism and absorption were also significantly negatively correlated with batting average (a longitudinal trait-like marker of performance) in females indicates stability or consistency relative to associations between these measures and both a hypothesized state (line bisecting) and a trait marker of performance (batting average). One could argue that this consistent pattern of responding indicates a trait-like relationship between PHO factors (neuroticism and absorption) and performance. A lack of response (as was the case in males) might indicate the same. From this perspective, differential responses to competitive situations may be a stable marker (trait) of gender differences (i.e., gender interacting with performance).

Other evidence also indicates that line bisecting may reflect a stable neuropsychological trait, especially when examined in relationship to personality measures that were not investigated in this study. For example, Drake and Ulrich (1992) and Drake and Myers (2000) reported that line-bisecting performance was associated with positive affect, personal optimism, and risk-taking—left hemisphere-based personality measures—and importantly, they found that these relationships were stable (i.e., reliable) over a 60-day test–retest period.

Drake (2000a) argues that line bisecting reflects a trait-like propensity, pointing out that he would expect athletes to be high in positive affect, personal optimism, risk-taking behavior, and other measures (self-descriptors) that have been investigated in the context of this paradigm (line bisecting), including feelings of being strong, dominant, determined, powerful, and mighty (Drake and Myers 2000). In fact, there is evidence indicating that athletes are higher in many of these and related characteristics than are nonathletes (Eysenck et al. 1982; Edwards 1995; Jones et al. 1996; Newcombe and Boyle 1996; Curry et al. 1997; Grove and Heard 1997; Petersen 1997; O'Sullivan et al. 1998).

In light of these studies, one could posit that the relative left hemispheric predominance overwhelmingly exhibited by athletes may be mediated by left hemisphere-based positive affect. Had this study measured this trait and other left-based personality measures, additional support for the trait perspective may have emerged (positive affect, a left-based trait, was studied in a follow-up investigation that will be reported later in this section).

In this context, it should also be noted that neuroticism, a right hemisphere-based trait, was significantly negatively correlated with line bisecting (in females), in line with what one would expect on the basis of previous neurophysiological evidence (Davidson 1984). This finding appears to extend on the finding by Drake and Myers (2000) that positive but not negative affect was associated with line bisecting, in support of the trait view. Because high neuroticism was linked to less rightward and more leftward errors, this finding appears to partially fill a gap in the Drake and Myers (2000) study, in which a left hemisphere-based trait was associated with line bisecting, but a right hemisphere one was not (negative affect). Neuroticism and negative affect are considered closely related constructs (Watson and Clark 1984).

Moreover, it is interesting to note that a recent study of neuroticism extending on previous right hemisphere findings associated with this PHO measure reported not only that neuroticism and depression appear to be linked to right frontal brain activation but also that right cerebral activation may also be associated with reduced thresholds for pain in depressive neurotics (Pauli et al. 1999). This finding is consistent with the anecdotal notion that athletes have a higher threshold for pain than do nonathletes and fits the data showing that the vast majority of athletes appear to be left-brain hemisphere predominant. Athletes also have been found to have a lower incidence of general psychopathology and depression (Brewer and Petrie 1996).

It should be noted that the above findings could have resulted as a function of singular PHO factors and of and constellations of PHO factors exerting their effects on performance and relative cerebral activation, and not necessarily because of gender. What is more important regarding predictions from the TCM regarding constellations of PHO factors is that absorption and neuroticism interacted to influence performance and relative cerebral activation as predicted. The same pertains to the findings on repressive coping. As a consequence, although gender differences existed in relationship to the effects of PHO factors on performance and relative brain activation, the effects of sex on line-bisecting performance may not be as important as the effects of PHO factors/constellations. Conceivably, PHO factors may have mediated the observed gender differences and not the underlying gender specific biological, genetic, or developmental predispositions per se.

PHO Factors and Relative Brain Hemispheric Activation

Absorption, Neuroticism, and Repressive Coping

Absorption was significantly negatively correlated with rightward errors in line bisecting in females, indicative of less left-brain hemispheric activation in persons high in absorption. Because absorption has been associated with bilateral cortical processing (Taylor et al. 1997), this finding indicates that the right-brain hemisphere-based visual and imaginative components of absorption may have been more predominant before or during line bisecting in females. Considering that absorption was also negatively correlated with performance in females, it is conceivable that in combination with high neuroticism (negatively correlated with line bisecting and batting average), the imaginative components of absorption were focused on negative intrusive thoughts and images. Females who were high in absorption may have maintained both an experiential set and negative cognitions associated with neuroticism and with decreased performance.

Because these effects were not evident in males, it is possible that baseball players who were high in absorption were more capable of suspending their experiential set in favor of an instrumental one, perhaps, as previously suggested, with the help of repressive coping. The fact that neuroticism had no effect on performance (in baseball players) indicates that in males, potential negative aspects of absorption remained dormant, with negative thoughts either not surfacing or being blocked by repressive coping from adversely affecting performance.

The data on absorption in females indicative of relative right hemispheric activation is inconsistent with the Athlete's Profile, in which relative left-brain hemispheric activation shifts to right hemisphere activation before the initiation of an athletic task. Thus, athletes who are concurrently high in absorption and neuroticism may exhibit a neurophysiological profile opposite to the ideal one, whereby right-brain hemisphere-generated negative cognitions and images transfer to and remain active in the left hemisphere before action, thereby blocking or disrupting a shift to the right-brain hemispheric activation associated with preaction preparation (heightened visuoperceptual activity) and consequent better performance. By contrast, in males, repressive coping appeared to function to suppress and prevent the interhemispheric transfer of negative intrusive thoughts associated with neuroticism. This facilitated the emergence of the Athlete's Profile, whereby the cognitive preparatory function of the left brain hemisphere seamlessly gave way to the right brain hemisphere and regulation of visuoperceptual components associated with a sport-specific task immediately before the initiation of action. The fact that repressive coping was significantly correlated with performance in males lends support to this explanation.

The above analysis is an important aspect of the TCM. It attempts to account for the effects of negative intrusive thoughts on cortical functioning and performance and proposes how cognitive processes are mediated by PHO factors. This is a starting point for investigating the yet to be adequately explained anecdotal conjecture surrounding the effects that negative and superfluous cognitions are thought to exert on flow and zone states and, ultimately, on performance (Gallwey 1974; Waller 1988).

Implications and Future Research: Cerebral Activation and Performance

One of the contributions of this study to our understanding of cortical processes in highly skilled athletes is that PHO personality and behavioral factors appear to influence relationships between brain functioning and sport performance. This is something more sophisticated EEG studies have not revealed (nor have they attempted to) with the results of this research confirming with a high degree of empirical certainty that highly skilled athletes overwhelmingly exhibit baseline (trait) and situational (state) relative left-brain hemispheric predominance or activation. Considering that all of the cited EEG studies contained small sample sizes, the fact that this investigation quasi-replicated certain EEG findings on athletes on a large scale is noteworthy and significant (Hatfield et al. 1984; Salazar et al. 1990; Landers et al. 1994; Etnier et al. 1996). This may seem surprising because the Line-Bisecting Test may appear to be a crude measure of cerebral activity. Nevertheless, despite not being sensitive to specific "time-locked" episodes (e.g., preparing to shoot) or capable of illuminating neurophysiological activity at the microlevel, the Line-Bisecting Test may have an advantage over more sophisticated methods used to measure brain function (e.g., EEG, ERP); namely, the ability to efficiently assess relative brain hemispheric predominance longitudinally, situationally, and in relation to PHO factors/constellations.

This is not to say that EEG could not be used in longitudinal designs in which personality and performance measures were involved, just that it would be more difficult to test hundreds of athletes on relationships between these variables with more sophisticated methods.

As a consequence, the robust findings on cerebral laterality attest to the functionality and utility of the Line-Bisecting Test, indicating that it can be used and possibly refined to concurrently validate EEG and ERP studies of cerebral laterality in athletes, similar to clinical settings in which it is frequently used to evaluate brain function in neurologically impaired patients (Cowie and Hamill 1998).

Future research must determine to what extent the Line-Bisecting Test can be used to more precisely assess brain functioning in athletes and to predict performance on the basis of state and PHO trait-mediated changes in relative cerebral activation before and during competition (see Chapter 12). If this method proves reliable, one scenario might involve having an athlete take the Line-Bisecting Test immediately before competition. Considering that line bisecting may reflect affective states (Drake and Myers 2000), this test may be a simple and efficient way to evaluate an athlete's emotions before competition and to intervene accordingly. It may also be interesting to concurrently administer the state version of the Positive Affect Negative Affect Schedule or Profile of Mood States scales to determine to what extent the Line-Bisecting Test is correlated with self-report of affective states before competition (McNair et al. 1971; Watson et al. 1988).

If line-bisecting error reflects a state-like condition or reaction, interventions could be attempted to manipulate emotion in a direction more conducive to better performance. In particular, if left hemisphere activation is found to reflect a state of positive affect or repressive coping, it may be important for an athlete to activate the left hemisphere before or even during competition. Research indicates that brain laterality can be manipulated to achieve a more positive emotional state. For example, Drake (1987) and Merckelbach and van Oppen (1989), by manipulating the direction from which persons were forced to view photographs, found that gazing to the right resulted in more positive evaluations of pictures. In addition, Reuter-Lorenz and Davidson (1981) reported faster response times to faces expressing positive emotions that were presented to the left hemisphere, a finding that may have implications for athletes (e.g., manipulating emotions using directional stimuli to elicit faster reaction times; effects of facial expressions of opponents as a function of direction of attention).

Although the manipulation of attention in the above studies may seem contrived and far removed from the playing field, Schiffer's (1997) research extending on the basic theoretical premise of this body of literature indicates that laterality-based interventions can benefit patients and may be applicable to athletes. Using goggles that were obstructed to promote visual intake by the right visual field of an eye (right or left eye) so as to activate the contralateral hemisphere (left hemsiphere), Schiffer (1997) found that certain patients experienced significantly less anxiety when stimuli were presented to the left hemisphere (right while the left visual field was blocked). Essentially, patients experiencing major depression and posttraumatic stress syndrome reported a significant attentuation of symptoms in conjunction with this goggle-laterality-therapy (Schiffer 1997). Schiffer's (1997) findings are consistent with literature dating back to Dimon, Farrington, and Johnson (1976), associating the left hemisphere with the processing of positive affect.

Obviously, it remains to be seen whether laterality manipulation interventions will work on athletes. Nevertheless, because competitive anxiety is prevalent in sports, this intervention modality should be explored (Crocker et al. 1995). Future research might involve having athletes high in neuroticism and absorption (hypothesized right hemisphere-based) prime themselves before action (e.g., batting) by manipulating their gaze to the right. For example, before stepping into the batter's box or between pitches, baseball or softball players who are high in these traits, while visually scanning the pitcher, would either turn their head to the left so that the right eye would be dominant or would temporarily close their left eye while preparing to hit (to induce activation of the left hemisphere). Recalling Reuter-Lorenz and Davidson's (1981) finding that reaction times were associated with the hemisphere in which facial expressions were processed, a baseball or softball player might use gaze-manipulation while in the batter's box to come to perceive the pitcher in positive terms rather than to fear him or her as a negative adversary. Such a right gaze-generated positive emotion may facilitate reaction time, something that is crucial when trying to hit a ball often traveling over 90 miles per hour. Similarly, athletes could wear goggles blocking the left eye before action in an attempt to create positive emotions and to reduce fear and anxiety.

The goal of such laterality interventions would be to induce a state of positive affect and to potentiate the hypothesized role of repressive coping (Tomarken and Davidson 1994) in preventing the interhemispheric transfer of negative affect in an attempt to block intrusive negative thoughts associated with neuroticism from adversely affecting performance.

In addition to helping facilitate positive emotions, activating the left hemisphere may help generate the Athlete's Profile of neurophysiological functioning that has been observed in a number of studies, independent of emotions or personality factors. As previously noted, left hemispheric predominance is associated with efficient learning, successful preparation, and performance outcome in highly skilled athletes (Etnier et al. 1996; Hatfield et al. 1984; Landers et al. 1994; Salazar et al. 1990).

Limitations and Issues: Line Bisecting and Cerebral Laterality

Although it is widely accepted that numerous hypothesized measures of cerebral laterality including the Line-Bisecting Test reflect relative brain hemispheric predominance, one must consider that there is little psychometric or neurophysiological data to support this belief (Schwartz and Kirsner 1984).

Because virtually no information or data on criterion-related or concurrent validity of line-bisection tests could be found, one could call into question whether the line bisecting actually measures what it purports to (Schwartz and Kirsner 1984). Because it is even difficult to precisely interpret more sensitive measures of hemispheric asymmetries such as EEG, one must be cautious about reaching conclusions on the basis of more simple indices of neurophysiological activity such as the Line-Bisecting Test (Bradshaw et al. 1987; Sarter et al. 1996; Schwartz and Kirsner 1984; Tomarken et al. 1992b).

Ideally, considering the large body of literature on line bisecting (Jewell and McCourt 2000), researchers in this area would have measured brain activity (EEG) concurrent with these instruments to determine whether direction and magnitude of error corresponds with, or exhibits a specific electrophysiological profile that is consistent with, what is assumed about tendencies in line bisecting.

In the case of the Drake paradigm used in this study, in which eight alternating lines of varying lengths are bisected, no published data on the concurrent or criterion-related validity, internal consistency, or reliability of this instrument could be found, possibly calling the interpretations and hypotheses of this study on personality measures and line bisecting into question. One might ask, can conclusions be reached or justified if they are based on assumptions about line bisecting that have yet to be validated? For example, relative to absorption, neuroticism, and line bisecting, is it reasonable to assume that athletes who are high in these traits exhibit right hemispheric predominance on the basis of their correlations with line-bisecting error without knowing to what extent magnitude and direction of error reflect incremental or hemispheric changes in cortical activity? The same could be asked of all conclusions reached on relationships among personality, performance, and line bisecting.

These questions have yet to be unequivocally answered, pointing to the need to validate the Line-Bisecting Test. Although the data are suggestive, further research must determine whether "true" relationships exist between the personality measures of this study, performance, and relative tendencies in brain hemispheric predominance.

In defense of the line-bisecting paradigm, it should be noted that tendencies in bisecting were first studied in the context of patients with brain damage in whom it was discovered that lesions in the right hemisphere resulted in neglect or rightward error when bisecting a line, whereas intact persons tended to err to the left (Brain 1941; Fuji et al. 1995). This led to the extrapolation that direction of error represented activation of the brain hemisphere contralateral to the point of bisection, giving this paradigm a quasi-concurrent or criterion-related validity by default (Drake and Myers 2000; Jewell and McCourt 2000).

Although the line-bisecting model has not been more precisely delineated in term of its neurophysiological correlates or properties, it is nevertheless accepted as a measure of relative cerebral hemispheric predominance (Drake and Ulrich 1992; Drake and Myers 2000; Jewell and McCourt 2000). Moreover, irrespective of the validity of line-bisecting error as a measure of relative hemispheric predominance, as Drake (2000b) has argued, this test can be considered a standardized instrument. Reliabilities calculated in this study and in an unpublished study of substance abusers (Fortino 2000), representing some of the first psychometric information on Line-Bisecting Tests (revealing alphas ranging from 0.70 to 0.80, respectively) tends to support Drake's view, indicating that his paradigm has acceptable internal consistency (Anastasi 1988; see Reliabilities section). As a consequence, it appears that the Drake model can be considered and used as a standardized instrument at least for measuring how persons bisect a line, regardless of the validity of this test as a measure of cerebral laterality. Drake and Myers' (2000) study showing that behavior could be predicted on the basis of line-bisecting performance 6 weeks after initial testing further attests that this instrument's test–retest reliability.

It should be noted that the above caveats, although cautioning against reaching premature and unjustified conclusions on line bisecting, personality, performance, and laterality relationships, do not diminish the robust finding that highly skilled athletes made significantly more and greater rightward errors in line bisecting than did nonathletes. This tendency in line bisecting very likely reflects relative left-brain hemispheric predominance despite the noted limitations.

Athlete's Profile: Limitations

Certain conclusions on cerebral laterality and personality relationships reached in this study were based on a relatively small body of research on cortical functioning in athletes (Hatfield et al. 1984; Salazar et al. 1990; Landers et al. 1994; Etnier et al. 1996). Although overall these studies implicated the left hemisphere as being more predominant in the preparation phases of sport-specific tasks, these findings were not consistent across all sports. For example, this profile did not emerge in golfers while putting or in weightlifters doing arm curls (Gannon et al. 1992; Crews and Landers 1993). Crews and Landers (1993) suggested that differences in EEG profiles between golfers and marksmen were the result of biomechanics specific to each sport, with Gannon et al. (1992) attributing EEG changes across sport-specific tasks to varying cognitive styles or demands associated with processing potentially incongruent stimuli (e.g., looking at the golf ball vs. focusing on internal thoughts before an arm curl).

Thus, although athletes in this study across the sports of baseball, softball, tennis, soccer, golf, and basketball, on the basis of line-bisecting performance, appear to be relatively left-brain hemispheric predominant, one cannot with absolute certainty assume that they would all exhibit the Athlete's Profile proposed by the TCM. However, the assumption that virtually all athletes in this study exhibited the left predominant EEG profile could be seen as central to the interpretation of the data on PHO factors, line-bisecting performance, and cerebral laterality relationships. For example, when positing that repressive coping prevents the transfer of negative thoughts associated with neuroticism from the right to the left hemisphere, thereby facilitating the Athlete's Profile, one must assume that this ideal left profile really exists in baseball or softball players. Otherwise, without knowing with certainty whether these athletes exhibit such a left-biased EEG profile, how can one explain the effects of repressive coping, if the ideal profile turns out to involve predominantly the right hemisphere? In fact, such a scenario exists in the literature, with Kline, Allen, and Schwartz (1998), in contrast to Tomarken and Davidson (1994), reporting that men who were high repressors were relative right-brain hemisphere predominant.

As a consequence, findings running counter to the Athlete's Profile, indicating that EEG profiles vary as a function of sport-specific task or PHO factors, caution one not to assume that this ideal profile is universally present. This may limit the extent to which one can extrapolate on the PHO-cerebral laterality relationships.

Nevertheless, the fact that the vast majority of athletes from all sports made more and greater magnitude rightward errors in line bisecting strongly indicates that highly skilled athletes are relatively left-brain hemispheric predominant regardless of the EEG profiles the athletes have exhibited in previous research, especially when line-bisecting performance and the emerging Athlete's Profile reflect a longitudinal (trait) and baseline (trait) profile of cortical functioning. On the basis of the strongly supportive data of this study, there appear to be at the very least an Athlete's (Behavioral) Profile of Cerebral Laterality (rightward error in line bisecting) irrespective of what EEGs have or might reveal.

As a consequence, it may not be necessary to validate the relationships found in this study on the basis of concurrent indices of cerebral laterality (e.g., EEG/magnetic resonance imaging) if a standardized behavioral measure (line bisecting) establishes its own body of associations among personality, performance, and hemispheric predominance (e.g., between line bisecting, neuroticism, and performance).

Because most neurophysiological measures have been shown to be relatively unstable (Cacioppo and Tassinary 1990; Sarter, Berntson, and Cacioppo 1996) varying significantly temporally and as a function of even slight changes in a stimulus, the line-bisecting task may actually be a more reliable indicator of relatively stable longitudinal tendencies in cerebral laterality than is EEG.

It may be faulty to assume that EEG activity, which reflects responses that are time-locked and linked to specific stimuli, can be reliably used to concurrently validate certain behavioral measures that reflect more global parameters of cortical activity not necessarily associated with a specific stimulus or temporal pattern. For example, it may be possible that athletes who are found to be left predominant on the basis of the Line-Bisecting Test are shown to be right hemispheric predominant when engaging in a sport-specific task that activates the right brain for a brief period of time. Such a finding would not necessarily call into question a hypothesized global and longitudinal measure of cerebral laterality indicating left predominance, as there may not necessarily be a one-to-one correspondence between line bisecting and EEG.

PHO Factors and Performance Relationships

There were nine significant findings between PHO factors/constellations and performance. Although at first glance one might question the consistency and generalizability of such divergent findings across sports, multiple findings are reconcilable and consistent with the TCM. For one, the TCM maintains that hypnotic ability/absorption, neuroticism, and repressive coping will emerge as PHO factors on the basis of their singular and combined ability to influence performance situationally, at baseline during routine phases of competition, and as a function of level of criticality of an outcome measure. Thus, the more significant findings that can be established between PHO factors/constellations and outcome measures the better. A plethora of significant findings support the TCM tenet that hypnotic ability/absorption, neuroticism, and repressive coping are indeed PHO factors. Multiple findings based on the above PHO factors help distinguish these measures from secondary lower order and other psychological variables in terms of their ability to affect performance. Because psychological factors have yet to explain much of the variance in the performance equation, multiple findings attest to the primacy and potency of the selected PHO factors.

As previously mentioned, the strongest finding between PHO factors and performance occurred relative to free-throw shooting percentage in basketball, where neuroticism and repressive coping accounted for 0.44 of the variance in this performance measure (criticality level 5). Neuroticism alone achieved a correlation of 0.54 with free-throw shooting, whereas repressive coping was strongly (0.50) negatively correlated with free-throw shooting. Although these findings on neuroticism and repressive coping may appear inconsistent with their hypothesized function, one must recall that each PHO factor can exert a facilitating or disruptive effect on performance singularly or in combination, depending on the competitive situation and outcome measure used, yet they will influence performance as originally predicted during critical moments. The original and primary predictions made by the TCM regarding constellations or interactions of PHO factors and their effects on performance are expected to hold up in the context of the highest level of criticality or the most critical moment.

It must be reiterated that although free-throw shooting percentage in basketball was deemed to reflect the highest level of criticality in this study, when compared with customized operationalizations of critical moments, free-throw percentage in itself does not necessarily reflect "real" critical moments, only an approximation. As a consequence, a wide array of diverse findings involving PHO factors can emerge without calling the primary TCM predictions into question.

Nevertheless, PHO factors and performance relationships in this study, despite being based on a hybrid hierarchy of critical moments statistics, still emerged as predicted. The strongest relationships occurred at the highest levels of criticality and were supportive of the TCM criticality tenet, despite this study not having access to "real" critical moment statistics.

It is again emphasized that the primary TCM PHO predictions address complex three-way interactions among specific levels of hypnotic ability/absorption, neuroticism, and repressive coping and performance during critical moments. Secondary predictions advance the contention that independent or combined effects of PHO factors can affect performance outside the context of critical moments, conceivably in a direction that runs contrary to what is expected. Findings running contrary to primary TCM predictions that involve only one or two PHO factors or their combination are likely, as any given PHO measure is multidimensional in nature and is capable of exerting facilitating and disruptive effects on performance.

As a consequence, the seemingly contradictory findings on neuroticism and repressive coping and free-throw shooting can be explained as follows: Free-throw shooting is a technically and psychologically challenging task. It demands a high level of focus or concentration and control over mind–body processes. It is also predicated on having good technical skills. Although high neuroticism is associated with negative intrusive cognitions during periods of heightened stress (e.g., critical moments), these thoughts may not necessarily manifest themselves during the more routine phases of competition on which the free-throw statistics in this study were based. As a consequence, the arousal component of neuroticism, a potentially performance-facilitating characteristic of this PHO measure, may have exerted its effect to help basketball players maintain a level of physiological reactivity high enough for optimum concentration when shooting free throws. At the same time, the potentially negative cognitive component of neuroticism remained relatively dormant.

How, though, can one account for the negative effect of repressive coping, the supposed moderator of cognition and suppressor of negative intrusive thoughts, on free-throw shooting? Recall that repressive coping, at baseline, during routine phases of competition and off the playing field, is associated with enhanced self-esteem and confidence. The high levels of repressive coping that facilitate optimism and heightened motivation can also work against certain athletes by making them overconfident. Such athletes may have a distorted and inflated self-image to the point of being unable to recognize their technical flaws and psychological weaknesses. These athletes, instead of working on technical elements of their game, ignore or deny that they have any weaknesses, preferring instead to "will" their way to victory by subscribing to the "just do it" motto, when indeed, major technical training is indicated. Because the mean free-throw shooting percentage in this study's sample was quite low (64%), technical factors very likely contributed to such poor performance. Here, repressive coping exerted a negative effect on performance. Paradoxically, the very characteristics associated with repressive coping that can facilitate performance can also have a detrimental influence on performance.

It should be noted that although neuroticism may help maintain an athlete's ZOF during routine phases of competition (e.g., routine free throws), once critical moments occur, the negative intrusive thoughts associated with neuroticism are expected to drive levels of physiological reactivity upward and out of the ZOF or to disrupt motor performance, especially in athletes who are high in hypnotic ability/absorption and low in repressive coping. Although the technical considerations associated with athletes who are high in repressive coping may not be resolved, athletes who are high in repressive coping will perform at their best during critical moments of competition, whereas athletes who are low in repressive coping and concurrently high in neuroticism and hypnotic ability/absorption, despite possibly having good technical skills, will be more likely to falter. In other words, even though neuroticism may facilitate free-throw shooting, a basketball player who normally shoots 80% during routine phases of competition but who is high in neuroticism may experience significant performance decrements during critical moments.

By contrast, the basketball player who is technically weak when shooting free throws, but who is high in repressive coping, will not perform worse during critical moments; in fact, such a player may shoot for a higher percentage than during routine phases of competition. Essentially, the 80% shooter who is high in neuroticism becomes a 45% shooter during critical moments, and the 50% shooter who is high in repressive coping becomes a 70% shooter during critical moments. Although he has not been assessed for PHO factors, Shaquille O'Neil, who is known for being a poor free-throw shooter in the technical sense, has a history of making free throws when they count the most—which is consistent with an athlete who is high in repressive coping.

Interestingly, neither neuroticism nor repressive coping had an effect on basketball field-goal shooting, and the same was true for any other PHO factor or constellation. This implies that free-throw shooting is more psychological in nature than field-goal shooting and that the statistics used in this study, although macro or global in nature, still contained some critical moment data.

The fact that select PHO factors accounted for 44% of the variance in the performance equation for one and 0% for another task in the same sport attests to the need to investigate psychological–performance relationships in a multidimensional manner and supports the TCM criticality and PHO tenets.

Gender

Gender was found to influence relationships between select PHO factors and outcome measures, indicating that psychological variables can mediate and affect performance as a function of sex. Especially interesting was the finding that repressive coping, considered a protective or facilitative PHO factor, was significantly correlated with performance in males (baseball players), whereas neuroticism and absorption, which are potentially disruptive factors, were significantly negatively correlated with performance in females (softball players). The finding in males is consistent with what one would expect on the basis of the literature, where it has been found that repressive coping appears to prevent the transfer of negative affect or intrusive thoughts associated with neuroticism from the right to left hemisphere (Tomarken and Davidson 1994). Both greater rightward error on line bisecting and high repressive coping were significantly correlated with better performance in males, indicating that neurophysiological processes associated with repressive coping may have been active in facilitating their performance. The fact that neuroticism was not correlated with performance in males lends additional support to the hypothesis that repressive coping may have a protective influence on certain athletes.

Gender-specific findings on performance also indicate that males may benefit more from the facilitative properties of potentially positive PHO measures (in sports) than females, who, based on the data, appeared more vulnerable to potentially negative manifestations of select PHO measures. The fact that a protective PHO factor (repressive coping) was not correlated with performance in females, whereas potential negative trait manifestations (neuroticism and absorption) were, supports this interpretation. Both neuroticism and absorption were negatively correlated with batting average, indicating that repressive coping could not override the potential deleterious effects of these PHO measures in females.

Because mean scores on repressive coping, neuroticism, and absorption did not differ significantly as a function of gender, it appears that males and females may indeed respond differently psychologically before and during more routine phases of competition.

Absorption, Neuroticism, Repressive Coping, and Performance

The most important overall finding on PHO measures was that athletes were significantly lower in absorption than were nonathletes (TAS mean score = 16 vs. 20, $d = 0.57$; hypothesis 8), independent of the between-group differences. The athlete's mean score of 16 is on the cusp of a commonly used cutoff (15) that separates low from medium levels of absorption (Wickramasekera and Price 1997), with 44% of all athletes being low, compared with only 11% (89% of all athletes scored in the low or medium range) being high in absorption—further evidence of the predominately low trait levels of absorption in athletes.

Although absorption was significantly negatively correlated with line bisecting and batting average in females, the fact that most athletes were low in absorption independent of gender and performance measure indicates that athletes may be less likely to develop the type of attentional style commonly associated with high absorption, a propensity that may not be conducive to peak performance in sports.

It is possible that over the course of their athletic development, athletes become more reality focused or task oriented (i.e., less absorptive), learning to sublimate or eliminate certain or all aspects of absorption that may not facilitate optimum attention (contextually [e.g., outside the context of "mental training"] or situationally [e.g., during a competitive moment]), including the ability to summon vivid and suggestive images (possibly negative ones), the ability to have "cross-modal" experiences, the ability to become absorbed in one's own thoughts and imaginings (including negative thoughts and images), and the ability to vividly reexperience the past (including remembering losing experiences; Tellegen and Atkinson 1974; Roche and McConkey 1990).

As previously mentioned, in a study of hypnotic ability Hilgard (1968) reported that most of her successful athletes were low in hypnotic ability (a correlate of absorption; Kirsch and Council 1992; Shames and Bowers 1992) and tended to engage a reality-oriented style of attention or focus-orientation. Even athletes who were high in hypnotic susceptibility used a similar approach to attending as did lows, whereby during competition they learned to block out superfluous mystical or imaginative intrusive thoughts that are often associated with absorption. Hilgard's investigation provides some of the only documented insight (outside of this study) into mental processes associated with absorption in athletes, with the findings from my investigation appearing consistent with her conclusions (Hilgard 1968).

The fact that absorption was significantly negatively correlated with line bisecting and batting average in females partially supports the hypothesis that high absorption may be detrimental to performance. It should be remembered and emphasized that gender differences associated with absorption and performance may be mediated by trait levels of neuroticism because both absorption and neuroticism were negatively correlated with batting average. Again, persons high in absorption are thought to be more vulnerable to intrusive negative and catastrophizing cognitions associated with high neuroticism (Wickramasekera and Price 1997). Athletes who are high in both of these traits may experience levels of physiological reactivity or competitive anxiety that adversely affect performance.

Because neither absorption nor neuroticism manifested themselves relative to personality–performance and personality–laterality relationships in males, one could speculate that in men, repressive coping (which was significantly associated with higher batting averages) protected against intrusive thoughts associated with neuroticism, thereby facilitating absorption in the sport-specific task at hand instead of the rumination on negative cognitions that is associated with neuroticism. Thus, in the presence of repressive coping, the performance-enhancing qualities of absorption are likely to emerge. By contrast, in the absence of repressive coping and the presence of neuroticism, the disruptive side of absorption is likely to affect performance negatively.

A paradox surrounding these findings on absorption–performance relationships (e.g., batting average) and how this construct is conceptualized is difficult to reconcile, especially because many of the components of the absorptive experience are considered to be an integral part of optimum performance. The anecdotal literature of sport performance is replete with references to "peak-like" experiences, "intense focus," or "unawareness" of distracting stimuli (e.g., Gallwey 1974; Waller 1988; Carlstedt 1995)—states that have been associated with absorption (Tellegen and Atkinson 1974; Kihlstrom et al. 1989).

On the basis of these descriptors, one might expect most athletes to be high in absorption. However, the data show this not to be the case. Revisiting the concept of "sets" (Tellegen 1981) may be a good starting point for addressing this paradox and helping to explain why most athletes were low in absorption. Previously, it was hypothesized that sports having an instrumental set (e.g., baseball) involving continuous and incremental action, with success being contingent on constant attention and goal-orientation, would favor athletes who are low in absorption. In contrast, it was posited that sports involving an experiential set (e.g., long-distance running) that have minimal external demands on attention may favor highs.

Because the sports in this study all fall into the former category, it is possible that a different profile for absorption would emerge in, for example, track and field and distance runners or in athletes from other sports in which one competes more against oneself or time (e.g., skiing, gymnastics, weightlifting, shooting) than against an opponent.

In fact, opponents who are constantly trying to disrupt the attention and flow of athletes may be an important variable that hinders achieving the peak-like experiences associated with high absorption. Although highs may be able to enter a flow-like state more readily than lows, the hypothesized instrumental nature of most sports, coupled with the potentially distracting influence of an opponent or even the noise from the crowd, may render highs incapable of sustaining the experiential set they need to maintain high absorption during sports.

External noise may negatively exert its influence in a manner analogous to the biofeedback signal in certain laboratory experiments, whereby the instrumental nature of this noise (signal) interferes with the experiential set highs seem to need to achieve relaxation (Qualls and Sheenan 1979).

It is also possible, especially in sports like baseball and softball, where players often are not involved in any action for longer periods of time, that highs may more likely become absorbed in thoughts and images that are not relevant to the actual game (i.e., have a "wandering mind"). Such a loss of sport-specific concentration might explain unexpected blunders or errors in normally highly skilled athletes who have become "lost in their own thoughts" at the wrong moment (total immersion or absorption to the point of forgetting the actual game at hand).

By contrast, highs who do succeed in instrumentally oriented sports may be those athletes (highs) who are more capable of dissociating from their experiential set in favor of an instrumental one, as Hilgard (1968) suggested.

As a consequence, the ability to experience the peak-like experiences or "flow" associated with optimum performance and absorption may be contingent on matching sets with an athlete's level of absorption. When matched with an instrumental set, lows may be just as capable as highs of achieving states of sport-specific absorption that facilitate performance. Conversely, highs who normally are expected to be more capable of readily accessing deep states of attention may not achieve heightened levels of focus when attempting to attend within a set that is not ideal for their type of absorption (i.e., they may be involved in a sport that is not ideal for their "absorptive style").

Future research must determine whether sports that are hypothesized to be favorable for the experiential set are composed more of athletes who are high in absorption and whether high absorption is associated with better performance in these sports.

Hypothesis 8: Repressive Coping and Neuroticism

In addition to establishing relationships between relative cerebral activation, PHO factors, and performance, this investigation also found that athletes exhibited levels of PHO measures that differed significantly from other samples of nonathletes (students) independent of performance, partially confirming hypothesis 8. As previously reported, athletes were significantly lower in absorption than were nonathletes. Although no differences in repressive coping and neuroticism were found, it should be noted that the most frequent combination of personality traits included high repressive coping, low neuroticism, and low absorption, with 92 out of 699 athletes falling into the high repressive coping, low neuroticism, and low absorption cell (only 25 would be expected by chance alone; $P < 0.001$). In addition, 48% of all athletes were high in repressive coping (Marlowe Crowne score of 16 or above; only 33% would be expected by chance alone; $P < 0.01$), with 72% of all athletes being medium or high in repressive coping. The data and findings on absorption and repressive coping are the first on these measures to be obtained on athletes.

Implications: PHO Factors and Performance

Absorption

Because it appears that athletes are disproportionately low in absorption, it may be advisable to "red-flag" athletes who are high in this trait. Highs may be more vulnerable to fluctuations in sport-specific attention and, despite having the potential to more readily achieve flow-like concentration, may have to be guided toward such an attentive state using specific interventions (Tellegen 1981). As a consequence, it may be important to assess absorption in athletes and especially to identify highs, who, ironically, may not only have the most potential for achieving highest levels of attention but also could be most susceptible to losing their focus.

Research indicates that imagery-based interventions and hypnosis may be better suited for highs, with lows responding more favorably to cognitive–behavioral interventions and biofeedback (Wickramasekera and Price 1997). Unfortunately, high–low differences in absorption are rarely, if ever, assessed in athletes.

The tendency to apply mental training interventions en masse irrespective of a person's psychological profile may contribute to some of the inconsistent results associated with mental training (Morgan 1997). For example, one of the most popular interventions in sports, imagery, assumes that virtually all athletes are capable of effectively using visualization, when, in fact, wide variability may exist relative to who can potentially benefit from this modality (Morgan 1997).

Because high absorption has been associated with an increased ability to visualize and use imagery, with lows being less capable of accessing this cognitive mode, the rationale for implementing one of the most used approaches to the enhancement of performance may be fundamentally flawed (Gould and Damarjian 1996). The fact that as few as 11% of athletes were found to be high in absorption indicates that only a small portion of athletes may actually be capable of benefiting from imagery or other visualization techniques. Considering that 89% of athletes in this study were low to medium in absorption, should such persons indeed to be found less capable of using imagery, the field of sport psychology may have to discard the prevalent assumption that this intervention modality will help most athletes and have to revise the manner in which it applies this method.

Assessing absorption in athletes may be crucial for determining who will most likely benefit from one of the most widely taught and used methods of mental training (Gould and Damarjian 1996).

Repressive Coping

Although it was hypothesized that repressive coping may differentially affect an athlete's ability to deal with intrusive thoughts during competition, it has yet to be established whether this type of coping can be manipulated. Because repressive coping appears to occur on an unconscious level (Schwartz 1990), we may be dealing with a firmly entrenched behavioral propensity that cannot be accessed through conscious attempts or managed using specific interventions.

If repressive coping cannot be manipulated, then athletes who are high in this trait may have an intrinsic advantage over lows when it comes to being able to block negative and intrusive thoughts from consciousness during competition. However, even if this behavioral mechanism cannot be directly manipulated, it is conceivable that lows could learn to consciously prevent negative intrusive thoughts from disrupting performance. Cognitive strategies such as thought stoppage, countering, or self-talk (Williams and Leffingwell 1996) could be used by lows in an attempt to fend off intrusive thoughts.

Moreover, because high repressive coping appears to be a left hemisphere-based mechanism (Tomarken and Davidson 1994), it is also possible that the previously mentioned laterality–manipulation interventions (Drake and Ulrich 1992; Merckelbach and van Oppen 1989; Schiffer 1997) could be used to induce states of positive affect in lows. Because positive affect and repressive coping appear to involve similar adaptive mechanisms or styles of information processing (Bonanno and Singer 1990), the activation of positive affect through a laterality intervention may help override the hypothesized reduced capability of lows to suppress negative intrusive cognitions.

Assessing repressive coping may help identify athletes who are more susceptible to the potential deleterious effects of faulty thought patterns. Especially in male athletes, where it was shown that high repressive coping was associated with better performance, it may be important to know who is more or less capable of suppressing negative intrusive thoughts. Athletes identified as low in repressive coping could also be taught the above-mentioned cognitive interventions to recognize and counter unwanted thoughts.

Although repressive coping was not directly associated with performance in females, the fact that absorption and neuroticism were suggests that repressive coping could not overcome negative and intrusive thoughts. As previously hypothesized, absorption and neuroticism may have prevented repressive coping and left hemisphere activation from emerging to facilitate performance.

As a consequence, cognitive strategies or laterality interventions could also be used to help female athletes high in absorption and neuroticism attain the left predominant state associated with high repressive coping, positive affect, and better performance.

Neuroticism

Neuroticism appears to have fulfilled its hypothesized role in the performance equation, at least in females (softball players), where it was associated with less-rightward errors on the Line-Bisecting Test and with lower batting average. As such, it appears to be a trait that can affect performance particularly in the presence of high absorption and low repressive coping. Although males were not affected by this trait, as previously argued, this may have been the result of the protective influence of repressive coping.

Because this study advances a theory that intrusive and negative thoughts associated with neuroticism are likely to disrupt performance, it may be important to routinely assess neuroticism in athletes. As with athletes who are high in absorption, neurotics (athletes high in neuroticism) should be screened and dealt with in a preemptive manner. Interventions could be used to help monitor and regulate psychophysiological functioning of highs. Biofeedback may be the intervention of choice to reduce the hyperreactivity commonly observed in highs along with cognitive strategies for countering the propensity of neurotics to engage in negative thought patterns (Wickramasekera 1988). The decision on what intervention strategy to use in athletes high in neuroticism should also take an athlete's level of absorption into account.

Limitations and Issues: Personality and Performance

Certain results from this study may not have captured the "real" essence of personality–performance relationships, possibly leading to an underestimation of effect sizes and variance explained. In this study, the effects that personality measures could exert on performance may have been constrained by physical (e.g., speed, reflexes, power), technical (e.g., form, technique, biomechanics), and important situational factors (e.g., influence of opponents, teammates, preparation, training). For example, personality measures may have been more likely to exert their influence in the context of critical moments, when an athlete is more likely to experience greater psychological stress. However, because it was not possible to obtain data on the criterion variable (batting average) during critical moments, certain small effect sizes and variance explained resulted from examining relationships between the predictor and criterion variables during routine phases of competition, a more global context that is considered less than ideal for isolating the effects of personality on performance. Malatesta and Wilson (1988) maintain that personality and emotions exhibit themselves most clearly under stressful conditions (e.g., critical moments). Thus, had it been possible to investigate personality and performance during critical moments, stronger results may have been obtained.

It should also be noted that sports involve opponents who are constantly attempting to disrupt or hinder the performance of an athlete. As such, even persons possessing "ideal" levels or combinations of certain personality traits may be vulnerable to an opponent's stellar defensive or offensive play. In such cases, a criterion or dependent variable (performance indicator) may not accurately reflect the influence that personality may have on performance, potentially resulting in a distorted correlation coefficient, effect size, or variance explained.

Nevertheless, even if the variance explained or effect sizes reported in this study accurately reflect the statistical extent of a relationship, as Cohen (1988, p. 535) argues, "the meaning of any given effect size (or variance explained) is in the final analysis, a function of the context in which it embedded." Eysenck, Nias, and Cox (1982) agree, maintaining that accounting for only 7 to 10% of the variance in performance on the basis of personality measures (i.e., the total added variance; e.g., repressive coping + neuroticism + absorption = total variance) can be viewed as considerable even if the variance explained by each individual factor is small. Therefore, considering the lack of positive findings on certain personality–performance relationships in athletes, where traits have rarely been investigated in the context of specific operationalizations of performance, any significant finding may be meaningful regardless of the size of an effect or variance explained. Thus, even low variance explained at criticality levels 1 to 3 in this study can be considered significant and important and can attest to the selection of potent predictor variables in this study. Moreover, the high variance explained at the upper criticality levels show that successful prediction of performance depends on the dependent variables.

Additional Directions for Future Research

Because most of the hypotheses of this study were derived from research and findings in clinical and nonsport experimental settings, it may be important to investigate these measures in the context of sport-specific paradigms. For example, when studying the Athlete's Profile, it is recommended that researchers control for repressive coping, absorption, and neuroticism to ascertain whether these traits and measures are related to tendencies in relative hemispheric activation similar to those observed in nonsport EEG studies. Will athletes who are high repressors exhibit a relative left predominant profile in a sport-specific EEG paradigm (e.g., Hatfield, Landers and Ray 1984), as nonathlete repressors did in Tomarken and Davidson's (1984) laboratory studies? It would also be interesting to determine whether the hypothesized associations between absorption and neuroticism and cerebral laterality could be confirmed in sport-specific EEG studies.

Relative to relationships between personality and performance, sport-specific paradigms should also be created to directly test some of the hypotheses of this dissertation. For example, studies could investigate whether repressive coping affects the performance of athletes in sport-specific experiments. One way of doing this might be to subliminally interject negative stimuli (words or pictures delivered below auditory or visual thresholds) while athletes engage in a reaction-time task or play a video game to determine whether and how this behavioral response (repressive coping) affects performance. Similar experiments could be structured to investigate the effect absorption and neuroticism may have on performance.

The effects of absorption could be tested by requiring highs and lows to engage in a repetitious sport-specific task; for example, hitting a ball over the net as many times as possible. Error rates would then be analyzed to determine how highs and lows differentially attend when engaged in a monotonous task.

Neuroticism and performance relationships could be studied by monitoring physiological systems while athletes perform a stressful task (e.g., while they play a road racing video game), or even during actual competition (Carlstedt 1998).

The combined effects of these measures should also be studied in the context of sport-specific paradigms. All measures should also be investigated in the context of interventions to enhance performance as well. It may be important to determine to what extent absorption is related to an athlete's ability to benefit from imagery, hypnosis, and biofeedback. These and the previously proposed directions for future research may lead to more robust findings and concurrently help validate some of the suggestive findings of this book.

Conclusions

One of the major strengths of the investigation is that it was multidimensional and longitudinal by design, allowing for the testing of multiple hypotheses involving predictor–criterion relationships across time, sports, sport-specific task demands, and numerous statistical categories at the intraindividual level. Such a multifaceted approach resulted in revealing findings that would have gone unnoticed had the study been limited to one sport, a single statistic as an outcome measure, or a small sample size.

Although this study employed a multidimensional approach to the study of psychological factors and performance outcome, it should be noted that this research was still limited by its dependence on performance statistics made available by participating teams. These statistics were not conceived of specifically to measure psychological influences on performance. As a consequence, the depth of microlevel of criterion variables in this study was not as great as desired had customized critical moment statistics been available. However, the fact that levels of variance explained spanned a wide range as a function of diverse criterion measures indicates that even at "more," the macrolevel, or "less," the microlevel, of the criterion variable, the deeper or more micro the level of a performance outcome measure is, the greater influence psychological variables can be shown to have on performance. In other words, the criterion measures used in this study, despite not being customized critical moments statistics, still were "deep" or microlevel enough to reflect psychological influences on performance. Three seasons of performance statistics led to the discovery of significant correlations between and among predictor variables and performance outcome measures that would not have been apparent on the basis of one season of performance statistics or other more global criterion measures. This supports using a longitudinal design when studying psychological–performance relationships.

It has been pointed out that although the TCM has isolated specific predictor variables as being PHO psychological variables, conceivably, future research that adheres to the TCM's criticality tenet (the more microlevel the criterion measure, the greater the probability of finding psychological–performance relationships) may also discover significant relationships between psychological predictor variables not identified by the TCM. Reanalysis of previous research using new microlevel criterion measures may also lead to new discoveries, retrospectively.

Such findings would be welcome even if they were to call into question the TCM's hypothesis that hypnotic ability/absorption, neuroticism, and repressive coping will modulate virtually any psychological–performance relationship during critical moments of competition. Should important new relationships between psychological and performance measures be discovered on the basis of objective microlevel criterion variables, researchers are still cautioned and urged to control for the PHO variables the TCM has identified, as they are expected to influence psychophysiology and psychological and behavioral factors that have been associated with performance, especially outside of baseline or routine phases of competition.

The results of this investigation supported the TCM's tenet that the greater the level of criticality of a competitive moment, the greater the probability that significant relationships between psychological predictor variables and performance outcome will exist.

Thus, for future research on psychological factors and performance to be most revealing, outcome measures will need to center on critical moments of competition, which will require the development of special critical moment statistics that go much beyond the deepest microlevel criterion variables used in this study (longitudinal—three seasons of performance statistics).

8

Psychophysiological Concomitants of Primary Higher Order Factors and the Athlete's Profile: Ambulatory Psychophysiology

A theory develops and gains credibility as a function of supportive findings from the research it stimulates and to the extent that initial results can be replicated and validated concurrently on the basis of multiple outcome measures. Because the Theory of Critical Moments (TCM) advances a mind–body model of sport performance, it is essential that physiological concomitants or correlates of primary higher order (PHO) constellations can be isolated, especially during critical moments of competition. The presence of consistently manifested trends of physiological responding during crucial phases of competition would serve to concurrently validate the effects that psychological variables (PHO factors) have been shown to exert on performance. The following study on heart rate variability (HRV), using methods in ambulatory psychophysiology, was carried out in an attempt to validate concurrently certain psychophysiological components of the TCM.

Ambulatory Psychophysiology: Athlete Monitoring and Analysis

Ambulatory psychophysiology involves the continuous physiological monitoring and observation of athletes during real competition (Carlstedt 2001). It is particularly valuable to the study of athletes, where it is imperative that research findings have a high degree of ecological validity (i.e., the data must be procured from and reflect conditions encountered in context-specific situations; Fahrenberg and Myrtek 1996). For example, it is not sufficient to assume that shifts in relative brain hemispheric activation that were observed in an experimental situation will transfer to the playing field without measuring brain functioning during real competition. Similarly, because the ecological validity of physiological responses induced in the laboratory has been challenged, it cannot be assumed that an analysis of HRV in vitro will be predictive of an athlete's autonomic balance during real competition (de Geus and van Doornen 1996; van Doornen et al. 1994).

Although strong relationships were established between PHO factors and performance, it is still important to determine to what extent psychological and behavioral measures that were derived from self-report instruments fulfill their hypothesized roles in mediating psychophysiology. Ultimately, lawful tendencies in physiological responding that are observed during real competition will help explain the dynamics of PHO factors/constellations in the performance equation. As a result, it is necessary to leave the laboratory to obtain a more ecologically valid assessment of athletes by determining whether the predicted effects of PHO on physiological responding are manifested during real competition (critical moments).

Although the value of ambulatory psychophysiological assessment has been recognized, it is a relatively unexplored and underused procedure in sport psychology despite the fact that many of the central constructs and theories of sport performance have physiological and psychophysiological components (Heil and Henschen 1996; Taylor 1996). For example, Yerkes and Dodson's (1908) Inverted-U Theory proposes that a curvilinear relationship exists between physiological reactivity and performance, whereby increases in reactivity result in incremental improvement in performance, but only to a certain point, after which excessive reactivity disrupts performance. The psychophysiological concomitants of the Inverted-U Theory are delineated in

Duffy's (1972) description of activation theory and include increasing levels of heart rate (HR), blood pressure (BP), muscle tension, skin conductance, and desynchronization of electroencephalographic (EEG) alpha activity. In extending the Inverted-U Theory to account for individual differences in physiological reactivity, Hanin's (1980) Zone of Optimal Functioning theory is also based on similar physiological markers of activation or intensity. Catastrophe Theory, the most recent postulate of intensity, similarly alludes to physiological processes (Hardy and Fazey 1987). This theory advances the idea that cognitive anxiety mediates the effects of physiological arousal on performance (Hardy and Fazey 1987).

Unfortunately, many of the physiological measures to which these theories allude have not been operationalized beyond the theoretical. Little is known about the psychophysiological functioning of athletes during actual competition. Attempts to delineate physiological functioning during real competitive events have been nonexistent, with the field of sport psychology still relying on imprecise operationalizations of key physiological elements of sport performance. This is illustrated in Taylor's (1996) view of intensity, to which he refers as the most crucial factor during competition because, no matter how confident, motivated, or technically or physically prepared athletes are to perform, they will simply not be able to perform their best if their bodies are not at an optimal level of intensity, accompanied by the requisite physiological and psychological changes (Taylor 1996, p. 75). In viewing Taylor's notion of intensity, one must ask what "confident" and "motivated" mean. Also, what is an "optimal level of intensity," and what are "requisite physiological" and "psychological changes" that accompany intensity? These questions have yet to be answered. Without studying the components and effects of physiological and psychophysiological processes on performance, assumptions about intensity or states of activation and performance remain speculative. The ultimate goal of ambulatory psychophysiology in sports is to establish performance relationships that have a high degree of ecological validity as well as to derive methods for testing the efficacy of interventions and replicating laboratory data that have implications for performance. To date, the use of ambulatory psychophysiology in studying performance has been neglected, despite the potential it holds for acquiring data that may be vital to the validity of many of the theories and interventions of sport psychology. In the following study, relationships between PHO factors, psychophysiology, and performance were investigated using methods in ambulatory psychophysiology.

Background and Review of the Literature

Heart Activity: An Ideal Measure of Psychological Performance

Research has revealed significant interactions between the cardiovascular system, the central nervous system, and the somatic nervous system (Andreassi 1995). One line of research has established relationships between cardiac activity and reaction time (RT), with Lacey and Lacey (1964); Obrist, Webb, and Sutterer (1969); and Webb and Obrist (1970) reporting decreased heart rate (HRD) during the fixed foreperiod of simple RT experiments. It has also been shown that greater magnitudes of HRD are related to faster RTs (Lacey 1967). It has been suggested that HRD represents a preparation to respond when an individual expects a significant stimulus (Andreassi 1995). Another line of research has focused on power spectral density analysis (PSD) or spectrum analysis of HRV to assess sympathetic vs. parasympathetic influence on the heart (i.e., autonomic balance; Akselrod et al. 1981; Jorna 1992; Porges and Byrne, 1992; McCraty and Watkins 1996). As a sensitive noninvasive test of autonomic nervous system function, spectrum analysis of HRV has been used in clinical settings to investigate stress-related disorders, such as hypertension and cardiovascular disease (McCraty and Watkins 1996). Clinical research has found that lowered HRV is associated with aging, depressed hormonal responses, and increased incidence of sudden death (Malik and Camm 1995). In addition, spectrum analysis of HRV has shown that depression, panic disorders, anxiety, and worry affect autonomic function and can reduce the protective influence that parasympathetic activity exerts on the heart (Malik and Camm 1995).

The TCM predicts that constellations of PHO factors that have been shown to drive physiological hyperreactivity and resulting clinical complaints in patients can disrupt motor performance in athletes (Taylor 1996; Wickramasekera 1988). By contrast, it is predicted that athletes who possess ideal constellations of PHO factors are more likely to reach their zone of optimal functioning and to maintain peak performance, especially during critical moments of competition. Because both physiological reactivity and autonomic balance are reflected in spectrum analyses of HRV and HRD, heart activity is a valuable measure of physiological reactivity (intensity), emotions, and attention in athletes and may reflect the dynamics of PHO factors on these measures (Akselrod et al. 1981; Tiller et al. 1996; McCraty et al. 1995).

Heart activity can be viewed as the window into mind–body interactions. In addition to reflecting physiological reactivity and emotions, heart activity has also been found to be an important measure of attention and cognitive activity (Sandman et al. 1982). In reviewing the literature, Sandman et al. (1982) concluded that HR and BP were the physiological parameters that best differentiated the cognitive–perceptual process. Their observation was based on the Lacey's (1964, 1967) work, which discovered that HR decreased during tasks demanding attention to the environment and increased during tasks requiring mental concentration (or rejection of the environment). This phenomenon has been explained on the basis of brain–heart interactions, whereby HRD has been found to release the cortex from the inhibitory control of the baro-receptors, as reflected in fast-frequency (i.e., beta waves in the 23 to 38+ Hz range) EEG activity (23 to 38+ Hz EEG activity has been associated with vigilant or attentive behavior; Lindsley 1969; Sandman et al. 1982). Conversely, heart rate acceleration (HRA) has been shown to stimulate baro-receptor activity and thereby inhibit cortical activity. This is reflected in slower-wave EEG (8 to 12 Hz), which has been associated with decreased perceptual processing (Sandman et al. 1982; Wolk and Velden 1987).

Galin (1974) maintains that heart activity is more useful than EEG for analyzing attentional processes, because EEG represents only activity at the dorsal convexity of the brain but does not reflect activity in deep medial brain areas such as the hippocampus and the amygdala. Pribam and McGuiness (1975) have proposed that the hippocampus and amygdala (deep, medial brain areas) play an important role in attentional processes.

Not surprisingly, attention and cognitive activity play central roles in the anecdotal literature and research of sports performance (Gallwey 1974; Waller 1988). As might be expected, attention (e.g., focusing on the ball) is considered a desirable psychological state, whereas cognitive activity (e.g., thinking about winning during a point) is thought to disrupt sport performance. For instance, Gallwey (1974), in his classic book *The Inner Game of Tennis,* advocates letting things flow, or happen naturally, by focusing on the ball and warns of thinking too much about the consequences of hitting the ball. These notions appear to have found acceptance, with Ravizza (1977) reporting that 95% of the athletes he surveyed believed that thinking hinders performance. In addition, Waller (1988) reported that reduced levels of cognitive activity were experienced by athletes during peak performance episodes. Because heart activity has been shown to reflect many psychological states (e.g., attention and cognition), its importance to concurrently validating predictions of the TCM is emphasized. It is an ideal measure for operationalizing psychological constructs that have yet to be defined beyond anecdotal conjecture in sports (e.g., attention, cognitive activity, physiological reactivity, or intensity). Given that there have been no studies on psychologically mediated HRV during real competition, research exploring the dynamics of PHO–brain–heart interactions and their effects on performance is presented here. In extending research on HRD and HRV to the field, this study investigates some cardiovascular concomitants of constellations of PHO factors during actual competition, in this case, official tennis tournament matches.

HRV

To understand how HRV can reflect psychological processes (PHO factors) and performance, it is necessary to review how the heart responds to autonomic nervous system activity. HRV represents the net effect of parasympathetic (vagus) nerves, which slow HR, and the sympathetic nerves, which accelerate it (Porges and Byrne 1992).

At rest, both parasympathetic and sympathetic nerves remain tonically active, with vagal effects being dominant (Obrist 1981; McCraty and Watkins 1996). Stimulation of the vagus nerves slows the heart. This slowing occurs almost immediately, within one or two heart beats after the stimulation begins. After vagal stimulation ceases, HR quickly returns to its previous level. An increase in HR can result from a reduction in vagal activity. Therefore, sudden changes in HR are initiated by parasympathetic activity (Lacey and Lacey 1978). Increases in sympathetic activity cause HR to rise above the intrinsic HR level produced by the sinoatrial node. After sympathetic stimulation begins, there is a delay of up to 5 seconds before a progressive increase in HR occurs, reaching a steady level in 20 to 30 seconds (McCraty and Watkins 1996). The slowness of HR response to sympathetic stimulation is contrasted to vagal stimulation, which produces immediate HR deceleration (McCraty and Watkins 1996).

Blood Pressure, Baro-Receptors, and HRV

BP regulation is of primary importance to cardiovascular function. The factors that control BP also regulate HRV (Obrist 1981; McCraty and Watkins 1996). Short-term regulation of BP is achieved through an intricate system of pressure-sensitive baro-receptors located throughout the heart, aortic arch, and carotid artery (Lacey and Lacey 1978; Obrist 1981). Afferent impulses (i.e., signals transmitted to the brain) from the baro-receptors travel via the glosso-pharyngeal and vagal nerves to the vasomotor centers in the medulla oblongata, where they regulate sympathetic nervous system transmissions to the heart and blood vessels. Some modulation of parasympathetic nervous system transmission also occurs in the medulla oblongata (Obrist 1981; Porges and Byrne 1992). Baro-receptors regulate HR, vasoconstriction, venoconstriction, and cardiac contractility to maintain BP (Obrist 1981).

The regulation of BP by baro-receptors is hypothesized to differentially facilitate or inhibit cortical activity and attentional efficiency (Lacey and Lacey 1978). Specifically, elevated HR and BP are thought to inhibit cortical activity, thereby decreasing attention, whereas HR deceleration and lowered BP are thought to facilitate attentional processes (Lacey and Lacey 1978; Sandman et al. 1982).

In summary, autonomic nervous system (sympathetic and parasympathetic) activity along with afferent signals from the baro-receptor produces the beat-to-beat changes that characterize HRV (Obrist 1981; Porges and Byrne 1992).

Measures of HRV

Time and frequency domain measures are used to analyze HRV (Leiderman and Shapiro 1962; Akselrod et al. 1981). The most common method for obtaining these measures is to plot the sequence of time intervals between the R-waves of the heart period (HP; such data can be obtained using ambulatory HR-monitoring equipment, e.g., Holter and Polar systems). The resulting graph of HR changes (i.e., HRV) is called a tachogram (Andreassi 1995). The tachogram reflects the autonomically mediated HRV signal and beat-to-beat changes in HR (Andreassi 1995; McCraty and Watkins 1996).

With both methods, the time intervals between consecutive R waves of the HP are calculated first (Andreassi 1995). Thereafter, HRV measures of interest are delineated and analyzed accordingly (e.g., HR deceleration or PSD analysis).

Time Domain Measures

Time domain measures of HRV express changes in heart activity that occur within a single cardiac cycle (i.e., HP, or interbeat interval [IBI], and are expressed in milliseconds [ms]; Andreassi 1995). Time domain measures of interest include HRD and, to a lesser extent, HRA. HRD is the progressive slowing of one or more successive IBIs (i.e., HR slowing from R-wave to R-wave of the HP). For example, IBI values of 555, 560, 570, 575, and 580 ms reflect HRD between four IBIs (increasing values reflect a longer HP, or slowing of the heart; Andreassi 1995). In contrast, IBI values of 580, 575, 570, and

565 ms reflect HRA between three consecutive IBIs (decreasing IBI values indicate a shorter HP or acceleration of the heart).

Time domain measures of HRV have been used to study RT, task performance, complex motor activity, perception, mental imagery, attention, motivation, emotion, and operant conditioning of HR (Elliott et al. 1970; Hahn 1973; Obrist et al. 1973; Elliott 1974; Lacey and Lacey 1974; Schell and Catania 1975; McCanne and Sandman 1976; Carriero and Fite 1977; Jennings and Wood 1977; Lang et al. 1983).

Frequency Domain Measures

Frequency domain measures refer to PSD or spectrum analysis measures of HRV (McCraty and Watkins 1996). PSD shows how the power of heart activity is distributed as a function of frequency (McCraty and Watkins 1996). The PSD of HRV is obtained by filtering and extracting the different-frequency components of HRV that are discernible in the tachogram. The HRV power spectrum contains three main frequency ranges: very low frequency (VLF, 0.033 to 0.04 Hz), low frequency (LF, 0.04 to 0.15 Hz), and high frequency (HF, 0.15 to 0.4 Hz; Akselrod et al. 1981; Porges and Byrne 1992; McCraty and Watkins 1996). The HF range reflects rapid changes in beat-to-beat variability (i.e., HRV) caused by parasympathetic or vagal stimulation (Akselrod et al. 1981; Porges and Byrne 1992; McCraty and Watkins 1996). The VLF range is thought to reflect predominantly sympathetic stimulation (Akselrod et al. 1981; Porges and Byrne 1992; McCraty and Watkins 1996). The LF range reflects a mixture of both sympathetic and parasympathetic stimulation of the heart (Akselrod et al. 1981; Porges and Byrne 1992; McCraty and Watkins 1996). The LF/HF ratio is used to quantify the overall balance between the sympathetic and parasympathetic systems and is a measure of special interest in this study (McCraty and Watkins 1996). Frequency domain analysis of HRV (i.e., PSD or spectrum analysis) provides reliable measures of the effects that stress and emotions exert on autonomic function. To date, PSD analysis of HRV research has been limited mostly to clinical and organizational settings (Jorna 1992; McCraty and Watkins 1996; Myrtek et al. 1996). It has not been used to analyze psychologically mediated HRV during sports.

HRV Research

This study is based on two lines of research. The first line is traced to Lacey and Lacey's (1964, 1978) studies of cardiac deceleration

(HRD) in the simple reaction time paradigm. The second line can be traced to Axelrod et al.'s (1981) mathematical quantification of the physiologic mechanisms of beat-to-beat HR fluctuations, or spectrum analysis of HRV. Research of HRD and spectrum analysis has been numerous, although at present, interest in HRD appears to be waning, whereas interest in spectrum analysis of HRV has been increasing. This is attributable to the fact that psychologically mediated HRD is no longer disputable, and spectrum analysis, which is more relevant to clinical, educational, and work place issues, has yet to be comprehensively studied (Sandman et al. 1982; Andreassi 1995; McCraty and Watkins 1996).

Although there is literature covering HRD research in sports, it has been limited to static, nonaction types of sports such as shooting, archery, and golf (Hatfield et al. 1984, 1987; Boutcher and Zinsser 1990). However, HRD has not been studied during real competition or in action sports where little is known about the effects of cardiac deceleration, especially during critical moments. Furthermore, no studies of athletes have investigated HRD in the context of PHO factors. There are no previous studies on spectrum analysis of psychologically mediated HRV in athletes.

Heart Rate Deceleration Research

This study classifies research of HRD into two categories: first, mechanistic studies are investigations that have detailed the properties of HRD within experimental variations of the simple RT paradigm. These studies have demonstrated the existence of HRD. Simple RT time and choice RT paradigms are presented in some detail to illuminate components of the simple RT model that have been adapted to this study and other investigations of HRD in sports. Second, performance studies have investigated the effects of HRD on performance. These studies have associated HRD with differential RT and task performance, both in the laboratory and in sport settings.

Mechanistic Studies of HRD

HRD has been demonstrated in a variety of studies, with Lacey and Lacey (1964) being the first to show that HR decreased in response to an imperative (i.e., imminent or impending) stimulus. The Laceys' work introduced the simple RT paradigm in which subjects were required to press a key after the appearance of a ready signal (a green circle in a display box), hold the key down until the imperative signal (a white cross) was superimposed on the green circle, and respond as quickly as possible to the white cross by releasing the key. The so-called fixed foreperiod, or time offset, between the time of initial key depression and the presentation of the imperative signal lasted 4 seconds. Results of this study showed a progressive slowing of the heart (i.e., HRD), from the time of the ready signal (i.e., pressing the key) to when the imperative signal was presented (as reflected in the lengthening of successive IBIs before the imperative signal).

In an extension of their original research, the Laceys (1978) measured HP as a function of time in which the imperative stimulus was presented in the cardiac cycle. They found that the magnitude of HR deceleration during the fixed foreperiod depended on where in the cardiac cycle the imperative stimulus was presented: it was significantly greater early (4th decile) in the cycle than later (10th decile).

The Laceys (1970) also reported anticipatory slowing (i.e., HRD) in experiments requiring self-initiated responses (choice RT paradigm). For example, subjects having a prior knowledge of the onset of a significant stimulus tended to exhibit increasingly greater HR slowing (HRD) as the time of voluntary motor response approached.

The simple RT paradigm and variations thereof (e.g., choice RT paradigm) lend themselves well to studying HRD in settings in which persons are waiting to respond to a stimulus, including before certain sport-specific tasks (Edwards and Alsip 1966; Nowlin et al. 1970; Surwillo 1971; Walter and Porges 1976; Heslegrave et al. 1979). For example, in measuring heart activity as a function of task demand, the Laceys (1968) measured HRD during a 6-second interval before the foreperiod, for 6 seconds of the foreperiod, and for 6 seconds after the response. In tennis this would amount to a player waiting 6 seconds before entering the ready position to receive serve, after which 6 more seconds pass before the ball is served (stimulus presentation–response), followed by action lasting 6 seconds (time period from when the serve was returned to when the point ends). Similar intervals occur in golf, baseball, softball, and basketball—sports that were investigated in study 1.

The Laceys' original mechanistic studies of HR deceleration have been replicated numerous times (e.g., Webb and Obrist 1970). In essence, these replication studies support the validity of HRD as a species-wide response, in anticipation of an imperative stimulus.

Performance Studies of HRD

The mere fact that HRD has been empirically validated as a species-wide response is of minor importance to athletes if HRD cannot be linked to within- or between-subject differences in performance.

Thus, if HRD does not distinguish good from poor performance, why should it be studied? This question is in part answered by performance studies of HRD that indicate that within- and between-subject differences in HRD are associated with differential task performance and level of skill. For example, Wang and Landers (as cited in Boutcher and Zinsser 1990, original source unavailable), comparing highly and moderately skilled archers, reported HRD in both subject groups before shooting (i.e., in the preparation phase before arrow release). In addition, they found differences in HRD between groups. Although both groups exhibited HRD patterns, during the aiming phase, highly skilled archers demonstrated significantly greater HRD in comparison with lesser skilled archers.

In a similar study involving golf, Boutcher and Zinsser (1990) replicated the basic findings of Wang and Landers. In a comparison of elite and beginning golfers during putting, they reported individual differences in HRD–performance effects. Specifically, they showed that both elite and beginning golfers exhibited significant HRD compared with baseline HR before putting. In addition, elite golfers were found to experience significantly slower HR than beginning golfers immediately before, during, and after the ball was putted. Hatfield et al. (1984) also reported that elite rifle shooters exhibited HRD before shooting. Although this study did not differentiate performance proficiency, it did provide evidence in support of previous electrophysiological and neurocardiologic explanations of psychologically mediated HRV (e.g., Lacey and Lacey 1978; Sandman et al. 1982; Armour 1994; McCraty and Watkins 1996). These researchers reported that increased right-hemispheric EEG activity was a concomitant of HRD before shooting. This finding is in line with previous research associating HRD with increased cortical activity (as observed in increased EEG alpha activity; Lacey and Lacey 1978; Sandman et al. 1982). The authors proposed that elite marksmen have developed attentional focus to the extent that they are unconsciously capable of reducing cognitive activity in the left hemisphere (i.e., the left half of the brain). Left-hemisphere cognitive activity has been associated with the disruption of motor performance (Hatfield et al. 1984; Langer and Imber 1979).

The above studies are important because they clearly establish that the magnitude of HRD during self-paced sports is associated with a performer's level of skill. They provide evidence that HRD is not only a species-wide physiological response but also that it reflects individual differences in athletic ability. However, they did not investigate within- or between-subject differences in HRD as a function of personality traits or behavioral measures (e.g., PHO factors/constellations). Recent research by Hassmen and Koivula (2001) showing that anxiety (a secondary lower order [SLO] factor) can disrupt HRD trends supports the TCM hypothesis that personality and behavioral factors can affect physiological responding and should be considered in all psychophysiological research.

Case Study: Hypotheses

Hypothesis 1: Total HRD

Hypothesis 1 predicted that HRD patterns during tennis matches would resemble deceleration trends observed in previous research of self-paced sports. For example, it was hypothesized that during the preaction phases of matches, IBIs would progressively lengthen (i.e., become slower) up to the point when action commences.

Hypothesis 2: HRD and Successful Performance

Hypothesis 2 predicted that more and greater magnitudes of HRD would occur in a match that was won compared with a match that was lost.

Spectrum Analysis of HRV

A spectrum analysis of HRV was performed for exploratory purposes to determine whether differences in HRV existed between matches.

Participant

This study involved a 16-year-old male who was a nationally ranked tennis player. He was assessed on PHO factors and found to have the constellation high absorption, medium neuroticism, and low repressive coping. It should be noted that this is considered a relatively negative constellation is the context of critical moments of competition.

Research Design

The study used a single-case research design and was carried out in the field during an official U.S. Tennis Association tennis tournament. The player's heart activity was monitored using ambulatory equipment during his first-, second-, and third-round matches. Because the goal of this study was to establish differences in HRD and HRV between matches that were won and lost, match 1 (won) was compared with match 3 (lost). Match 2, which was won, was not analyzed because it was played on the same day as match 1. All the matches were videotaped in their entirety. Performance measures in the matches were obtained using qualitative and quantitative methods of content analysis. The exploratory nature of this field study precluded the manipulation of variables.

Instrumentation

Heart activity was recorded using the Polar Vantage Heart Rate Monitoring System. The Polar system uses a noninvasive wireless and telemetry system to transmit heart signals from a chest strap (housing electrodes) to a wristwatch for data storage. Data are then transferred to a computer by an interface for analysis. IBIs of each HP were extracted using Polar HR analysis software (Polar Corporation 1996). HRD and HRA measures were also obtained using the same software. The Polar system has been tested to be accurate to within +3 ms.

Video Analysis

Matches were videotaped using a Sony camcorder. Tapes of the matches were time coded using a Sony video-editing system to establish a timeline between match events and heart activity.

Procedure

This study was carried out at an official U.S. Tennis Association men's tennis tournament in central California. Before the tournament the subject was familiarized with the Polar equipment. This involved learning how to start the receiver (wristwatch) and how to read its data display. A practice session was also carried out in which it was established that the equipment would not hinder the player's stroking ability and mobility. On arriving at the tournament venue, preparation to carry out the study commenced. The Sony camcorder was placed on a platform overlooking the court on which the player's matches would be played. A computer station for receiving data was set up in the clubhouse. Approximately 10 minutes before the beginning of the first match, the subject was fitted with the Polar chest strap. The wristwatch was attached to the player's left arm. The player was instructed to start the watch immediately before the first point. The camcorder was started just before the end of the warm-up session before the match. These procedures were repeated before both matches.

Treatment and Analysis of Data

The heart activity–performance timeline was calibrated from the time on the videotape when the watch was started. That time was compared with the heart activity timeline of the watch to discern HRD trends before, during, and after action. Videotapes of the two matches were analyzed to obtain performance data. HRD and HRV data were extracted using computer-generated data sheets that sequentially listed all IBIs stored in the watch.

A questionnaire was used to debrief the subject. The purpose of this questionnaire was to obtain self-report feedback on the player's perceived psychological state during the matches.

Statistics

T-tests were used to analyze the HRD data. They were performed on preaction IBIs within and between matches. The exploratory spectrum analysis generated descriptive data on HRV between matches. Tests for the difference between two proportions were carried out to examine between-match differences in HRV.

Results

Match Outcome

The player won match 1 by a score of 6–4, 6–1. He lost match 3 by a score of 6–0, 6–1 (the score of match 3 is the second-worst score possible in a best-of-three-set match).

Self-Report of Psychological State during Matches

The player reported that he was very attentive in match 1 (5 on a 5-point Likert-like scale) and not very nervous (2 on a 5-point scale). He further described himself as very motivated and confident of winning every point in the match (4 on a 5-point scale). The player also mentioned not having "much respect for the game of his opponent." During changeovers, the player stated that he visualized how he would play the upcoming game, something a player high in absorption would be likely to do and benefit from. In general, the player reported highly positive emotions and cognitive activity in match 1. As would be expected, the player described vastly different emotions before and during match 3. He reported a high degree of nervousness (4 on a 5-point scale) and a low level of attention (2 on a 5-point scale) during match 3. He also stated that after being unable to make his best shots throughout the match, "negative thoughts" tended to dominate. He frequently thought about losing, lost motivation (1 on a 5-point scale), and eventually resigned himself to being defeated.

This feedback is highly consistent with what would be expected to occur in an athlete having a PHO constellation of high absorption, medium to high neuroticism, and low repressive coping, especially once performance becomes disrupted during competition.

Qualitative Observations

The first match was won easily. At no time was the player in danger of losing control of the match, and he appeared motivated as well as psychologically stable throughout. In addition to remaining both calm and attentive (high absorption) from beginning to end, the player conveyed the impression that he had confidence in his technical abilities and was not afraid to attempt difficult or risky shots. The first match was routine in nature, and he was obviously better than his opponent from a technical standpoint. Critical moments did not emerge in this match, with the average criticality level for all points being between 1 and 2. As a consequence, potential negative manifestations of his PHO constellation did not emerge. The player appeared to benefit from his high intrinsic level of absorption because the overall low level of stress associated with this match was low. This facilitated focus on the task at hand as opposed to internal cognitions that might have emerged to disrupt performance during a more demanding match. Essentially, potential manifestation of the player's neuroticism remained dormant, allowing for full absorption in the tasks at hand.

The player's behavior and performance in the third match visibly contrasted with that of the first. In facing the number one–seeded player, a 31-year-old veteran of the professional tennis tour, the player appeared nervous from the beginning of the match. His agitation was reflected in poor movement and technique, which resulted in numerous unforced errors. The player also displayed displeasure with his performance by frequently chiding himself. These emotional displays stood in stark contrast to the calmness he exhibited in the first match. However, after it became apparent that the match would be very difficult to win, the player reverted to a state of emotional indifference, indicative of an athlete who is resigned to losing.

Although points in match 3 only averaged about 3 on the criticality scale, it should be noted that the player lost all criticality level 5 points. This was to be expected on the basis of his constellation of PHO factors, whereby it appeared that the player's medium level of neuroticism emerged under the stress associated with match 3 to drive excessive physiological reactivity. The heightened stress and resulting physiological hyperreactivity in match 3 (as reflected in decreased HRD) coincided with the player's self-report of negative intrusive thoughts. Associated with high neuroticism, such cognitions are the kind that people high in absorption tend to ruminate on during times of increased stress. As a consequence, the player's increased ability to focus on tasks at hand, an ability associated with high absorption (which was exhibited in match 1) shifted from sport-specific tasks to internal negative thoughts in match 3, leading to poor performance. The fact that the player was low in repressive coping allowed for the unmitigated interaction of absorption with neuroticism. In accord with predictions from the TCM, the player's low level of repressive coping and high absorption made him especially vulnerable to negative intrusive thoughts associated with neuroticism, which is more likely to occur during critical moments of competition.

Match Statistics

The subject committed 10 unforced errors and 16 forced errors and hit 16 winners in the first match. Forced errors are considered unavoidable and a result of an opponent's forcing shot. Thus, a winners-to-unforced errors ratio of 16:10 is consistent with matches that are well played and won. In contrast, the subject committed 28 unforced errors and three forced errors and hit four winners in match 3. The low winners-to-unforced errors ratio of 1:7 reflects a match that was poorly played and lost and underscores the above qualitative observations. Conversely, statistics from the first match support the contention that the player was psychologically in control of his game in match 1.

HRD and HRA Phases

There were 51 action phases in match 1 and 27 in match 3. Action phases were identified in the videotapes of the matches. These phases corresponded with heart activity data extracted from the computer analysis data readout.

Episodes of HRD before action were identified 51 times in match 1 and 27 times in match 3. In contrast to laboratory research in which a prespecified number of IBIs were studied before action, a field study cannot predict in advance how many IBIs will occur before action. Thus, the number of IBIs before each action phase was variable. In match 1 there were 283 decelerating IBIs before the 51 action phases, or a mean of 5.55 IBIs per preaction phase. There were 112

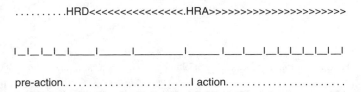

Figure 7. Sample selection of preaction, action, and postaction interbeat intervals (IBIs) in match 1. Notice that the IBIs become proressively longer leading up the response IBI. Thereafter, the IBIs become progressively shorter during the action phase. After action ceases, the IBIs again become longer in the postaction recovery phase. Longer IBIs indicate a slowing of the heart; shorter IBIs indicate an acceleration of the heart or a shorter and faster heart period.

decelerating IBIs before 27 action phases in match 3, or a mean of 4.15 IBIs per preaction phase.

Hypothesis 1

An examination of all preaction IBIs in match 1 and match 3 revealed HRD in all IBIs before action. The presence of HRD in the IBIs before action supported the hypothesis that HRD trends during tournament tennis would resemble decelerative trends observed in previous laboratory and field studies (Figure 7).

Hypothesis 2

Hypothesis 2 was tested by comparing various combinations of IBIs in preaction phases of matches 1 and 3. The following IBI combinations were examined to determine whether greater magnitudes of HRD would be evident in a match that was won compared with a match that was lost: the difference in the rate of HRD between all IBIs before action in match 1 compared with that in match 3 (Figure 8), the difference in the rate of HRD between the last IBI before action in match 1 compared with that in match 3 (Figure 9), and the difference in HRD between the second-to-last IBI and the next-to-last IBI compared with the difference between the next-to-last IBI and the last IBI before action in match 1, compared with those of match 3.

The following significant effects in support of hypothesis 2 were found: first, total IBIs before action in match 1 compared with those in match 3 revealed more preaction HRD in match 1 than in match 3 (mean IBI = 6.79 vs. 5.57; $P = .05$; second, HRD in IBIs before the last IBI before action in match 1 compared with match 3 revealed more HRD in match 1 (mean IBI = 6.37 vs. 5.42; $P = .085$); third, the

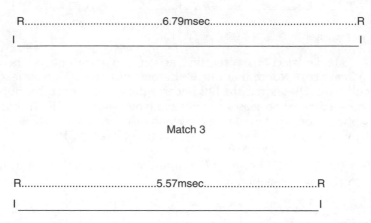

Match 1

R..............................6.79msec...R
I_____I

Match 3

R..............................5.57msec....................................R
I_____I

Figure 8. Mean rate of heart rate deceleration for all interbeat intervals before action in match 1 compared with match 3 (*P* < .045).

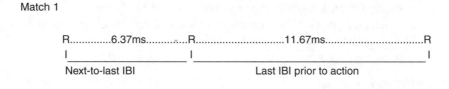

Match 1

R...............6.37ms..............R...............................11.67ms.................................R
I_____I_____I
Next-to-last IBI   Last IBI prior to action

Match 3

R...........5.42ms...........R......................8.67msec................R
I_____I_____I
Next-to-last IBI   Last IBI prior to action

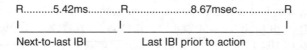

Figure 9. Mean difference of the rate of heart rate deceleration between the last interbeat interval (IBI) before action compared with the next-to-last IBI in match 1 (*P* < .008) and mean difference of the rate of heart rate deceleration between the last IBI before action compared with the next-to-last IBI in match 3 (P < .079).

next-to-last IBI, compared with the last IBI before action in match 1, revealed significant HRD between the last two IBIs (mean = 11.67; *P* = .008); fourth, the next-to-last IBI, compared with the last IBI before action in match 3, also revealed significant HRD between the last two IBIs (mean = 8.67; P = .079; Figure 9); and fifth, the IBI decelerative trend between the second-to-last IBI and the next-to-last IBI, and the next-to-last IBI and the last IBI before action in match 1, compared to those of match 3, revealed more HRD in match 1 (mean = 3.86 vs. 1.67; P = .037).

Although a comparison of the next-to-last IBI with the last IBI before action in match 1 with that of match 3 did not reveal significant differences (mean = 11.67 vs. 8.67; P = .16) more HRD did occur in the last IBI before action in match 1. This is important in the context of within-match performance, where significant HRD in the last IBI before action was demonstrated.

Spectrum Analysis of HRV: Exploratory Data

A spectrum analysis was performed to determine whether matches could be distinguished on the basis of autonomic nervous system activity. The spectrum analysis of match 1 revealed the following values: 5-minute total power = 1573.4 (power in the band < 0.40 Hz), 5-minute VLF = 1378.6 (power spectrum range from 0.0033 to 0.04 Hz), 5-minute LF = 180.6 (power spectrum range from 0.04 to 0.15 Hz), 5-minute HF = 14.3 (power spectrum range from 0.15 to 0.4 Hz), and LF/HF = 12.7. Spectrum analysis of match 3 revealed the following values: 5-minute total power = 2288.7, 5-minute VLF = 2094.5, 5-minute LF = 174.6, 5-minute HF = 19.6, and LF/HF= 8.9.

Discussion

The results of this study showed that varying magnitudes of HRD preceded action phases during both tennis matches. These findings are the first to demonstrate HRD during an action sport. Moreover, the general hypothesis of this study, which predicted that more HRD would occur before action phases in a match that was won compared with in a match that was lost, was supported. Although both matches were marked by progressive HRD leading up to action, match 1 showed significantly greater HRD in all configurations of IBIs before action. A particularly noteworthy finding was that the last IBI before the action response was significantly longer than the IBI preceding the action response (i.e., more HRD) in match 1 compared with in match 3. This finding is consistent with studies by Lacey and Lacey (1978) and Jennings and Wood (1977) that reported the greatest amount of HRD in the last IBI before the presentation of a stimulus. In addition, when comparing the last three IBIs before action in match 1 with those of match 3, it was found that HR slowing was significantly greater between IBI 2 and IBI 1 (last IBI before action) in match 1 than between IBI 3 and IBI 2 in match 3. These data also replicate studies reporting that successive IBIs, before the imperative stimulus, become progressively slower as the time of response nears (Jennings and Wood 1977; Lacey and Lacey 1978).

It should be noted that significant HRD occurred both within matches and between matches. However, this study marks the first time that significant within-subject differences between HRD and performance outcome have been reported. Previous research has focused either on between-subject differences in performance or did not report significant within-subject results as a function of performance (Nowlin et al. 1970; Boutcher and Zinsser 1990).

This study also marks the first time that HRD has been demonstrated at higher HR levels. For example, in previous research, HRD was observed in the 70 to 90 bpm range, whereas in this study, HRD occurred at levels as high as 150 bpm (Boutcher and Zinsser 1990). This is noteworthy because experiments of operant conditioning of HR have only been successful in slowing HR below resting baseline or slightly elevated HR (McCanne and Sandman 1976). Although the HRD observed at higher HRs in this study could be attributed to the exercise recovery response, this is only a partial explanation because HRD here resembled HRD trends in other laboratory and field studies (Obrist 1981; Boutcher and Zinsser 1990). These trends were thought to be mediated by constellations of PHO factors.

The results of the spectrum analysis indicate that, in general, there was more sympathetic activity in match 1 and more parasympathetic activity in match 3. This is reflected in the LF/HF ratio of each match (LF/HF ratio = 12.7 in match 1 vs. 8.9 in match 3). Although parasympathetic dominance was evident in match 3, it is pointed out that VLF, which is also thought to reflect sympathetic activity, was higher in match 3 than in match 1. Because there are no norms for, or studies of, spectrum analysis during tennis or any sport, there is much room for interpretation and speculation when analyzing these results. Thus, the results of spectrum analysis can only be addressed in the context of the comprehensive data of this study.

The results of this study become more meaningful when interpreted in relationship to the diametrically opposed performance and outcome of the two matches. These extreme differences are reflected in quantitative performance data (e.g., match score and statistics) and qualitative impressions of the match (i.e., psychological performance) and are consistent with the player's constellation of PHO factors. The player's self-report of experiencing major differences in attention, emotions, self-confidence, cognitive activity, and reactivity (SLO factors) between matches strongly indicates that his PHO factors influenced the above SLO factors, HRD, and performance.

Of these SLO factors, attention is considered by many to be the most central to performance because it is directly related to observing and processing environmental stimuli (Boutcher and Zinsser 1990). Relative to the findings of this study, it was hypothesized that this player's level of attention was mediated by his constellation of PHO factors negatively exerting their effects on cognitive activity and the resultant HRD in the match he lost.

In match 1, PHO factors may have potentiated vagal activity and resultant greater HRD before action. This could have increased attention by limiting competing sensory feedback such as negative intrusive cognitions from reaching the left-brain hemisphere (Carlstedt 2003; Sandman et al. 1982). In essence, limiting superfluous and disruptive feedback to the brain prevents sensory flooding from diverting attentional resources from a significant stimulus (Klemm 1996). As a consequence, heart–brain feedback loops marked by increases in HRD may have facilitated attention in match 1 by efficiently taking in stimuli that were significant and by excluding stimuli that were potentially disruptive (intake-rejection hypothesis; Lacey and Lacey 1964). These dynamics were thought to occur because of the positive influences of high absorption in match 1, which allowed for optimum focusing.

Paradoxically, although HRD was significantly greater in match 1, this match was marked by less total parasympathetic activity. This may be attributable to an overall higher level of sympathetic activation during action phases of the match, indicative of motivated performance and greater intensity. Thus, levels of sympathetic activity associated with greater motivation, activation, and energy expenditure in match 1 may have skewed the spectrum analysis data to underreflect the parasympathetic activity associated with increased HRD and attention (Jorna 1992; Porges and Byrne 1992; McCraty et al. 1996).

Match 3 was marked by a major decrease in overall performance and HRD. Self-report indicated that the player was more nervous, less motivated, and less attentive in this match. In addition, the player reported a loss of confidence and a sense of helplessness as the match progressed. He also admitted to frequent negative cognitions. Thus, it was hypothesized that the negative intrusive thoughts associated with the player's increased levels of neuroticism interfered with his attention during preaction phases of match 3 by diverting focus away from (external) sport-specific tasks toward disruptive (internal) cognitions. Because negative cognitive activity has been associated with decreased attention, it was posited that focus on internal thoughts before action disrupted the priming of neuronal networks responsible for initiating motor responses and HRD, leading to more errors in match 3 (Ravizza 1977; Waller 1988; Klemm 1996). The player's tendency to fixate on negative intrusive thoughts was believed to have been facilitated by his high level of absorption.

Match 3 was marked more by parasympathetic than sympathetic activity. Because it was believed that losing a match would be marked by greater emotion, stress, and hyperreactivity, the data on spectrum analysis from match 3 were surprising. However, because the player revealed that after recognizing that the match could not be won he became more relaxed, it was to be expected that parasympathetic activity would increase. Thus, it was hypothesized that the stress and effort associated with a difficult match was attenuated once the subject gave up hope of winning, leading to increased parasympathetic activity in match 3.

The fact that performance and outcome between matches were highly incongruous indicates that HRD is not only a species-wide physiological response to an impending stimulus but also varies as a function of specific tasks, performance demands, and psychological factors (PHO and SLO factors). This contention is based on a comprehensive evaluation of the data. Although initial P values were set at less than .10 for this exploratory study, most HRD effects were demonstrated to be significant at $P < .05$, with the most important effect being significant at $P < .008$ (next-to-last IBI, compared with last IBI in match 1) and $P < .038$ (comparing last three IBIs in match 1 to match 3). Even though statistical procedures and their results can be broadly interpreted to suit a particular hypothesis, the quantitative results of this study lend additional support because of their extreme differences in match scores, performance statistics, data on content analysis, and self-report feedback (Denzin and Lincoln 1994; Gall et al. 1996). As a consequence, there was a high degree of qualitative certainty that HRV effects in this study were not random.

It can be argued that because an athlete's constellation of PHO factors does not change over time (i.e., it is stable and trait-like), it should have the same effect on performance regardless of match outcome. However, one is again reminded that PHO factors are not static. Constellations of PHO factors are dynamic and are predicted to affect performance the most during critical moments of competition by mediating physiological responses and subsequent motor performance. Because HRD has been shown to reflect physiological reactivity, attention, and cognitive activity, the changes in HRD that were observed between matches having highly incongruent performance and outcome may have been mediated by PHO factors. The player's self-report between matches supports this interpretation because it was consistent with theoretical conceptualizations of PHO factors and how they can affect performance and physiology. These dynamics were also quasi-validated in the context of the observed HRD trends.

Although this investigation involved only one athlete, single case studies have an important strength in that a person serves as his or her own control. Such control is particularly important in psychophysiological studies. As a consequence, changes in physiological response tendencies across diverse conditions in the same individual may very likely reflect psychological influences. Single-subject ambulatory psychophysiological field studies such as this one also can have a higher degree of ecological validity than laboratory studies involving a larger population (Gall et al. 1996; Myrtek et al. 1996), making them very useful for exploratory and validation purposes.

Directions for Future Research

Future research must delineate the general HRD observed in this study more precisely. Should it be determined that HRD is unequivocally associated with performance and affected by psychological factors (PHO-SLO), interventions can be designed to help tennis players manipulate their HR in the desired direction. Because HR biofeedback has been successfully demonstrated both in the field and in laboratory studies, it is plausible that this mental training method could be used to enhance the psychological performance of athletes (Weiss and Engel 1971; Ludwick-Rosenthal and Neufeld 1985; Fahrenberg and Myrtek 1996).

Because this study also demonstrated that within-subject HRD varied situationally, individualized norms for HRD should be derived through future research (Lezak 1995). A large-scale study should be implemented to determine whether HRD can be used to distinguish and assess level of ability, attention, motivation, and activation in athletes (Fahrenberg and Foerster 1991; see Chapter 10) and to unequivocally determine to what extent PHO factors affect this cardiovascular response.

Although the results of the spectrum analyses were only revealing at the macrolevel, spectrum analysis of HRV still holds much potential for assessing states of activation in athletes. Spectrum analysis could be used to establish individual norms for activation and reactivity in athletes and to establish parameters of physiological reactivity beyond the hypothetical (Hanin 1980; Hardy and Fazey 1987; Taylor 1996). Doing so would have major implications with regard to preparing athletes for competition. In addition, spectrum analysis could be used to better discern to what extent specific psychophysio-logical processes are active during certain phases of competition (e.g., levels of attention, cognitive activity, autonomic nervous system activity). Such research could lead to a better understanding of how cognitive activity, and hence psychological variables, facilitates or disrupts motor performance during action phases of competition (see Chapter 16).

Applied Sport Psychology: Assessing and Mastering Critical Moments

9

Assessing Critical Moments

Because the statistics of most sports were designed primarily to assess or document physical and technical proficiency, they are of limited use for the analysis of psychological performance. Batting average, field-goal percentage, greens in regulation, first-serve percentage, and a plethora of other global indices of performance are interpreted more in terms of their relationship to the physical and technical abilities that directly influence these measures of proficiency. A baseball player who hits .200 or a basketball player who shoots 35% from the free-throw line is likely to be analyzed first from a technical or physical, and not necessarily a psychological perspective. Although one can infer psychological performance on the basis of global statistics of a sport, the fact that associations between psychological factors and sport-specific outcome variables have been weak indicates that new measures must be developed to better isolate relationships that may exist between psychological factors and outcome measures (microlevel statistics).

Operationalizations of Critical Moments

Outcome measures should be customized to increase the probability that they will reflect psychological influences on performance. Because the central tenet of the Theory of Critical Moments (TCM) maintains that primary higher order (PHO) factors are most likely to influence performance during critical moments of competition, it is crucial that outcome measures be reduced to the microlevel to reflect those moments as authentically as possible. This will maximize the probability that psychological influences on performance can be tapped or isolated on the basis of objective performance statistics.

The TCM approach to the assessment of critical moments is three-fold. The first approach involves using performance statistics that are integral to a sport to infer psychological performance. This involves using available global statistics or reducing these statistics to the greatest microlevel possible. For example, the sport of baseball uses an extensive battery of statistics that reflect performance over the course of a season. Embedded within these global statistics are some that pertain to the microlevels of performance on the playing field. These can be obtained by retrospectively analyzing available statistics to create new statistical categories that better reflect critical moments of competition. To illustrate, conventional global statistics might reveal that a baseball player had a batting average of .355 for the entire season, a measure of batting performance that, although impressive, is based predominantly on routine moments of competition. As a consequence, we must reduce this global measure to a greater microlevel by reexamining how this player hits in more pressure-invoking situations; for example, with men on base. Doing so might reveal that this player actually hits better in such a context, say .404. However, an even greater microlevel of criticality, such as batting performance with men in scoring position during playoff games, may reveal a significant drop-off in batting average, perhaps down to .285. The former statistics are obviously more global in nature, whereas the latter is a more microlevel statistic. It is hypothesized that the more a statistic approaches the micro level, the more likely psychological influences on performance will be revealed.

Using this example, it is apparent that the global statistic batting average, although indicating a high level of technical proficiency, might actually underestimate what the same player is capable of doing in a pressure situation. Thus, in this case, performance may be viewed more favorably when reexamined with the first microlevel reduction. However, improvement at this microlevel may have something to do with the pitcher who throws more cautiously with players on base, making it easier for the batter to get a hit. Although this situation is possibly more reflective of psychological influences than a global batting average would be, it may still not be the ideal microlevel for analyzing psychological influences on performance. We must dig still deeper to reduce statistics to even greater microlevels that reflect more critical than routine moments of competition. In this case, we observe a major decrement in performance in the postseason compared to the regular season, indicating that this player's batting average declined as the level of criticality increased.

Failing to reduce a performance outcome measure to the greatest micro- or criticality level can lead to faulty conclusions regarding an athlete's mental toughness. As this example illustrates, a high level of global proficiency does not necessarily mean an athlete will be mentally tough during the most critical moments of competition.

One drawback of trying to assess psychological performance on the basis of outcome statistics for any particular sport is that such statistics are mostly too global in nature and are more likely to reflect technical and physical elements of an athlete's game or performance. As a consequence, to adequately assess psychological performance, it is necessary to create an original battery of sport-specific, microlevel psychological or critical moment statistics. This can be achieved using a system of psychological performance assessment that weighs the level of criticality of all competitive events or moments. Such a system is dynamic and constantly changing not only as a function of the level of criticality of a competitive event but also in relationship to an athlete's technical and physical strengths and weaknesses, which can influence self-perception of criticality. In contrast to relying on common sport-specific statistics, even when extended to microlevels of criticality, this second approach to the assessment of psychological performance is much more dynamic and subtle in that mental performance can be observed and analyzed in the context of competitive events, situations, or moments that are neither necessarily directly linked to outcome nor available within the conventional statistics of a sport.

The TCM uses a system, the Carlstedt Critical Moment Psychological Performance Index (CCMPP-I), allowing for the documentation and evaluation of psychological performance during every competitive moment or event. Such a capability is important because it is often difficult to generate or find enough microlevel critical moments that an athlete has actually encountered, as most competitive situations are more routine in nature. For example, although free-throw shooting percentage when the championship game is on the line could be considered one of the highest microlevel or criticality statistics, most players would not have encountered this specific situation enough to allow for an adequate investigation of the influence of PHO factors on free-throw shooting. A lack of critical moment statistics can result in a reduction in statistical power, weakening findings on the basis of limited data. Thus, it is up to the practitioner to decide which method to use to assess and analyze psychological performance. If sufficient amounts of data are collected, one might opt to use commonly available statistics or their customized micro-derivatives. Otherwise, if one is interested in assessing continuous task- and situation-specific psychological performance, the CCMPP-I may be more revealing.

Carlstedt Critical Moment Psychological Performance Index

The CCMPP-I can be customized to assess psychological performance in virtually every sport. This system relies on expert raters (e.g., a team's coaching staff) to determine the level of criticality of competitive moments. Although there is an element of subjectivity involved in such an approach, converging evidence indicates that criticality ratings of experts are consistent with athletes' self-reports and concurrent physiological measures. In a retrospective analysis of the tennis matches in the section on heart rate deceleration, three expert raters achieved an interrater reliability alpha of 0.90, which is very high. Expert criticality ratings also correlated highly with a tennis player's self-report regarding perceptions of criticality ($r = 0.82$). In a separate study of heart activity (see study on decreased heart rate [HRD] trends; study 3) there were more HRD trends of at least four or more interbeat intervals in a match containing fewer critical moments compared with a match containing more critical moments. This indicates that critical moments can disrupt mind–body interactions associated with peak performance, including reductions in amount and magnitude of HRD.

Although these data are preliminary, they are consistent with central tenets of the TCM, which maintain that encountering high levels of criticality of competitive moments can disrupt psychophysiological processes associated with peak performance, especially in athletes possessing the most negative constellations of PHO factors. In study 3, the tennis player was high in absorption, high in neuroticism, and low in repressive coping, making him more vulnerable during critical moments of competition.

Following is an analysis of an actual tennis match between a former number one tennis player and a very successful junior player just starting his professional career, using the CCMPP-I. This will be followed by a brief description of assessment approaches and templates that can be used to analyze psychological performance in a few other sports and in relationship to the use of technical skills as a performance outcome measure.

Tournament: Cincinnati, ATP Men's Tennis Tour
Player: Neophyte professional (our player)
Our player's PHO psychological factors: Medium/high hypnotic ability/absorption, high neuroticism, and low/medium
Surface: Hard court/outdoors (slow to medium speed)
Pre-match point weighting adjustments: None
Score: 6–4, 6–7, 2–6 (our player lost to the champion)
Expert raters: A former captain of a European Davis Cup Champion Team, a television commentator (and former professional player), and Roland A. Carlstedt, Ph.D.

The following psychological performance statistics were generated from a tennis professional's second-round match against a multiple Grand Slam winner. Note that there were no prematch point weighting adjustments because neither player had a major advantage or disadvantage because of the court surface. In instances in which the surface or other factors favor a particular player's technical or physical game, the level of criticality of a point can be raised or reduced as a function of such factors (e.g., a "big" or powerful serve on a fast court [grass court] would reduce the criticality of certain moments for the server [e.g., break point]). It is thought that exceptional technical or physical skills can attenuate stress and pressure and boost confidence in certain situations.

The analysis that is interspersed between the matches Point Progression Protocol is based on a postmatch debriefing of the player and expert raters. It provides the rationale for the applied criticality weights.[1]

Set 1

Game 1
PPS/W or L: S 1L, 2W, 2L, 4W, 3W–2W
Total Level of Criticality/Pt. Won/Score: 14–11/1–0

Our player served the first game. The first point received a criticality rating of 1. Our player lost the first point. The fact that a player

---

[1] *Key:* R = receiving; S = serving; level of criticality/psychological significance range: 1 to 5 (low to high); W = won point; L = lost point; CW = criticality weight. Game information is in the order of game number/Point Progression Protocol/W or L, followed by total level of criticality/points won/score. After each game, the total criticality weight is calculated by totaling the CWs attached to each point. The CCMPP-I Psychological Performance Proficiency Quotient (PPPQ) is obtained by dividing the total CW won into the total CW. The CCMPP-I for game 1 was 14–11, meaning that the game had a total of 14 criticality points, of which 11 were won. The average CW per point was 2.3 (14/6 points; PPPQ = 0.79).

serving against a good return player loses the first point was thought to slightly increase pressure and the need to win the next point. Otherwise the player is one point away from game point and close to losing the first game. As a consequence, the second point was given a CW of 2. Our player won this point, making the game score 15–15. The third point of the first game was also given a CW of 2 because losing this point would again put our player close to break or game point. Our player lost this point, bringing the score to 15–30. Being one point away from break or game point resulted in the next point receiving a CW of 4. Our player won this point, bringing the score to 30–30. This score reduced the pressure slightly, leading to a CW of 3. Our player won the 30–30 point, giving him a game point. Having the advantage of serving and at game point early in the set reduced the pressure further, giving the 40–30 point a CW of 2. Our player won this point and the first game.

Game 2
PPS/W or L: R 1L, 1W, 2L, 1W, 3W, 3L, 2L, 2W, 2L, 2L
Total Level of Criticality/Pt. Won/Score: 19–7/1–1

CW in this return game remained low to moderate. Although our player achieved break point opportunities twice in this game, these points were deemed not to be critical moments because the serve was not thought to be a factor in this match. Both players were not considered powerful servers. Breaks of serve were expected. As a consequence, at this early stage of the match, break-point opportunities were not expected to raise the level of stress or pressure. Our player won seven of 19 criticality points during this game. The average CW of each point in this game was 1.9.

Game 3
PPS/W or L: S 1W, 1L, 3W, 2W, 1L, 3L, 2L, 2W, 2L, 2L
Total Level of Criticality/Pt. Won/Score: 18–13/2–1

This was another routine game in terms of psychological significance or criticality. As the server, our player had a slight advantage that helped keep the pressure down, especially during CW 3 points when our player could have run into trouble.

Game 4
PPS/W or L: R 1W, 2L, 2L, 2L, 1L
Total Level of Criticality/Pt. Won/Score: 8–1/2–2

This was a routine return game devoid of significant psychological or critical moments. Routine refers to moments, situations, or events that evolve as expected. When returning serve, most players are at a distinct disadvantage because the server usually dictates play and the progression of a point. This advantage is mitigated if the server does not get the first serve in. In games in which the returner wins few points, it can be assumed that the opponent is serving well and that technical and physical factors outweighed psychological influences on the point.

Game 5
PPS/W or L: S 1W, 1L, 2W, 2W, 1L, 3L, 5L, 5W, 4L, 5L
Total Level of Criticality/Pt. Won/Score: 29–10/2–3

Our player faced critical moments in this game. Although he was serving and had a lead of 40–15, his opponent got the game back to 40–40. At this stage, the 40–40 point was given a CW of 5 because losing this point would lead to a break/game point against our player. He won this critical point but lost the next two points. The point immediately after winning the 40–40 CW 5 point was reduced to CW 4 because it was thought that winning a critical point would slightly reduce the pressure of the subsequent point. This may have led to a letdown, because our player proceeded to lose this point and the next break point, which had a CW of 5. Our player lost the game, winning only 10 of 29 criticality points (average CW this game, 2.9).

Game 6
PPS/W or L: R 2L, 2L, 2L, 1W, 2L
Total Level of Criticality/Pt. Won/Score: 9–1/2–4

This was another routine return game. Our player lost the game to go down 2–4 in the first set.

Game 7
PPS/W or L: S 2W, 2L, 3W, 2W, 1W
Total Level of Criticality/Pt. Won/Score: 10–7/3–4

This was a routine service game that was easily won.

Game 8
PPS/W or L: R 2L, 2L, 2W, 3W, 4L, 3W, 4W, 5W
Total Level of Criticality/Pt. Won/Score: 25–17/4–4

Our player needed a break of serve to even up the set. He played very well, staving off a game point against serve after being down 0–30 to go on to win three consecutive points of increasing CW. Our player won 17 of 25 criticality points. Points in this game had an average CW of 3.1, and set score is now 4–4.

Game 9
PPS/W or L: S 2W, 2L, 3W, 4L, 5W, 4W
Total Level of Criticality/Pt. Won/Score: 20–14/5–4

This was an important and challenging game for our player. After losing a CW 4 point, our player won a CW 5 and a CW 4 point to hold serve and go ahead in the match (average CW per point, 3.2)

Game 10
PPS/W or L: R 2W, 3W, 4W, 3W
Total Level of Criticality/Pt. Won/Score: 12–12/6–4

Our player, surprisingly, easily broke serve to win the first set without losing a point in this game. Notice that the 30–0 point received a CW of 4. The rationale here was that winning this point would give our player a set point; once this point was won our player led 40–0, giving him three set point possibilities. As a result, the first of these three points was allotted a CW of only 3 because, although this was an important point, the fact that he had three chances to convert a break point attempt was thought to reduce the pressure.

Set 1: 6–4 to Our Player

Our player won the first set despite being down 2–4 and one service break, indicative of good psychological performance (PPPQ = 0.580).

Set 2

Game 1
PPS/W or L: S 1W, 1W, 1L, 2L, 4L, 4W, 4W, 3W
Total Level of Criticality/Pt. Won/Score: 20–13/1–0

Our player came close to losing his first service game. At 30–30 he lost a CW 4 point to face break point. However, he went on to win this and subsequent CW 4 points and finally to win the CW 3 game point.

Game 2
PPS/W or L: R 1L, 1W, 3L, 2L, 1W, 3L
Total Level of Criticality/Pt. Won/Score: 11–2/1–1

Our player faced a CW 3 point early in this return game but could not win it. Eventually, he encountered another CW 3 point that he failed to convert. CW 3 points were points of heightened psychological significance and could have led to opportunities to break serve and place more pressure on the opponent. However, the opponent used his serve to win these important points and the game.

Game 3
PPS/W or L: S 1L, 1W, 3W, 2W, 2W
Total Level of Criticality/Pt. Won/Score: 8–7/2–1

Our player faced a CW 3 point. Had he not won this point, our player would have been one point away from facing a break point.

Game 4
PPS/W or L: R 1W, 3L, 2L, 2W, 3L, 3L
Total Level of Criticality/Pt. Won/Score: 14–3/2–2

Our player got to 30–30 and was in a position to reach break point. However, the next and subsequent CW 3 points were lost. A potential opportunity was squandered.

Game 5
PPS/W or L: S 2W, 2W, 2W, 1L, 2W
Total Level of Criticality/Pt. Won/Score: 9–8/3–2

This was a routine service game having minimal psychological significance.

Game 6
PPS/W or L: R 1L, 2L, 2L, 1W, 2L
Total Level of Criticality/Pt. Won/Score: 8–1/3–3

This was another routine game more reflective of physical and technical than psychological influences.

Game 7
PPS/W or L: S 2W, 2W, 2L, 3W, 2W
Total Level of Criticality/Pt. Won/Score: 11–9/4–3

Our player won a CW 3 point to prevent reaching a 30–30 point and potential CW 4 point. Points that are 30–30 late in a set when serving can take on heightened psychological significance because the loss of this point would lead to a break point (CW 5).

Game 8
PPS/W or L: R 3L, 3L, 3L, 1W, 2W, 4L
Total Level of Criticality/Pt. Won/Score: 16–3/4–4

Here our player, after being down 0–40, won two consecutive points against serve, giving him the opportunity to get to 40–40/deuce. This resulted in facing a CW 4 point, which he lost.

Game 9
PPS/W or L: S 2W, 2L, 3W, 3L, 4L, 5L
Total Level of Criticality/Pt. Won/Score: 19–5/4–5

The 4–4 game can be a pivotal game in a set, especially when serving. If you lose this game (when serving) your opponent is in a position to serve out the set. Here our player fell back to 30–30 after being ahead 30–15 and faced a CW 4 point. He lost this point and the subsequent CW 5 point (break point). A break point when serving has major psychological significance and is a classic critical moment. Such a moment is highly likely to elicit manifestations of PHO factors on performance.

Game 10
PPS/W or L: R 3W, 4L, 4W, 5W, 5L, 5W
Total Level of Criticality/Pt. Won/Score: 26–17/5–5

You will notice that the CWs of all points in this game are elevated. This was a crucial game for our player, who needed to break serve to stay in the set. Our player rose to the task, winning this important game, including two CW 4 and CW 5 points against serve, a major psychological achievement.

Game 11
PPS/W or L: S 3W, 3W, 3L, 3W, 2W
Total Level of Criticality/Pt. Won/Score: 14–11/6–5

Our player won this serve game in a relatively routine manner. Notice that each point had an elevated CW weight (3) until the game point, where it was thought that psychological pressure had abated.

Game 12
PPS/W or L: R 3W, 4W, 4L, 4L, 4L, 3L
Total Level of Criticality/Pt. Won/Score: 22–7/6–6

CWs were elevated from the beginning of this important return game. Our player was in a very good position to win this game (break serve) and the match by going ahead 40–0. Had he won the 30–0 point (CW 4), our player would have reached match point. Instead, he lost three consecutive CW 4 points and the game. One might ask why such crucial points were allotted a CW of 4 and not 5. The reason for this was that in the opinion of the expert raters, the serve still had a physical and technical advantage in this situation. The returner, although in a position to win the point, was still at a statistical disadvantage. As a consequence, the returner was not expected to experience the highest level of pressure (CW 5) here because he was not physically or psychologically in control of these return points. However, note that advanced applications of the CCMPP-I allow for midpoint changes in the CW of a point. For example, if a returner faces a second serve (less powerful and fast), the CW 4 attached to the significance of a first serve return may increase to CW 5 because the second serve is easier to return. Similarly, during a rally, if a player who was on the defensive has an offensive opportunity to dictate play, the CW of a point could be increased or decreased in midaction as a function of the situation and of the athlete's technical, physical, and psychological tendencies.

Game 13
PPS/W or L: Tie breaker. S4L (0–1), R4L (0–2), R4L (0–3), S4L (0–4), S4L (0–5), R5W (1–5), R5L (1–6), S5W (2–6), S5W (3–6), R5L (3–7)
Total Level of Criticality/Pt. Won/Score: 45–15/6–7

Perhaps the most psychologically significant episode in a tennis match is the tie breaker. From the very beginning of the tie breaker, each point has a heightened level of criticality. If our player could win the tie breaker he would win the match with a 2–0 lead in sets (two out of three sets constitutes a winning match). Unfortunately, our player got off to a bad start, falling behind 0–5 before winning his first point. Once his opponent reached 5 points, every point thereafter received a CW of 5. A loss of a point would lead to set point against our player. At 1–6, our player faced 5 consecutive set points. He managed to win two CW 5 points before losing the 3–6 point and the tie breaker.

Set 2: 7–6 to the Champion

Our player had an opportunity to win the match by winning the tie breaker. Although he lost the set, he performed well earlier in the set when he managed to rebreak after losing his serve. This gave him the opportunity to stay in the set and reach a tie breaker. Our player's PPPQ was 0.408.

Set 3

Game 1
PPS/W or L: R 1L, 1L, 1W, 3L, 1W, 4W, 4L, 4L
Total Level of Criticality/Pt. Won/Score: 19–6/0–1

Our player had an opportunity to reach break point against serve after being down 15–40. During this process he won one and lost two CW 4 points.

Game 2
PPS/W or L: S 2W, 2W, 2W, 1L, 2W
Total Level of Criticality/Pt. Won/Score: 11–10/1–1

Our player won his serve in a routine manner.

Game 3
PPS/W or L: R 2L, 2W, 3L, 3W, 4W, 5L, 4L, 4W, 4L, 4L
Total Level of Criticality/Pt. Won/Score: 35–13/1–2

Our player lost this return game after having a game point at 40–30. In the process he lost one CW 5 and two CW 4 points. Breaking serve at this point in a match would have given our player a psychological boost and statistical advantage in this match. Notice that the average CW in this game was 3.5 with our player well under (0.371) his first set's PPPQ of 0.580.

Game 4
PPS/W or L: S 2L, 3W, 3L, 4W, 4L, 5W, 4L, 5W, 4L, 5L
Total Level of Criticality/Pt. Won/Score: 39–17/1–3

Our player struggled with his serve, getting into trouble by losing a CW 4 point at 30–30. He did manage to win 2 CW 5 break points. Unfortunately he lost both CW 4 deuce points. This repeatedly put him in critical situations that he eventually could not master, losing a CW 4 and 5 points and his serve.

Game 5
PPS/W or L: R 2L, 2W, 3L, 3W, 4L, 4L
Total Level of Criticality/Pt. Won/Score: 18–5/1–4

Being down a service break in the final set of a match can create enormous psychological pressure. Although our player again played well in another return game in this set, he could not win crucial CW 4 points to break his opponent's serve.

Game 6
PPS/W or L: S 3W, 3L, 3W, 3W, 2W
Total Level of Criticality/Pt. Won/Score: 14–11/2–4

At 1–4 down in the final set, a player can frequently count on his or her opponent to let up slightly psychologically. This was reflected in this game that our player won easily. The psychological dynamic here is that the opponent who is in the lead needs only to win his serve to win the match. As a consequence, there is a tendency to focus more on the service game and less on the return game.

Game 7
PPS/W or L: R 3L, 3L, 3L, 1L
Total Level of Criticality/Pt. Won/Score: 10–0/2–5

Our player lost this game without much of a struggle. Notice that the last point (game point for the opponent) dropped to a CW of 1. This reflects resignation on the part of our player. Resignation has been shown to accompany reductions in sympathetic nervous system activity (Carlstedt 1998). Our player sensed he was going to lose and would not be able to break serve in this game.

Game 8
PPS/W or L: S 3L, 3L, 5L, 5W, 5W, 5W, 5L, 4W, 5L, 5W, 5L, 5L
Total Level of Criticality/Pt. Won/Score: 55–24/2–6

Sensing that our player was struggling psychologically (perhaps being aware of the lost opportunities in set 2) the opponent jumped out to a 40–0 lead and three break/match points. Our player fought back to deuce, winning three CW 5 points in a row. However, he then proceeded to lose the deuce point (CW 5) and face match point against him. Again he won this point (CW 4) to get back to deuce, only to lose the next CW 5 point and again face match point. After getting back to deuce one more time (CW 5), he went on to lose the next 2 points (CW 5) and the match. Notice that the average CW for points in this game was 4.7.

Comments

Our player seemed to have been worn down psychologically by early into the third set. As is frequently the case, players on the verge of victory who do not take advantage of an opportunity to win subsequently falter (PPPQ = 0.428).

Match Summary

Set 1

PPPQ (avg./pt. CW = 2.8): 96 out of 164 = 0.581
PPPQ for CW levels 4 and 5: 7 out of 12 = 0.583
PPPQ for CW levels 3, 4, and 5: 16 out of 24 = 0.667

Our player's PPPQ in the first set was relatively high for all levels of critical moments (CWs), as might be expected in a set in which he beat one of the top players in the world.

Set 2

PPPQ (avg./pt. CW = 2.8): 101 out of 223 = 0.408
PPPQ for CW levels 4 and 5: 9 out of 24 = 0.375
PPPQ for CW levels 3, 4, and 5: 18 out of 44 = 0.409

In set 2 we observe a significant drop in psychological performance with a relatively low PPPQ for CW levels 4 and 5. This was a set our player could have won, considering he broke his opponent's serve and reached the tie breaker. In the tie breaker, our player's PPPQ fell to 0.333 in a game that had an average CW over 4. Interpreted in the context of the TCM-PHO tenet, one would predict that a player who is high in hypnotic ability/absorption, high in neuroticism, and low in repressive coping is likely to falter psychologically in the highest-pressure situations. Our player, who was on the cusp of being medium/high hypnotic ability/absorption and low/medium for repressive coping, and who was high in neuroticism, appeared to lose concentration in the tie breaker, falling behind 0–5. Remember, although athletes can benefit from individual or constellations of PHO factors during routine macro/global phases of competition, negative constellations of PHO factors are most likely to disrupt psychological performance during microlevel critical moments.

Set 3

PPPQ (avg./pt. CW = 3.3): 86 out of 201 = 0.428
PPPQ for CW levels 4 and 5: 11 out of 27 = 0.407
PPPQ for CW levels 3, 4, and 5: 17 out of 42 = 0.381

Our player lost set 3 quickly and, as was apparent from his PPPQ during CW levels 3, 4, and 5 in this set, did not recover mentally from his poor psychological performance during the second-set tie breaker. As is frequently the case, poor psychological performance carries over or is perpetuated once poor play sets in, especially in athletes who are high in hypnotic ability/absorption and neuroticism and low in repressive coping. Our player appeared to ruminate on negative images and cognitions associated with the second-set tie breaker, and was unable to summon up the mental toughness needed to remain competitive in the third set.

Match Totals

PPPQ (avg./pt. CW = 2.8): 283 out of 588 = 0.481
PPPQ for CW levels 4 and 5: 27 out of 63 = 0.429
PPPQ for CW levels 3, 4, and 5: 51 out of 110 = 0.467

When using the CCMPP-I to analyze psychological performance, it is important to look beyond the PPPQ for the entire match or individual sets. It is necessary to go to the microlevel and to interpret differences between the mean PPPQ and the PPPQ for specific instances or moments of competition. For example, although our player had a PPPQ of close to 50%, it dropped to as low as 33% during the most critical moments of the match (in the tie breaker). In this match, the low PPPQ in the tie breaker clearly reflected poor psychological performance on the part of our player at a critical juncture. Isolating an athlete's PPPQ in the context of the most critical moments is crucial to the analysis of psychological performance.

Percentage of Criticality Weight Level Won

Table 2 also reflects a more micro analysis of psychological performance (CWs). Although we observe decrements in CW success rates across the sets, notice that our player still had a 56% success rate for

Table 2 Percentage of Criticality Weight Level Won

Points Won	Total (%)	Set 1 (%)	Set 2 (%)	Set 3 (%)
5	54	60	56	46
4	39	57	25	36
3	53	75	45	40

CW 5 points in set 2. This statistic could mislead one to think that our player, although losing the set, was still mentally tough; after all, he won 56% of CW 5 points. However, our player won only 25% of CW 4 points, or 40% of combined CW 4 and CW 5 points in this set. This set of statistics, although being a higher microlevel than overall mean PPPQ for a complete match or set, must also be viewed with caution because one could still overlook critical moments that were pivotal to the outcome of a match (such as the tie breaker in the second set.)

As a general rule, for the purposes of research that attempts to associate psychological variables with statistical outcome measures of performance, it is recommended that at least three PPPQs be used. The PPPQ should reflect increasing microlevels or critical moment episodes. For example, in this case we would analyze the relationship between constellation of PHO factors with mean PPPQ for the entire match, each set and the tie breaker. We would also observe these relationships in the context of PPPQs that are obtained on the basis of CWs 1–5; 3, 4, and 5; and 4 and 5.

The goal of such a multifaceted analysis is to isolate the greatest microlevel critical moment or moments and to use the PPPQ relative to these moments as the benchmark for mental toughness or psychological performance. In this case, the greatest microlevel critical moments occurred during the tie breaker. Conceivably, even though our player possessed a potentially detrimental constellation of PHO factors, analysts who relied only on his mean PPPQ for the entire match would have deemed him to have a good level of mental toughness. However, a further microanalysis revealed that during the most critical moments of the match, his psychological performance was poor and consistent with predictions from the TCM. Again, the key to isolating relationships between psychological variables and especially TCM-PHO factors lies in reducing statistical performance outcome measures to the greatest microlevel possible.

Table 3 is presented for readers who are not tennis experts to illustrate that statistics need to be customized to deal with the physical, technical, and psychological realities of a sport. For example, in men's tennis on most court surfaces the server has at least a slight and at most a major advantage over the returner. As a consequence, psychological statistics (CWs) and PPPQs in tennis must reflect this inherent advantage. Expert raters need to consider such a factor when

Table 3   Serving When Returning

Points Won	Serving (%)	When Returning (%)
5	50	44
4	47	35
3	67	38

establishing CW, and analysts must generate PPPQs when a player both serves and receives. Here, the statistics reveal higher PPPQs when serving than returning. Because the server is in a position to control a point from the outset, the failure to do so can signal psychological influences on technical performance. In this particular match, losing 50% of CW 5 and 53% of CW 4 reflects poor psychological performance when serving, whereas a 44% success rate for CW 5 points when returning could actually reflect good psychological performance when returning serve. An analysis of the tie breaker CW statistics revealed that our player won two out of five CW 4 and 5 points when serving and won one out of five CW 4 points when returning.

Using the CCMPP-I in Other Sports: Examples

Complete sport-specific analysis protocols and training (in CCMPP-I use) for analysts are available for coaches, sport psychology practitioners, and organizations/teams. It should be noted that analysts must have expertise in the sport being analyzed and, ideally, use at least two or three expert raters to assess psychological performance to optimally apply the CCMPP-I. If this is impractical, one analyst will suffice provided he or she has expertise in a sport. However, for research purposes it is mandatory that at least two expert raters be involved in the analysis process.

Assessment of Psychological Performance Using Technical Outcome Measures

Another approach to the assessment of psychological performance involves using technical factors as the performance outcome measure. Using technical measures in place of outcome-oriented statistical indices (win–lose, success percentage, etc.) has an advantage in that the PPPQ is an independently controlled outcome measure. The technical PPPQ (PPPQ-T) is based on deviations from an established individual norm for technical proficiency/style/tendencies during moments of competition of varying levels of criticality (CW). Maladaptive or negative deviations from an athlete's technical norm are hypothesized to reflect psychological influences on motor performance. In contrast to the PPPQ-I that is based on winning or losing points during competition, and that ultimately can be influenced by the performance of an opponent, the PPPQ-T is not directly affected by a competitor's actions. Obviously, if an opponent is capable of dictating play, this could disrupt an athlete's technical performance. However, this would be an indirect influence on technical performance, with consequent negative technical deviations (tds) being attributable to psychological influences on motor performance and not to the stellar performance of an opponent per se. For example, in tennis, a forcing shot by an opponent can lead to unforced errors.

From a strictly statistical perspective, the PPPQ-T exclusively reflects an individual measure of performance that is relatively free from measurement error, whereas the PPPQ-I contains measurement error that can be directly attributed to an opponent's performance. For example, if an athlete has a PPPQ-T of 0.750 during CW 5 moments of competition, this means that he or she exhibited technical deficiencies (tds) 25% of the time during this microlevel 5 critical moment. However, when examining the athlete's PPPQ-I in the same situation, his or her psychological performance proficiency might drop to 0.450. Such a decrement in an athlete's PPPQ-I when compared to their PPPQ-T usually can be attributed to the influence of an opponent on statistical outcome measures and not just psychological factors.

The PPPQ-T approach emanated from my work with an ATP tour tennis coach interested in documenting the psychological performance of a player he coached, who later went on to win Wimbledon. During our initial consultation we both came to the conclusion that his player exhibited subtle changes in technique throughout the course of matches, especially against higher-ranked opponents. It was felt that the player had to overcome the tendency to deviate from ingrained technical patterns associated with peak performances if he were ever to win a major championship. It should be noted that although this player was not assessed for PHO factors, the above tendency would be consistent with athletes who are medium to high in hypnotic ability/absorption, medium to high in neuroticism, and low to medium in repressive coping because persons with this constellation tend to be overly aware of their environment and the people they encounter, which can lead to hypervigilance and excessive physiological reactivity. Such a dynamic can disrupt motor performance in athletes.

Assessing Technical Performance: A Case Study

Over the course of about 6 months, numerous tournament matches of our player were analyzed from a technical perspective. I would sit next to the coach during matches, documenting every point with the CCMPP-I system. CWs were attached to every point, but instead of correlating points won–lost with CW, technical parameters were analyzed in relationship to the CW of a point. We soon observed that our player's most glaring flaw occurred when returning serve in the ad-court on a fast service. Here we observed a consistent breakdown in footwork and movement, resulting in his stabbing at the return as opposed to attacking it by quickly moving into the shot. Although he could win points despite a negative td, in accord with the CCMPP-I system, our player was only credited with success whenever his technique was perfect.

The following is a sample outtake from a point progression protocol from an ATP tour match in Stuttgart Germany, where our player reached the finals.

Game 1

1. *S, CW 1, first serve fault (1f) = td, second serve fault td L (toss) score: 0–15; point statistics: two attempts/two tds.* This point progression line is interpreted as follows: Our player had two attempts at carrying out the serve. He missed both. His missed serves were attributed to poor ball tosses by his coach, which is notated as "toss." A result of two for two equals a PPPQ-T of 0.000.

2. *S, CW 2, S1n, forehand volley crosscourt, td (split step), Ohw, W, 15–15; point statistics: three attempts/one td.* On this point our player hit a first serve in, a forehand volley crosscourt, and a winner overhead. Notice that although our player won the point, he was still penalized by his coach for doing a poor split step. Normally, on a fast surface our player would have put away the initial volley for a winner. However, because of his poor footwork he allowed his opponent a chance to stay in the point, increasing the odds that our player would lose this point. The PPPQ-T system penalizes all observable negative tds regardless of the outcome of a stroke or point. The PPPQ-T of this point was equal to 0.667.

3. *S1 net, td (toss), 2 S1n, FIIcc, BHsl, td (slow fw), L, 15–30; point statistics: four attempts/two tds.* On this point our player missed his first serve because of a poor ball toss (td). He hit in his second serve, followed by a forehand crosscourt and a backhand slice down the line that was long. The backhand error was attributed to slow footwork (td). Our player got off to a slow start on one of his favorite surfaces. When forced to stay in the backcourt, usually after a missed first serve or when returning, technical problems were seen to surface. At this point we should not necessarily

attribute technical problems to psychological influences, although one could argue that slow starts can be caused by inadequate mental preparation. However, because the CW of this point was only 2, we will attribute tds to the long-standing technical problems our player has. The PPPQ-T of this point was equal to 0.500.

4. *S, CW 4, BHVll, td (short), FHVcc, td (short), OH, td (long, pronation), L 15–40; point statistics: four attempts/three tds.* On this point, our player displayed tds on a backhand and a forehand volley that he hit short, indicating poor forward progression of the racket from the contact point. He also failed to follow through properly on the overhead, resulting in an error. The PPPQ-T of this point was equal to 0.250.

5. *S1l, td (pronation) CW 5, S2in, FHl, BHtcc, td (too much TS), BHp, td (weak TS), L game, 0–1; point statistics: five attempts/ three tds.* This point had a CW of 5, a psychologically significant point, especially because a loss of a service game on a fast surface can lead to losing the set. The fact that our player did not get his powerful first serve in and made a very weak backhand passing shot attempt indicates that his technical deficiencies were mediated by psychological factors. Our postmatch debriefing of the player confirmed our suspicions. Our player mentioned he was consciously concerned about getting his first serve in at 15–40. The game score was 0–1, with the PPPQ-T of this point equal to 0.400.

The PPPQ-T for this game (11 tds out of 18 attempts [tennis strokes] = 0.390) is consistent with what one would expect on the basis of his technical performance. Considering that our player had 11 tds out of 18 attempted tennis strokes, it is no surprise that our player lost the first game of the match.

The following game was quite different from the first game. In game 4 you will notice that our player won the game, yet his technical performance was quite weak. The CCMPP-I system of analysis is concerned with technical performance in relationship to the CW of a point and not the outcome of a point. As a consequence, one can win more points than one loses but still have a psychological performance rating indicating a player did not perform well mentally despite winning the game.

Game 4 of the First Set (Score at this Point: 1–2 against Our Player)

1. *R (receiving), CW 1, BHr1sl, td (no step), opponent volley error, 15–0; point statistics: one attempt/one td.* Although our player

won this point, he was penalized for poor technique on the backhand return of serve. The td occurring at this moment was likely not caused by psychological influences because the CW of the point was only 1. The PPPQ-T of this point was equal to 0.000.

2. *R, CW 2, BHr2cc, td (short return weak step), BHp, td (weak floater), opponent volley error, 30–0; point statistics: two attempts/two tds.* Our player appears to have gotten lucky again: After exhibiting a td on the return of serve and follow-up backhand passing shot attempt, his opponent made another easy volley error. Again, although our player is now leading 30–0 in an important game, he still is not performing well technically. The CW of this point was a 2, indicating that his poor technique was still more physically than psychologically driven. Notice that despite leading in this game by a score of 30–0, our player has a technical proficiency quotient of 0.000. The PPPQ-T of this point was equal to 0.000.

3. R, *CW 4, BHrcc, td (weak slice) BHpl, td (weak slice), Fhplwinner, 40–0; point statistics: two attempts /three tds.* Although our player hit a forehand passing shot winner, he was lucky to get a second opportunity to hit a passing shot because his weak return of serve or first passing shot attempt, a weak backhand slice, should have been put away for a winner by his opponent. As a result, although he won this CW 4 point, the tds that he exhibited revealed psychologically mediated weaknesses. In the context of the CCMPP-I system, rather than reward a player for winning a CW 4 point that in all actuality should have been won by his opponent, our player was again penalized for displaying tds. Note again that despite leading 40–0 in this game, our player's PPPQ-T until now in this game is only 0.088. This quotient reflects our player's only exhibiting correct technique in one out of eight attempts (tennis strokes). The PPPQ-T of this point was equal to 0.333.

4. *R, CW 5, BH2cc, td (no step), opponent FH error, game to our player, score 2–2; point statistics: one attempt/one td.* The progression of this game was quite rare, especially on a fast surface where the server usually dominates. Here, again, although our player hit a weak service return off the second serve, he was not punished for it. Instead, his opponent made another easy error. In contrast to the CCMPP-I, the PPPQ-T is less likely to mistakenly reflect psychological influences. In the case of this point, the former assessment system would have credited our player with winning a CW 5 point, even though in reality this point was lost by his opponent. Coupled with the fact that our player was technically deficient in this game, it would not have been valid to credit our

player for being mentally tough in this situation (CM). The PPPQ-T is concerned with psychological influences on technical performance and not outcome per se. This game illustrates how a player can win a game and still be a "loser" in terms of psychologically mediated technical performance. The PPPQ-T of this point was equal to .000.

The total PPPQ-T for game 4 was eight tds out of nine attempts (tennis strokes), or 0.088 (a very low PPPQ-T despite his winning the game).

Conversely, a player can also lose a game and yet exhibit excellent psychological performance, as reflected in a high PPPQ-T. This is illustrated in game 9 of the first set. In such a scenario, a player may successfully hit a variety of shots with excellent technique but still lose the point because of an opponent's stellar play, ending a point with a winning shot. The CCMPP-I would not capture such a dynamic because it only credits players psychologically when they win a point.

Game 9 of the first set was very important and psychologically significant, with high CWs being allotted to all the points in this game. After making up the lost-service game (first game of the match) our player was at 4–4 in the first set. It was crucial that he hold serve and take a 5–4 lead or else he would face set game returning serve.

Game 9

1. *S, CW 3, S1cc, FHcc, opponent wins shot with an incredible passing shot, 0–15; point statistics = two attempts/zero tds.* Here our player hit a good first serve that he followed up with a volley hit deep into his opponent's court. His technique was good with no tds. However, his opponent hit a spectacular passing shot to win the point.
2. *S1n, CW 4, td (low toss), S2m, FHl, BHl, FHcc, BHp, opponent volley winner, 0–30; point statistics = six attempts/one td.* Our player lost this point despite playing well technically. Although he missed his first serve because of a td, he proceeded to hit a good second serve followed up by a forehand down the line, backhand down the line, and forehand cross-court, at which point his opponent attacked the net. Our player made a backhand passing shot attempt that was well hit. However, his opponent intercepted the shot and hit a volley winner. Our expert raters determined that the backhand passing shot attempt was hit with good technique and speed. Our player exhibited good mental performance even though he lost this critical point.

3. *S1ace, CW 5, wins point 15–30; point statistics = one attempt/zero tds.* Our player hit a service ace to win this CW 5 point.

4. *S1, CW 5, opponent hits a winner off the serve 15–40; point statistics = one attempt/zero tds.* Our player hit a very powerful serve. However, it was returned for a winner by his opponent, leading to break point against our player.

5. *S1, CW 5, BHvcc, Bhol, BHvcc, FHvccd, opponent dives for ball making an incredible passing shot, opponent wins game and breaks serve to go up 5–4 in the first set; point statistics = 15 attempts/one td.* This game was not meant to be for our player. Although he played nearly flawlessly in the technical sense, his opponent came up with successive winning shots that would not have been expected. Although CWs of all points in this game were high, our player did not succumb mentally. He was able to maintain control over his technical game and motor skills despite the inherent pressure associated with every point in this game. It appeared though that our player's opponent had a physical (speed) advantage once the ball was in play and was capable of making shots a lesser player would not have made.

Our player only had one td out of 15 attempts (15 tennis strokes in the game), indicating a high level of mind–body motor control despite the high CW of each point in this game. For game 9, the PPPQ-T was 1 tds out of 15 attempts (tennis strokes), or 0.937 (a very high PPPQ-T despite the loss of the game).

Total Match Statistics

Set 1

The match score was 4–6, 7–5, 6–1 (our player won the match two sets to one), with the PPPQ-T of set 1 being 40 tds out of 240 attempts (strokes), or 0.836. Although our player lost the first set, his overall psychological proficiency was very high, demonstrating that good mental performance is not intrinsically associated with winning or positive outcome. Moreover, poor psychological performance is not necessarily associated with losing, as the following statistic reveals.

Set 2

The PPPQ-T of set 2 was 85 tds out of 238 attempts (strokes), or 0.643. Although a PPPQ-T of 0.643 might not seem that low, it reflects poor technical performance for a professional tennis player. This quotient reflects a td almost every two strokes. In set 2, our player managed to win 7–5 despite performing weak technically. A postmatch interview with our player revealed that he was concerned with losing the set very early in the set, a cognition that stayed with him to the very end of the set. Such intrusive thoughts are consistent with our player's hypothesized profile of PHO factors. Although CWs early in this set were in the low to medium range (1–3), our player apparently attached more psychological significance to each point in this set than did the expert raters. This indicates that players should be debriefed after a CCMPP analysis or should be integrated into the CW rating process.

Set 3

Our player won this set easily (PPPQ-T of set 3 was 23 tds out of 112 attempts [strokes] = 0.750), to take the match in three sets. The statistics of the final set reflected technical and physical more than psychological influences on performance. The average CW of points (1.5) in this set attests to this. Although the third set in a two-out-of-three match is the decisive one, and as a result is usually more stress-laden, in this set, our player was able to dominate with his physical and technical skills (a powerful serve). Our debriefing revealed that our player, after winning the second set despite having played poorly both mentally and technically, saw the third set as an opportunity to regain control. He did just that, resorting to his technical weapons (serve and net game) to carry him to victory. It should be noted that our player did not encounter any CW level 3 and 4 points in the third set. By contrast, in set 2 he encountered 50 CW level 4 and 5 points, during which tds occurred.

Match Totals

The total PPPQ-T for the match was 0.749 (148 tds out of 590 attempts/strokes), and the PPPQ-T for CW 4 and 5 was 36 tds out of 60 attempts (strokes during CW 4 and 5 points), or 0.400.

As when analyzing psychological performance on the basis of won and loss or success vs. failure outcome measures, it is important to determine psychologically mediated technical performance (CCMPP-I) in relationship to the most microlevel CW (critical moments). Doing so reveals a significant drop in psychologically mediated technical performance from 0.749 during all levels of criticality (CW 1–5) to only 0.400 during the most critical moments of competition. This demonstrates that the analysis of psychological performance must be multifaceted to isolate relationships between psychological factors and performance outcome measures. Taken at face value, one could easily deem the psychological performance of our player to be quite good. After all, he won the match by taking the third set easily after "squeaking by" in the second set. On the basis of conventional outcome measures such as win–lose or success–failure, we indeed might conclude that our player was mentally tough during this match. However, a closer analysis of technical parameters associated with peak performance revealed a significant decrement as a function of the level of criticality of competitive moments. During the most critical moments of this match, our player essentially played his worst tennis technically, independent of the outcome of a stroke or point.

It should be noted that one can also use the CCMPP-I system to evaluate tactical performance concurrent to technical performance. Because tactics are formulated centrally and represent strategic planning, the strategy in which a player engages can be very revealing of a player's psychological state. Although I will not present an entire tactical analysis in this chapter, templates for the assessment of psychologically mediated tactical performance are available on request. However, I will show one point progression line containing a tactical component that was extracted from the previously analyzed match: game 7: S, CW 3, S1f, S2cc, FHcc, BHcc, tacd, BHp, opponent volley error.

Our player won the point. However, note that our player, a dominating serve and volley/net attacking type, never should have gotten himself in a position to potentially lose the point. Normally, based on statistical analyses, once an opponent is at the net on a fast surface, he wins the point 80% of the time. As a consequence, our player was lucky that his opponent made an error at the net on this point. Nevertheless, our player is penalized by the CCMPP-I system for making a tactical mistake. Notice the "tacd" after BHcc above. This indicates that our player made a tactical error on this shot. Instead of attacking the net, he stayed back, as can be inferred by his next shot (a backhand passing shot), which was a tactical error in this situation because the odds of winning a point on this surface increase when a player is at the net. By not including tactics in the analysis of a point's progression, one could easily overlook an important cognitive element of performance that is very revealing relative to the assessment of psychological functioning during competition.

Assessment of Critical Moments Using Physiological Measures

The third and potentially most objective approach to the assessment of critical moments is rating the psychological significance of competitive events using physiological measures. An advantage of this approach is that critical moments can be defined or will emerge on the basis of physiological responses during specific competitive moments an athlete encounters. Rather than rely on expert raters and post hoc debriefings of players to evaluate the level of criticality of a competitive moment, the psychophysiological approach defines a critical moment in terms of deviations from an individual norm for physiological responding during specific competitive situations.

The psychophysiological approach involves synchronizing physiological responses with competitive moments and determining the criticality of a competitive moment on the basis of these responses. For example, an expert rater might deem a particular competitive moment to have a CW of 1, yet the athlete exhibits excessive low-frequency heart rate variability (indicating heightened sympathetic nervous system activity) and less HRD compared to his or her normal heart activity responses during similar competitive moments. The exhibited excessive physiological response (low-frequency heart rate variability [HRV]) likely reflects psychological influences on physiology. In this situation, the athlete's actual physiological responding would determine the CW of the competitive moment, superseding the expert rater's CW rating. In this case the CW might be adjusted upward to a CW of 3 or 4 based on the magnitude of deviation from the athlete's physiological norm for HRV during similar competitive moments.

Although we would hope to observe strong correlations between expert ratings and physiological responses, one cannot assume that these measures will be congruous. As a consequence, one should use both expert raters and physiological responses whenever possible to determine CWs and PPP quotients. Once congruence is established between expert ratings and physiological responding, one has the option to rely solely on expert rating (for practical reasons). However, if possible, physiological measures should be integrated into the assessment process to validate expert ratings and self-report concurrently because physiological measures are expected to better reveal subliminal processes (e.g., thought processes, emotions) that expert raters and athletes may not be aware of.

Here is a sample outtake from a point progression line of a tennis match in which psychophysiological measures were integrated. The expert rater's CW is replaced (post hoc) by a CW based on an actual physiological response (HRD) during the competitive moment:

Score: 4–5 in the third set of a tennis match. The player is returning serve. Point 1, CW 1, heart rate increased to 127 instead of the expected heart rate deceleration, indicative of hyperreactivity (i.e., psychological stress) during preaction when preparing to return serve. As a result, the CW (expert rating) was raised from 1 to CW4. Although the expert raters determined that the first point when returning serve (even at 4–5 in the third set) was not psychologically stressful, the player's physiological response (heart rate) during this competitive moment revealed that the situation induced a physiological response that deviated from his norm. The manifestation of heart rate acceleration instead of the expected HRD clearly reflected increased psychological reactivity or stress in this situation, warranting an increase of the CW of this competitive moment. Although one might argue that increased physiological reactivity in this situation is appropriate because preparing to respond is associated with increased motivation and intensity, one should recall that during the preparation phase of a self-paced task or when waiting to respond, HRD is a species-wide response associated with attention. Heart rate acceleration during the preparation phase is a deviation from species-wide norms as well as most individual norms unless an athlete always exhibits HRA in the preparation phase, which most likely would lead to poor performance.

Obviously, the use of psychological measures to determine CWs and assess psychological performance requires an extensive database of physiological responses to establish an athlete's individual norms. However, some of my preliminary research indicates that one can assess psychological performance on the basis of more global indices of physiological responding, making it easier for practitioners to apply psychophysiological methods for assessing psychological performance during critical moments. One method involves monitoring heart activity over the course of a competition. At the end of a game or match, the obtained heart activity data is entered into an HRV and HRD analysis program (e.g., BioCom Technologies HRV/HRD analysis software).

This method is applied in the following exploratory study, in which an attempt was made to assess psychological performance on the basis of global HRD trends without precisely synchronizing heart activity to competitive events. Because HRD and HRA trends clearly distinguish competitive moments (e.g., longer HRD trends usually occur before the commencement of action, longer HRA trends usually occur during action), the goal of this study was to be able to evaluate psychological performance by analyzing HRD/HRA trends independent of game statistics, technical/tactical evaluation, and outcome.

Using a blind analysis in which heart activity was analyzed post hoc without knowledge of outcome, this research attempted to predict performance strictly on the basis of heart activity. It was theorized that HRD/HRA trends would distinguish psychological performance and help to more precisely define zone or flow states.

10

Toward a Global Physiological Marker of Psychological Performance and Critical Moments during Competition: Assessing Zone or Flow States

Because the psychophysiological approach to the assessment of critical moments can be laborious, a quick, efficient, and reliable method for assessing global psychological performance is needed. An emerging method that I am developing involves monitoring and analyzing heart activity over the course of an entire competition because it appears to be the physiological measure that best illuminates mind–body interactions. It is also the only measure that can be reliably monitored during actual competition in a relatively nonintrusive manner, making it ideal for assessing psychological performance during critical moments of competition.

Although it has been established that decreased heart rate (HRD) reflects heightened attention during competitive moments that are preceded by a mental preparation phase, it has yet to be determined to what extent HRD occurs over the course of an entire competition independent of mental preparation phases (i.e., during action phases). As a conseqience, in this exploratory study, a tennis player's heart activity was monitored during an actual match to not only isolate HRD trends before action but also delineate global heart activity over an entire competition.

Participant and Procedure

A German amateur men's 35 division-ranked tournament tennis player's heart activity was monitored during the first round of tournament competition using the Polar Vantage system. The player was assessed for primary higher-order (PHO) factors and cerebral laterality before the match and was found to be high in absorption, high in neuroticism, and low in repressive coping. He was also shown to be relative right-brain hemisphere predominant on the basis of a line-bisecting test. His cerebral laterality score was consistent with high neuroticism and low repressive coping (relative left-hemisphere hypo-activation and increased right-hemisphere activation). The player's constellation of PHO factors made him psychologically vulnerable during critical moments of competition.

Heart activity was monitored continuously but was not synchronized to specific competitive events. Set statistics included points played, preaction points, and action moments. Afterward, the match data were transferred from the Polar device into heart rate variability and HRD software for analysis.

Analysis of the Data

Previous research (Carlstedt 1998) indicates that "true" heart rate deceleration, as distinguished from heart rate slowing because of diminishing metabolic demands, consists of an uninterrupted linear progression of at least four interbeat intervals (IBIs; e.g., 468, 473, 480, 487). An HRD trend is considered to be over whenever its linearity is broken by an accelerating IBI (e.g., 468, 473, 465). Linear HRD trends of four or more IBIs were isolated and interpreted in the context of previous research, the Theory of Critical Moments (TCM), and set statistics (post hoc).

Match Result and Set Statistics

The player lost his first-round match 4–6, 7–6, 6–1. For the purpose of this analysis, set 1 was compared with set 3; these sets were highly incongruous in outcome and HRD trends. Set 1 consisted of 60 points, 60 preaction preparation moments, and 360 action moments (six strokes per point). Action moments are defined as strokes (hitting the ball) occurring during the course of a point including the serve or return of serve. Set 3 consisted of 35 points, 35 preaction moments, and 175 action moments (five strokes per point).

These results were blind (not known) to me until after the heart activity data were analyzed. The y-axis of the histogram (Figure 10) depicts the number of HRD trends listed on the x-axis. Considering that both sets consisted of only 95 points, it is obvious that HRD occurred in excess of actual preaction moments (preparing to serve or return serve). However, when one considers the amount of strokes (action moments) that correspond to each point (competitive moment), most of the HRD trends can be accounted for.

In set 1, there was an average of six strokes per point, or a total of 360 action moments within the 60 points. In set 3 there were 175 action moments within the 35 points played. When analyzing HRD trends without being able to precisely synchronize them with competitive events, it is important to rely on previous investigations for guidance. Because most studies of HRD (for a review see Carlstedt 1998) in sports and in the laboratory have revealed HRD trends of at least four IBIs, trends of three IBIs were eliminated from the analysis. Very short HRD trends (less than or equal to IBIs) were considered random, superfluous, and irrelevant to performance and were thought to occur mostly during phases of movement not having a direct effect on preparation or sport-specific task (e.g., walking to get into position, walking to the bench).

HRD trends of four, five, and six IBIs were considered relevant to performance, leading to a preliminary theory attempting to explain their presence during action, something that has not previously been considered or thought possible. Because of their high prevalence and inability to explain HRD during action on the basis of two, three, and eight or more linear IBI sequences, I hypothesized that HRD trends of four, five, and six IBIs had to have occurred primarily during action moments in which technical, tactical, or physical performance was consistent with or exceeded normative performance standards. These magnitudes of HRD trends are thought most likely to occur during action moments when an athlete does not experience negative psychological influences (e.g., PHO-mediated negative intrusive thoughts). Instead, they are hypothesized to reflect psychophysiological microevents during action

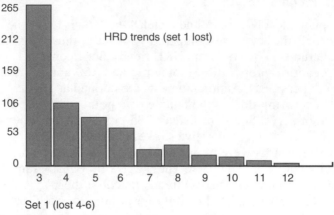

Figure 10a.

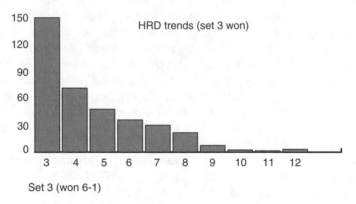

Figure 10b. Heart rate deceleration trends.

phases in which baro-receptor activity regulates flow of blood to the brain to facilitate task performance. I predict that athletes who are in control of mind–body processes (free from negative intrusive thoughts) will exhibit HRD not only before the initiation of a sport-specific task (e.g., preparing to putt) but also during action moments as well (e.g., shooting at a goal while moving). In contrast, athletes who experience negative intrusive thoughts during action will exhibit excessive or extra HR (heart rate acceleration [HRA]; Blix et al. 1974), exceeding metabolic demands that can disrupt motor performance or technical skills. When this occurs, baro-receptor activity permits more blood flow to the brain, activating cortical areas that should normally remain dormant during motor performance.

When comparing HRD trends of four, five, or six IBIs between sets, we observe that set 1 contained 240 such trends out of 360 action moments. This indicates that 120 action moments were devoid of HRD. In set 3, there were 155 HRD trends of four, five, or six IBIs and 175 action moments. Although we cannot be certain that these HRD trends corresponded to action moments, it is highly probable that they did, as lower- and higher-magnitude HRD trends are most likely to occur during other competitive and noncompetitive moments. As previously noted, HRD trends of two or three IBIs are most likely to occur in a random fashion, accompanying walking, slight movements, or resting, whereas HRD trends of seven, eight, nine, and ten IBIs have been shown to occur when preparing for action. Because it is unlikely that a linear trend of four, five, or six progressively slowing IBIs will occur randomly, action moments can be best accounted for on the basis of HRD trends of these magnitudes, with the ratio of HRD trends of four to six IBIs to total action moments being a potential index of psychological performance during action moments of competition (action moments/HRD trends = PPPQ-Phrd [Psychological Performance Proficiency Quotient-Psychophysiological Index/HRD]) in this study.

Using this formula, the player's PPPQ-Phrd was 0.667 in set 1 and 0.889 in set 3. This means that in set 1 it is probable that 120 action moments were not accompanied by HRD, indicating compromised technical, tactical, or physical performance when HRD did not occur. By contrast, in set 3 it is probable that this player experienced HRD during action moments approximately 89% of the time, or 155 out of 175 action moments. A PPPQ of 0.889 is very high and may reflect a level of psychophysiological functioning associated with a zone or flowlike state.

Preaction moments were also analyzed on the basis of HRD trends. In set 1 there were 75 HRD trends of eight, nine, or ten IBIs, 15 more than actual preaction moments. In set 3 there were 40 HRD trends in this range, five more than there were points or competitive moments (preaction phases). In the context of my preliminary TCM-HRD-action theory, whenever a range of HRD trends associated with a specific type of competitive moment exceeds the amount of actual preaction competitive moments or action moments, one can assume that technical, tactical, and physical performances were relatively free from negative psychological influences (intrusive thoughts) during those periods. Appropriately occurring HRD during any competitive moment is thought to increase the probability that motor performance will not be disrupted. Thus, in this match the player appeared to be psychologically in control during all preparation or preaction phases, as reflected in a 1:1 or greater ratio of competitive moments to HRD trends (eight, nine, or ten IBIs) in both sets.

Toward the Quantification of Zone or Flow States Using HRD

To date, most research has only documented HRD during nonaction phases of laboratory experiments, where it has been observed that HRD occurs before the initiation of an action response. Because it also has been observed that any movement occurring before responding disrupts the linear trend of consecutive slowing IBIs (HRD), few if any attempts have been made to study HRD in the context of action or during movement, because one would expect movement to disrupt HRD during sport-specific action tasks.

The effects of movement on HRD were elucidated by Obrist (1981), leading to the cardiac-somatic concept, which essentially contends that HRD is more a function of heart–muscle than heart–brain interactions. However, Lacey and Lacey (1978) took exception to the cardiac-somatic concept, attributing HRD more to attention and the orienting response as opposed to somatic quieting.

Thus, when interpreting HRD in the context of the TCM and sports, I hypothesize that HRD can occur during action moments of competition regardless of level of heart rate, metabolic demands, and muscular/motor activity during a sport-specific task because attentional and other cognitive components of focusing and orientation toward a stimuli during action very likely involve (or are unlikely not to involve) similar cortical and cardiovascular processes and interactions observed when focusing or orienting in a more static or nonaction situation. For example, when a tennis player is involved in an intense rally or a basketball player is trying to get open to shoot a jump shot, although having to maintain cardiac output associated with high metabolic demands, he or she is still expected to experience a brief episode of HRD (micro-HRD) when positive psychological processes involved in the initiation of a sport-specific action are manifested (e.g., attention, strategic planning).

Because it has clearly been demonstrated that HRD occurs before action when focusing on a stimulus (hole in golf, ball toss in tennis, hoop in basketball), it is reasonable to expect that HRD will occur even at high levels of heart rate. Such a micropsychophysiological moment is hypothesized to occur unconsciously or subliminally. If this moment is of the positive kind free from negative psychological influences (e.g., intrusive thoughts), the linear HRA that normally occurs with increased metabolic demands during intense action will briefly be interrupted precisely before the commencement of action (hitting a tennis shot while on the run, kicking a soccer ball, etc.). This temporary "freeze" in HRA is thought to facilitate neurophysiological processes underlying optimum motor control, including the baro-receptors and ensembles of neuronal units that function to block other "intrusive" neurons from interfering with performance (functional disconnection syndrome associated with high repressive coping). Relative to the TCM, the probability of achieving such a homeostatic peak performance state is more likely during innocuous routine action moments when psychological stress is minimal. However, once critical moments occur, depending on an athlete's constellation of PHO factors, an athlete will be more or less likely to experience a disruption of the delicate balance between the heart and brain.

Athletes possessing an ideal constellation of PHO factors or the Athlete's Profile are less likely to be affected by negative intrusive thoughts during critical moments as reflected in HRD, even during action phases of competition. By contrast, athletes possessing less than ideal constellations of PHO factors will more likely exhibit increases in HRA that exceed metabolic demands and that disrupt motor performance during critical moments.

Anecdotal notions such as "loss of concentration," "just do it," and being "in the zone" can be explained on the basis of, and are hypothesized to be reflected in, HRD trends, whereby remaining focused and free from intrusive thoughts is associated with micro-HRD trends of four to six IBIs during action phases and with greater-magnitude HRD trends (six or more IBIs) during preparation phases before action. It is hypothesized that so-called zone or flow states can be quantified on the basis of HRD trends, whereby consecutive HRD trends proportionate and appropriate to a specific competitive moment (action phase = four to six IBIs, preparation phase = six or more IBIs) will be an objective physiological marker of peak psychological or flow performance. Being in the zone or a flow state would be determined on the basis of a physiological measure (HRD) that correlates highly with successful technical and statistical performance outcome measures as well as self-report.

A zone or flow experience might look like this:

Return of serve: 450, 455, 468, 475, 488, 492, 495 ms (HRD); action phase: 467, 460, 445, 430, 423, 410, 400, 390, 378 (HRA), 385, 399, 403, 410 (micro-HRD prior to stroke), 391, 380, 370, 360, 345 (HRA), 366, 378, 382, 390, 399 (micro-HRD before stroke), 376, 369, 360, 355, 345 (HRA), 362, 366, 376, 384, 390 (micro-HRD); point ends.

In this point we observe one preaction preparation phase marked by a linear HRD trend of six IBIs (remember, increasing value reflects longer heart period or cardiac cycle; i.e., HRD) followed by an action phase. The action phase is delineated on the basis of commencement of a HRA trend (decreasing values, shorter heart period/cardiac cycle) consisting of nine linear, accelerating IBIs. HRA occurs as a function of increasing metabolic demands associated with running to the ball. After the 378 IBI, notice that there is a one decelerating IBI (385) followed by three more slowing IBIs. Another HRD trend starts with IBI 366 and 362. These are micro-HRD trends that are thought to reflect psychological influences involving strategic planning, priming of neuronal ensembles responsible for technical-motor action occurring at the millisecond level, long enough to maintain focus on the task at hand, but short enough to not disrupt cardiac output necessary to fulfill metabolic demands. Thereafter, HRA resumes until the next shot of the point occurring at IBI 366 and again at 362. This heart activity sequence depicts the hypothesized order of HRD and HRA acceleration trends during competitive moments of a tennis match. The observed trends are consistent with what research has revealed regarding HRD trends during preparation phases before the initiation of action and what is hypothesized to occur during actual action phases of competition. Approximations or variations of the above cycle are hypothesized to occur repeatedly whenever an athlete is in a zone or flow state.

Competitive moments and episodes consisting of appropriate HRD and HRA trends, like the above, that are sustained over the course of longer periods of time during competition are hypothesized to reflect optimum psychological performance or being "in the zone." It is expected that greater technical and physical performance will occur during phases of ideal heart rate variability (HRD-HRA) along with subjective feelings of well-being and mastery, and in many instances it will coincide with a winning performance. Once a series of ideal HRD trends comes to an end, it is predicted that a zone or flow state will also cease.

TCM-PHO factors play an important role in the HRD-zone/flow equation. Consistent with the TCM, it is expected that HRD trends are more likely to be disrupted during critical moments of competition in athletes possessing less than ideal constellations of PHO factors, and vice versa.

Although the HRD-zone/flow model needs to be further investigated, a preliminary analysis of heart activity data from this match is promising and indicates that HRD may indeed be the marker of psychological performance.

The TCM-HRD-action theory evolved from observing HRD trends in athletes, mostly tennis players, over the course of actual tournament competition and practice. Repeatedly, an analysis of heart activity revealed trends of HRD that could not be explained merely on the basis of metabolic demands or in the context of the cardiac-somatic concept, especially because many of these trends were observed to occur at high heart rate during action phases of competition, something that was not thought possible.

A recent functional magnetic resonance imaging study of golfers by Ross and colleagues (2003) indicates that cortical "quieting" occurs more frequently in skilled golfers compared with less skilled golfers. Fattaposta et al. (1996) also found more cortical effort expenditure in nonathletes attempting to learn a task never previously engaged in compared with expert marksmen. I hypothesize that reductions in cortical activity are marked by less blood perfusion to the neuron ensembles associated with specific motor activity and preparatory cognitions in expert or successful athletes. This reduction in cellular blood flow to specific neurons is regulated by baro-receptors that also induce concomitant heart rate deceleration that is seen in peak performance. By contrast, in novices or even skilled athletes who are disrupted by intrusive thoughts, more cellular blood perfusion is predicted to occur as a function of less baro-receptor control over regional cerebral blood flow, resulting in HRA or lessened HRD. Future research must determine to what extent HRD can be used to assess psychological performance and must quantify zone or flow states. Such research should precisely synchronize heart activity with competitive moments to discern whether HRD occurs lawfully as a function of psychological influences during competition.

11

Assessing and Predicting Psychological Performance during Critical Moments on the Basis of Psychophysiological Stress Testing: A Case Study

Although it is preferable to assess psychophysiological responding during actual competition, the nature of many sports can make on-the-field assessment difficult. Because of the intense movement associated with many sports, data can be compromised as motion and impact may cause electrodes to shift, resulting in artifact (faulty readings). Moreover, because physiological monitoring can be intrusive, some officials, coaches, and athletes may not be willing to participate in an elaborate system of physiological assessment. Although the credibility of psychological assessment of athletes is ultimately dependent on deriving ecologically valid data during real competition, an alternative first-step approach is to use psychophysiological stress testing (PST) off the playing field to assess response tendencies in the presence of induced stressors. These experimentally induced responses may help predict maladaptive physiological tendencies during actual competition and guide mental training interventions to counter them.

What is PST?

PST involves connecting a person to a physiological monitoring system, using electrodes and wires (or a telemetry system that does not require connecting wires) to observe the responses of various bodily systems under varying experimental conditions. Physiological responses that are frequently monitored during stress testing include heart rate/heart rate variability, blood pressure, breathing, electrodermal activity/skin conductance, muscle activity (EMG), peripheral temperature, and brain activity (EEG). The goal of PST is to assess a person's psychophysiological reactivity to stressors that are introduced during the course of monitoring. Stressors can include arithmetic tasks (e.g., counting backward from 100 by sevens), viewing disturbing photos, or self-creating negative images through visualization.

I routinely assess athletes I work with both off and on the field using physiological measures to gain insight into response tendencies that may mediate performance. Knowledge of these tendencies is crucial for designing interventions to improve psychological performance as well as for determining the efficacy of a specific mental training method. The following is a case study of a highly skilled tennis player who had major difficulties when confronting critical moments, which was consistent with what would be expected on the basis of his constellation of primary higher-order (PHO) factors (high absorption, high neuroticism, and low repressive coping).

A first step I incorporate into PST is videotaping athletes over the course of an entire real competition while keeping critical moment statistics using the Carlstedt Critical Moment Psychological Performance Index system. I use the videotaped competition as visual feedback, corresponding physiological responses to competitive moments that are being viewed, especially those having a high criticality weight (CW; 3, 4, and 5). Viewing a videotape of oneself during competition can be inherently stressful and can be expected to elicit hyperreactive physiological responses in vulnerable athletes (those with high-risk PHO constellations).

It should be noted that during a PST, many individuals are not necessarily reactive in all physiological systems being measured. However, most people do have what Wickramasekera (1988) refers to as a "window of maximum vulnerability"; that is, they exhibit excessive physiological responses in a specific bodily system. In some individuals, muscle tension may be the most revealing, whereas in others it may be peripheral temperature or heart activity, and in still others, excessive reactivity occurs in multiple systems. In certain individuals and situations, hypoactivation may occur in a specific system—an event that can have just as important implications for performance as can hyperreactivity. Thus, it is essential to measure multiple physiological systems simultaneously when stress testing.

Unfortunately, stressors encountered in the laboratory may not always elicit excessive physiological responses despite self-reports of anxiety or passivity during real-world activities or during competition. In fact, an extensive body of literature questions the validity of using PST results obtained in the laboratory to arrive at diagnoses because they have been shown not to correspond reliably to stress responses in the real world, leading to false-negative as well as false-positive readings (van Dooren, 1994). However, because most of this research failed to consider the effects of specific psychological factors and stimuli, especially constellations of PHO factors and critical moments in mediating stress responses, PST should still be administered as a first step in assessing psychophysiological reactivity. If a PST is revealing in terms of eliciting exaggerated physiological responses (compared with baseline responses), follow-up monitoring during simulated competition is indicated. If maladaptive physiological responses reoccur during simulated competition, there is a high probability that the observed response tendencies will emerge in real competition.

A Player's Window of Maximum Vulnerability: A Case Study

Because the athlete in this case study possessed a constellation of PHO factors that made him susceptible to psychological problems during competition, I suspected that merely observing critical moments he encountered in a previous match on a videotape of his performance would elicit excessive physiological responses. Being concurrently high in absorption and neuroticism and low in repressive coping predisposed him to focus and ruminate on negative intrusive thoughts under conditions of stress. In the absence of high repressive coping, which helps to suppress negative cognitions, athletes tend to use their inherently increased ability to attend to focus inward (on negative cognitions) instead of outward (on the task at hand), leading to technical problems and decreased performance, especially during critical moments of competition. Because high absorption is also associated with enhanced imaginative capabilities, a tendency that can lead to negative cognitions when combined with high neuroticism, I expected this athlete, even in the absence of the real stress of competition, to be capable of generating the same emotions he displayed in the actual match, along with physiological responses similar to those he exhibited during the match, just by watching the taped competition.

The player's heart activity, peripheral temperature, respiration, skin conductance (EDA) and muscle tension (EMG) were measured as he watched a videotape of a match he had just played and lost (within 24 hours). To make the PST more realistic, the player was instructed to hold his racket and to imitate the strokes he was observing in the videotape. Unexpectedly, all physiological parameters except for muscle tension remained relatively dormant compared with baseline. I expected greater reactivity, especially when it came to heart activity, because HRD has been shown to covary with muscle tension (Obrist 1981). Apparently, this player's window of maximum vulnerability was muscle tension, with greatest reactivity compared with baseline occurring during critical moments. The failure of HRD to covary with muscle tension during the PST indicates that the player may not have exhibited much HRD in the match, which he lost easily—2–6, 2–6.

Although this case study was intended to be illustrative, the fact that muscle tension stood out so prominently warrants taking a closer look at muscle tension and its relevance to the assessment of psychological performance during competition.

Background

The literature of EMG contains interesting findings that are relevant to sport performance. For example, Davis (1940) reported that subjects waiting to obtain a signal to respond exhibited increasing forearm extensor muscle tension, beginning about 200–400 ms after a ready signal was presented, up to the moment of reaction. In addition, the higher the muscle tension at the end of the foreperiod, the faster the reaction time. Furthermore, muscle tension was higher and reaction time quicker at the end of regular foreperiods as compared with irregular ones. This has implications for situations in sport when an athlete is preparing to respond. For example, in tennis, when returning serve, the phase before the serve can be seen as the fixed foreperiod. Increasing muscle tension in forearm muscles in a manner consistent with the above study might facilitate reaction time and help improve performance when returning serve. Because the return of serve is an important stroke in tennis, improving reaction time could contribute to successful outcome and performance.

Davis (1940) also reported that muscle groups not involved in the execution of a reaction time task showed a decrease in activity, presumably lessening the possibility of interference with the relevant motor response. Increases in task-specific muscles and decreases in task-irrelevant muscles may be psychophysiological concomitants of peak performance and may reflect the "choking" phenomenon in which athletes report feeling "tight" or "tense" muscles. As a consequence, athletes could possibly be trained to recognize and manipulate EMG activity in primary and secondary muscles to increase reaction time and prevent muscle tightening.

Muscle Tension and the Theory of Critical Moments

In line with the Theory of Critical Moments (TCM), it is expected that athletes will exhibit muscle tension response interactions between task-relevant primary muscles and task-irrelevant secondary muscles as a function of a constellation of PHO factors and of the level of criticality of a competitive event. At baseline, or in the context of more routine phases of competition, muscle tension responses are expected to be consistent with Davis's basic finding of increasing tension in primary muscles and decreasing tension in secondary muscles. However, in the context of critical moments, it is expected that athletes possessing less-performance-facilitating constellations of PHO factors will exhibit muscle tension increases in secondary task-irrelevant muscles, whereas athletes possessing the ideal Athlete's Profile of PHO factors will exhibit decreased muscle tension in secondary task-irrelevant muscles.

Procedure

Previous research (Carlstedt 1998) established that the dorsal extensor and flexor muscles of the forearm played the most important muscular role in the forehand and backhand ground strokes and volley. Thus, electrodes were placed over these muscles. In addition, electrodes were placed over the frontalis muscles of the forehead and the T-12 muscle of the back (paraspinals latismus dorsi). These latter placements were used to test the TCM prediction that increased tension in primary task-relevant muscles and decreased tension in secondary muscles would occur in athletes having the ideal Athlete's Profile of PHO factors and, relative to this case, that the player, based on a potentially negative constellation of PHO factors, would exhibit increased tension in secondary task-irrelevant muscles including the frontalis and T-12 muscles.

Prestress Test Measurement

The measurement of muscle tension during various simulated tennis strokes was carried out before starting the videotape to establish baseline EMG values independent of the introduction of stress stimuli (videotape of performance). Stroke simulations were measured as the player sat in a chair, standing up with arms hanging naturally, while in the ready position pose without a racket, and in the ready position with a racket. (The ready position is the position a tennis player assumes before preparing to hit the ball, and the position one returns to after hitting the ball.) Thereafter, comparison measures were obtained for a reaction response while actually preparing to return serve. Next, the backswing phase of the forehand was measured. After the backswing, the swing-to-contact phase was measured. Simulated tennis strokes were then compared with on-the-court measurements and found to be virtually the same at baseline.

Finally, measurements of stroke simulations were obtained while the player watched the videotape. All constellations of muscle tension were greater during simulated tennis strokes while watching the videotape compared with baseline.

The mean muscle tension for various conditions is presented in Table 4.

Discussion (Data Analysis)

All baseline conditions revealed significantly less EMG activity compared with active phases of the simulated strokes. As expected, sitting and in the standing position without a racket revealed the lowest EMG values. Surprisingly, the condition of the simulated ready position without a racket revealed higher flexor tension than the actual ready position condition with a racket (25.8 to 22.0 uV). Although holding a racket during the ready position phase of strokes placed more stress on the extensor than the flexor muscle of the forearm, it would not have been predicted that simulating the ready position without a racket would result in more flexor EMG activity than simulating the position while holding a racket. Interestingly, merely standing with arms at the side produced more EMG activity in the flexor muscle than when simulating the ready position either with or without a racket. The significance of these two findings is not clear at this time, although it appears that they are not relevant to EMG–behavior relationships.

The reaction response during the actual ready position while watching the videotape revealed the first major increase in EMG activity in both the extensor and flexor muscles from 83.8 and 22.0 uV,

Table 4 Integrated EMG Data (Mean Values in uV)

No Video/ Video	Extensor/ Video	Flexor/ Video	Extensor-Flexor/ Video	Frontalis/ Video	T-12/ Video
Baseline	13.3–15.5	4.8–6.2	7.8–9.70	7.3–7.5	24.8–26.8
Standing	31.0–33.6	37.8–42.9	26.3–28.8	7.8–9.7	46.0–50.2
Ready	27.8–28.4	25.8–29.6	19.5–19.9	7.5–8.7	68.5–69.2
Ready position	83.8	22	47	8.5	56.3
Racket back	131.8	172.5	131.3	4.5	53.3
Ready to swing	141.3	225.5	285.5	4.3	57.8
Swing to contact	146.3	219.8	214.3	4.2	56.3
Swing to contact-CM	213.7	264.4	364.6	15.8	78.3

respectively (ready position with racket), to 141.3 and 225.5 uV, respectively (reaction response). The reaction response is part of the preparation phase during which HRD has also been shown to occur. It is a relatively quiet moment free from movement. Increasing muscle tension in this phase can be attributed to psychological influences because metabolic demands do not increase appreciably during this period. The response of the player during this phase may have relevance to his psychological state if future on-the-court tests reveal that he has an optimum EMG activity range associated with faster reaction times doing specific strokes. For example, if Davis' (1940) findings apply to, say, the return of serve reaction time, it must still be determined whether ±140 uV is a muscle tension level associated with faster reaction time or whether an incremental rise in muscle tension before reacting is more important than an increase to an absolute EMG activity level in this player. If the former condition is found to be more important for faster reaction, players could be trained (using EMG biofeedback) to rapidly increase muscle tension to an ideal level, whereas if the latter condition is more important, players should be trained to incrementally raise tension to an ideal level before reacting.

After the reaction response in the ready position was measured, the forehand backswing was measured. Here we observed a decrease in EMG activity (from the ready response) to 131.8 uV in the extensor and 172.5 uV in the flexor muscles. It remains to be seen whether these values have behavioral significance.

During the swing to contact, EMG extensor activity increased to 146.3 uV and decreased to 219.8 uV in the flexor muscle, changing from 141.3 and 225.5 uV (during the initial reaction response), respectively. Interestingly, the reaction response in the ready position, revealing more flexor tension than during the backswing, and swing to contact would not have been predicted (225.5 vs. 219.8 uV) because swinging the racket is associated with greater metabolic demands than just holding it. This paradoxical response may be attributable to psychological factors leading to increased flexor activity when reacting. The expectancy of reacting, especially in a psychologically vulnerable athlete like this player, may lead to excessive levels of muscle tension analogous to exhibiting heart rate acceleration during the preparation phase. This may lead to a disruption of technical elements of strokes. However, future research must determine whether 225.5 uV reflects excessive muscle tension before this hypothesis can be confirmed. It is conceivable that forearm flexor activity in the 200 to 250 uV range facilitates faster reaction time, as opposed to slowing it down. Nevertheless, the flexor activity exhibited during the reaction response intuitively appeared disproportionate to metabolic demands (i.e., the reaction response is not as physically demanding as swinging the racket).

The concept of metabolic demands comes from cardiovascular psychophysiology, in which an algorithm is used to help distinguish between metabolic heart rate and nonmetabolic heart rate (Myrtek et al. 1996). Whereas metabolic heart rate reflects the physiological requirements of an organism, nonmetabolic heart rate reflects heart rate changes that are hypothesized to reflect psychological influences (Myrtek et al. 1996). I hypothesize that the metabolic demand concept is also applicable to other psychophysiological measures, including muscle tension. As a consequence, flexor tension exceeding or not reaching task-specific metabolic requirement levels during the reaction response may reflect the influence of this player's constellation of TCM-PHO factors on muscle tension activity.

Frontalis EMG ranged from 8.5 to 15.8 across all conditions. The highest frontalis tension occurred when the player was observing critical moments. During other nonbaseline conditions of the ready position, ready-to-swing, backswing, and swing-to-contact frontalis tension dropped, consistent with what one would expect and with what was previously observed by Goldstein (1972), and Obrist, Webb, and Sutterer (1969). These researchers reported that increased practice led to lower EMG activity in muscles not involved in a specific task. Their findings are reconcilable with what would be predicted on the basis of the TCM. Considering that this player was well practiced (an elite tennis player), it would be expected that reductions in muscle tension would occur in secondary task-irrelevant muscles like the frontalis, as was the case, except when the player observed critical moments. The increase in frontalis tension during critical moments to

12.8 strongly indicates that the player experienced emotional reactions consistent with his constellation of TCM-PHO factors during phases of competition in which he fared poorly. The excessive physiological reactivity he exhibited in the frontalis muscle while watching critical moments on the videotape very likely also occurred during actual competition because he failed to master the majority of critical moments he faced. The technical mistakes apparent in the videotape during critical moments were hypothesized to occur because of excessive muscle tension in a secondary muscle, the frontalis, interfering with the technical demands of various tennis strokes. This excessive tension and the resultant poor performance during critical moments can be attributed to negative intrusive thoughts being ruminated on because of an inappropriate absorption with internal as opposed to external stimuli. Because the player was also low in repressive coping, he was unable to handle the negative cognitive intrusions during periods of heightened stress, leading to breakdowns in his motor performance.

Measurement from T-12 of the back, also considered to be a secondary muscle, revealed the following: tension levels ranged from 24.8 uV when sitting to 68.5 uV when simulating the ready position without a racket, and to 56.3 uV with a racket. Interestingly, the reaction response elicited a rise in tension from 56.3 uV (ready position with racket) to 82.5 uV, a value that even exceeded simulated overreaction (78.3 uV). T-12 reaction response activity also exceeded the backswing (67.3 uV), and swing-to-contact (57.8 uV) levels. The above would not have been predicted. Again, intuitively, it would be expected that muscle tension in T-12 would be lower during the reaction response than when swinging to contact. In this case, a secondary muscle (T-12) revealed a tension level (82.5 uV), one that might have disrupted stroke performance. Recall that previous studies reported that faster reaction times were associated with increasing tension in primary muscles and with decreasing levels of tension in secondary muscles (e.g., Davis 1940). Thus, ideally, a player preparing to return serve should exhibit proportionately increasing forearm flexor tension (i.e., increasing tension from baseline to optimum reaction tension in primary muscles) but exhibit proportionately decreasing tension in secondary muscles (the T-12 should exhibit a tension level close to baseline). Again, in line with the metabolic demand hypothesis, tension levels in secondary muscles that exceed metabolic demands are thought to be mediated by psychological factors (TCM-PHO factors).

Although it might be argued that T-12 is a primary muscle relative to tennis ground strokes, the data show that T-12 is almost equally stressed during the swing to contact as during the ready position (57.8 vs. 56.3 uV). Thus, if T-12 is a primary muscle, its tension levels would be predicted to be greatest during the swing to contact, the most important and physically stressful phase of ground strokes, but this was not the case. Instead, the greatest T-12 activity occurred during critical moments—phases of competition associated with the most psychological stress.

Conclusion

The preceding findings reflect the first EMG data in an athlete obtained during the performance of real and simulated sport-specific tasks under conditions of PST. The results of this case study revealed that in predisposed athletes, it is possible to elicit psychological, emotional, and physiological responses on the basis of merely observing videotape of a previous performance. Consistent with this player's constellation of PHO factors, greatest levels of muscle tension were exhibited in secondary task-irrelevant muscles when simulating tennis strokes during the observation of critical moments of competition recently experienced in a real tennis match. On the basis of these findings one would expect this athlete to exhibit excessive physiological reactivity during critical moments of actual competition, to show less HRD because this measure covaries with decreasing muscle tension in secondary task-irrelevant muscles, and to demonstrate poor motor performance during critical moments.

These findings attest to the utility of using PST to assess athletes before and after competition, a necessary first step in determining what form of mental training intervention to use and in testing the efficacy of psychological interventions.

12

Mastering Critical Moments: The Carlstedt Protocol

According to the Theory of Critical Moments (TCM), athletes are predisposed to respond during critical moments as a function of their constellation of primary higher-order (PHO) factors. Athletes who are low or high in hypnotic ability/absorption, low in neuroticism, and high in repressive coping are thought to have a psychological advantage during the most crucial phases of competition, whereas those who are high in hypnotic ability/absorption, high in neuroticism, and low in repressive coping are most likely to fall victim to negative psychological influences during these same pivotal periods.

Although these theoretical tenets and supporting data may be reassuring to those who possess the ideal Athlete's Profile, they are likely to be deflating to athletes not so favorably predisposed. This latter class of athletes may feel that there is little that they can do to overcome ingrained negative psychological propensities, resigning themselves to the fact that they may have psychological difficulties during critical moments when peak performance is required. By contrast, psychologically endowed athletes may think that all they have to do is show up and their "mind-power" will do the rest. However, matters are not that simple. Although an athlete's constellation of PHO factors is expected to influence performance during critical moments, a 100% correspondence does not exist between psychological variables and outcome. This indicates that both positively and negatively predisposed athletes need to do specific things to increase the probability that they will benefit from facilitative psychological traits and behaviors or reduce the odds that potentially detrimental constellations of traits and behaviors will render them relatively helpless during critical moments.

Making sure an athlete is physically, technically, tactically, and nutritionally prepared for competition is an important first step in reducing the possibility that negative psychological factors will disrupt performance, or in increasing the probability that the potential positive effects of desirable psychological qualities will be manifested during critical moments. After all, even the most favorably predisposed athlete will have difficulty mastering critical moments if he or she is not physically fit or technically prepared.

By contrast, the most negatively predisposed athlete can do a lot to avert the potentially disruptive consequences of having a detrimental constellation of PHO factors by being well primed both physically and technically. If they are in possession of superior technical and physical skills, these kinds of athletes may be able to dominate to such an extent that critical moments when they are most vulnerable are simply not encountered, turning a potential psychological battle into a routine, technically driven competition. On the other hand, a psychologically superior athlete who is not prepared physically and technically may never be able to show his or her mental prowess if critical moments fail to occur in a competition that is dominated by a psychologically weaker opponent who is better conditioned and prepared. This dynamic may underlie "upsets" in sports, when a physically/technically superior athlete is defeated by a psychologically robust player who manages to win most of the critical points because the "better" athlete was not ready to compete. The more technically capable athlete normally is in a position to dominate precisely because of his or her more masterful physical skills and rarely faces critical moments, leaving his or her potential psychological weaknesses unexposed. However, when unprepared, this same proficient athlete in possession of a negative constellation of PHO factors becomes vulnerable whenever critical moments are encountered.

Thus, it is vital that the technically superior but psychologically labile athlete avoid critical moments by controlling play to the extent that psychologically significant moments rarely surface, lest he or she fall victim to the negative influences of their constellation of PHO factors on physiology and motor performance. The more critical moments encountered, the greater the likelihood that a technically inferior but psychologically superior athlete will master important competitive situations.

Assuming that an athlete is well-prepared physically and technically and is competing against an opponent with a similar level of skill, how can that athlete increase the probability of benefiting from a positive constellation of PHO factors or neutralizing the potential effects of a negative constellation of PHO factors? The obvious answer to this question is to engage in mental or psychological training. However there is much more to mental training than meets the eye. Mental training no longer just means engaging in imagery, goal setting, self-talk, or various other techniques to enhance psychological performance. In the context of the TCM, mental training strategies are highly individualized and are based on an athlete's constellation of PHO factors.

The failure to consider individual response tendencies associated with specific PHO factors or propensities in physiological responding (independent of PHO factors) can result in the application of an intervention technique that is not best suited to a particular athlete. It is no longer tenable to apply a particular intervention en masse, especially in light of findings from the High-Risk Model of Threat Perception showing that interventions should be used on the basis of an individual's specific constellation of risk factors (or TCM-PHO factors).

To this end, I have developed the Carlstedt Protocol (CP), a comprehensive individualized mental training approach that is based on an athlete's constellation of PHO factors and neuropsychophysiological response tendencies. The following is a listing of interventions that best correspond to a particular constellation of PHO factors.

Constellation of PHO Factors and Ideal Mental Training Intervention

1. High hypnotic ability/absorption, high/low neuroticism, and low repressive coping—active-alert hypnosis-imagery and esoteric cognitive therapy
2. Low hypnotic ability/absorption, low/medium neuroticism, and high repressive coping—biofeedback and realistic cognitive therapy

3. High hypnotic ability/absorption, high neuroticism, and high repressive coping—active-alert hypnosis-imagery combined with biofeedback and esoteric cognitive therapy

Cerebral laterality training can also be used regardless of constellation of PHO factors, although one can always expect resistance to mental training from athletes who are low in absorption and high in repressive coping. Furthermore, athletes who are high in hypnotic ability/absorption may benefit more directly from active-alert hypnosis, a modality that may facilitate immediate activation of intense task-specific focus that is observed during zone or flow states.

Imagery-based cognitive therapy involves traditional methods including self-talk, thought stopping, and restructuring. However, in contrast to reality-based cognitive therapy, the former method uses language and metaphors that appeal to a person who is high in hypnotic ability/absorption and who thus has a propensity to engage in imagery or imaginative activities. Accordingly, it appeals to this type of person's more visual cognitive style.

Rationale for Applying Specific Interventions

The rationale for applying a particular intervention can be traced to the High-Risk Model of Threat Perception's discovery that patients possessing specific risk factors were more or less amenable to certain forms of treatment. People high in hypnotic ability/absorption who are more fantasy prone and imaginative compared with lows were found to benefit more from hypnosis and imagery-based interventions than were therapies that are more reality based, such as rational-emotive psychotherapy. In contrast, individuals high in repressive coping who are more skeptical and reality oriented than lows benefited more from biofeedback, a modality providing objective feedback about mind–body interactions that they would otherwise not believe or would tend to ignore, as well as reality-based cognitive therapy. Those who were low in hypnotic ability/absorption were less likely to benefit from hypnosis and imagery and were also more likely to benefit from biofeedback, whereas individuals low in repressive coping were found to be amenable to hypnosis and imagery provided that they were not also low in hypnotic ability/absorption. Individuals exhibiting a rarer constellation of high hypnotic ability/absorption and high repressive coping were considered good candidates for both hypnosis/imagery and biofeedback.

The above interventions are used mostly before competition, the goal being to help athletes generalize intervention-induced cognitions and the physiological responding associated with peak performance that have been learned off the playing field to real playing conditions. This is most likely to occur if the selected intervention best suits the PHO constellation of an athlete. It should be noted that all the above methods except biofeedback are considered cognitive interventions and include self-talk (e.g., posthypnotic suggestion), talk therapy, goal setting, and motivational elements. However, just as the TCM hypothesizes that the psychological factors it has identified are PHO factors that mediate other psychological factors (secondary lower-order factors); it proposes that active-alert hypnosis/imagery and biofeedback serve as primary interventions, with other cognitive methods being integrated into these primary methods. Each primary intervention is most amenable to a specific PHO profile.

The selected intervention is for the most part determined by an athlete's constellation of hypnotic ability/absorption and repressive coping. Neuroticism is the PHO factor that one is trying to manipulate in the desired direction. In most cases, an attempt is made to attenuate the disruptive neuropsychophysiological manifestations associated with the negative and catastrophizing cognitions that accompany high neuroticism. In certain underactivated athletes (hyporeactive), at times, attempts to increase neuroticism to raise physiological reactivity might be indicated.

Repressive coping is considered the great moderator of neuroticism, in that it acts to suppress negative intrusive thoughts by functionally disconnecting the right- from the left-brain hemisphere during critical moments of competition. This prevents right-hemisphere-based negative cognitions from disrupting the sensitive psychological preaction preparation phase that occurs in the left hemisphere.

If neuroticism can be seen as the great disrupter and repressive coping the great suppressor and moderator, then hypnotic ability/absorption can be viewed as the great facilitator of focus, helping an athlete attend intensely to internal or external stimuli as a function of level of neuroticism and repressive coping. As a consequence, a mental training intervention strategy based on the High-Risk Model of Threat Perception and TCM is designed to suppress negative intrusive thoughts associated with high neuroticism from being manifested especially during critical moments. The goal is to facilitate the potential beneficial aspects of ideal constellations of PHO factors or to suppress the potential detrimental effects of these factors working together.

An attempt is also made to induce temporary state changes in athletes possessing undesirable constellations of PHO factors. This latter goal can be facilitated using an emerging intervention called cerebral laterality manipulation, a technique based on the research of Schiffer (1997), Drake (2002) and others. It is designed to alter states of relative brain hemispheric activation. Brain laterality manipulation is engaged in to induce increased positive affect, performance-facilitative cognitions, and visuo-perceptual processing free from the negative intrusive thoughts associated with high neuroticism. This method usually involves increasing activation in the left-brain hemisphere and a reduction of right-hemisphere activation, a cortical state observed in people who are high in repressive coping. This can be achieved using auditory, visual, tactile, and even nasal stimulation or deprivation, whereby a stimulus is presented in such a manner that activation in the left-brain hemisphere exceeds that of the right hemisphere. Goggles, ear-plugs, guiding visual orientation (looking to the right), nose-plugs (blocking the left nostril), and tactile stimulation (with eyes closed) can be used to engage the brain hemisphere contralateral to direction of stimulation or deprivation (e.g., blocking the right visual fields of the eyes will activate the left hemisphere). In addition, I have been experimenting with the use of a Line-Bisecting Test in the field to manipulate cerebral laterality during actual competition. I report on preliminary data from a case study below.

Neurofeedback, a form of biofeedback in which brainwaves are assessed and manipulated, can also be used in an attempt to achieve a more permanent shift toward relative left-brain hemispheric predominance, a state-trait propensity in cortical organization and functioning that has been shown to exist in athletes possessing the ideal Athlete's Profile of PHO factors (Carlstedt 2001). However, current sport neurofeedback protocols are exclusively concerned with enhancing attention and not with manipulating cerebral laterality to achieve hemispheric asymmetries associated with heightened positive affect and reductions in negative intrusive thoughts, under the assumption that increasing attention alone will facilitate performance. As with many psychophysiological interventions and assessment models in sport psychology, existing neurofeedback protocols fail to consider individual differences in traits and behaviors as potential mediators of attention, especially under conditions of stress or critical moments.

Although it is indisputable that keen attention is a vital performance ingredient, the TCM maintains that the ability to attend well, particularly when it counts the most, is to a large extent contingent on an athlete's constellation of PHO factors. As a consequence, a recommended strategy when using neurofeedback on athletes is to first attempt to induce state and, eventually, long-term trait levels of relative left-brain hemisphere activation to increase positive affect and to enhance visuo-perceptual and cognitive processing (strategic planning/preaction preparation) while suppressing negative affect or neuroticism, as opposed to merely attempting to increase attention in the context of contrived laboratory tasks. Gains in attention that are measured on the basis of laboratory paradigms that do not consider individual differences in constellations of PHO factors lack ecological validity and are unlikely to hold up during critical moments of competition.

Thus, the TCM approach to neurofeedback is to first help athletes generalize their self-altered cortical functioning to the playing field. This applies especially to psychologically vulnerable athletes who need to learn how to suppress negative intrusive thoughts during critical moments if they are to exhibit gains in attention during competition that they may have already achieved off the field (in the lab). Once state and trait levels of cortical functioning associated with ideal EEG activity before action (the TCM Athlete's Profile) are induced, attention should automatically increase even under stress, independent of neurofeedback protocols that are specifically designed to increase attention.

Neurofeedback may be the most promising intervention for changing maladaptive behaviors and cognitions associated with negative constellations of PHO factors and poor psychological performance. The successful application of neurofeedback in clinical settings indicates that it can be applied to enhance sport performance provided that it is used in the context of an integrative model cognizant of individual differences (PHO factors) that mediate attention. I predict that merely using neurofeedback in the laboratory to enhance attention will not be sufficient to achieve such an effect during actual competition.

Biofeedback also holds much potential for helping negatively predisposed athletes achieve psychophysiological states that positively predisposed athletes exhibit most of the time, including greater relative left-brain-hemispheric activation during the preaction phase and subsequent heart rate deceleration. Essentially, biofeedback provides a means for psychologically vulnerable athletes to achieve levels of self-regulation that occur more naturally in the ideal Athlete's Profile.

The Carlstedt Protocol

The Carlstedt Protocol is based on an initial assessment of PHO factors including hypnotic ability/absorption, neuroticism, repressive coping, and relative cerebral laterality. Once an athlete's profile has been established, psychophysiological testing is used off and on the playing field. An initial psychophysiological stress test is administered to determine whether physiological reactivity in the laboratory/ practice is consistent with what would be expected on the basis of an athlete's constellation of PHO factors and cerebral laterality. Thereafter, heart rate variability/heart rate deceleration responses are measured during both training and actual competition while analyzing physical/technical, tactical, and statistical performance with the Carlstedt Critical Moment Psychological Performance Index system. Assessment of physiological responding and psychological performance during actual competition is done in an attempt to concurrently validate psychophysiological stress test responses on the field. It is also carried out to determine the predictive validity of an athlete's PHO factors relative to on-the-field performance and physiological responding. Once a trait-like profile of psychophysiological reactivity/ responsivity is established on the basis of longitudinally acquired data (at least three to five complete measurement occasions), interventions are implemented to modify responding in the desired direction.

An important component of the Carlstedt Protocol is efficacy testing of interventions using the Carlstedt Critical Moment Psychological Performance Index to determine the extent to which an intervention affects outcome (physical/technical, tactical, physiological, or statistical success/won–loss outcome measures). If an intervention proves to be ineffectual, it is usually supplanted with an alternative method until an ideal mental training modality is found. Thereafter, mental training is routinely engaged in as a prophylaxis in an attempt to optimally prepare an athlete for competition. Mental training during actual competition includes affect monitoring and altering using cerebral laterality manipulation to activate the left brain hemisphere before action (gaze manipulation, etc.) and during time-outs (Line-Bisecting Test and PANAS schedule).

Whenever possible, athletes are also monitored during actual competition and training. The acquired data are then analyzed, discussed with the athlete and coaches, and stored. In this era of high-technology, replete with sophisticated computer analysis and psychophysiological monitoring devices, it is no longer tenable to administer interventions that have not been tested for reliability, validity, and efficacy. All sport psychology practitioners should be trained in psychophysiology and biofeedback and be equipped to monitor and assess the psychophysiology of athletes and teams.

Step-by-Step Overview of the Carlstedt Protocol

A step-by-step overview of the Carlstedt Protocol is presented here, followed by case studies of athletes involved in various stages of the protocol:

1. Assessment of PHO factors and cerebral laterality
2. Off-the-field psychological stress test
3. On-field heart rate variability/decreased heart rate analysis
4. On-field heart rate variability/decreased heart rate analysis with critical moment analysis
5. Postcompetition data analysis
6. Intervention selection, precompetition and on the field
7. Efficacy testing-intervention
8. Mental training using most efficacious intervention
9. Continual monitoring, data bank

13

Assessment and Intervention Using the Carlstedt Protocol: A Case Study

This chapter presents a case study of an athlete who was assessed and trained using my protocol. The client is a regionally ranked senior tennis player. He was assessed for cerebral laterality and PHO factors. Recommendations for mental training based on his profile were made and discussed below. Please note from the language that I am addressing the client directly. I used informal language and jargon to establish better rapport with this athlete as well as make to the findings more understandable.

Assessment Results

The Line-Bisecting Test previously described in this book was administered, followed by the Marlowe-Crowne Scale, Eysenck Personality Inventory, and Tellegen Absorption Scale. The Positive–Negative Affect Schedule was taken throughout the course of his assessment and intervention program. Cerebral laterality manipulation was applied as an on-the-court intervention, eventually emerging as the most effective intervention for this athlete. The report and comments follow.

Relative Brain Hemispheric Predominance: Mildly Right-Hemisphere Predominant

This finding is consistent with your self-report of frequently experiencing racing thoughts, negative cognitions, and self-defeating thinking, because negative emotions have been localized in the right-brain hemisphere. Relative right-brain predominance is found only in about 10% of elite athletes but in more than 50% of nonathletes, indicating that elite athletes may have a unique cortical (brain) organization and brain response system marked by less-negative thoughts.

Repressive Coping

Coupled with the fact that you are also low in repressive coping, a trait or behavioral (unconscious) tendency associated with enhanced self-confidence and high self-esteem along with the ability to shut out negative intrusive thoughts and to ignore physiological pain (considered a left-brain based trait), it becomes clear why you struggle with self-defeating cognitions (thoughts) and experience these intrusive thoughts even when playing well. The finding on repressive coping is consistent with your brain laterality assessment, as low repressors are consciously aware of negative internal (mental) and external (environmental) stimuli, tend to be right-brain hemisphere predominant, and fail to benefit from the psychologically protective and insulating properties of this trait. About 66% of elite athletes are medium to high in this trait.

You should know, however, that with regard to long-term morbidity and mortality, you are actually better off being low in repressive coping. Although repressive copers feel little psychological distress, they usually have an underlying physiology that is overreactive, especially in the context of nonexercise or sport situations. In athletes, the higher levels of activation seen in repressors may actually facilitate performance, but once these individuals are in a sedentary situation, high repression appears to mediate physiological hyperreactivity associated with psychosomatic symptoms and certain illnesses.

Neuroticism

Your neuroticism score is in the lower-middle range, indicating that your autonomic reactivity is in the normal range relative to sedentary or baseline conditions; that is, outside of sports or competition. This finding is consistent with your low repressive coping score. Based on your repressive coping and neuroticism scores, you may even have difficulty at times getting pumped up (perhaps just before a match). We should discuss this and verify later through a heart rate variability analysis whether this is the case. On the basis of your neuroticism score, it is doubtful that you will become hyperactivated during competition, even after an emotional outburst. However, if you do experience anger or excessive emotion, you are likely to recover faster than someone who is high in neuroticism. With your profile for repressive coping and neuroticism, I would suggest letting your emotions show during play to achieve higher levels of intensity. You mentioned in your video analysis that in a particular match when you got mad you actually played better. This would be predicted on the basis of your RC and N scores. Your natural tendency toward underactivation and openness, or your lack of repressive coping, may cause you to experience psychological but not physiological stress in competition. As a consequence, a surge of intentionally induced activation may help override your tendency toward hypoactivation and help you reach a level of intensity associated with peak performance

Absorption

Your level of absorption is in the middle range. Combined with low repressive coping, this may place you at risk for focusing on or becoming too absorbed in internal stimuli (e.g., negative intrusive thoughts), especially during critical moments of competition.

Positive Affect-Negative Affect Schedule Scores

Positive Affect-Negative Affect Schedule (PANAS) scores will be your main read on your emotional state and mood. PANAS will be an important diagnostic tool in conjunction with heart rate variability (HRV) analyses and the mental training stage of our plan to improve your performance. Your scores show very high positive affect or positive emotions across all situations. This is good in terms of general mental health. However, you are also concurrently high in negative affect (i.e., negative emotions). Negative affect probably manifests itself at times during competition, consistent with what you told me and with your relative right-brain-hemispheric predominance. You appear incapable at this time of overriding the potential positive benefits of your high trait (long-term) and state (short-term) positive affect. As a person who is relatively right-hemisphere predominant, you will need to guard against generating negative thoughts. We will discuss how to do this later in the report, and we will also discuss heart activity monitoring, which will incorporate specific diagnostics involving the Line-Bisecting Test and the PANAS.[1]

Summary

You exhibit the following profile of traits and behavioral tendencies relevant to attention/concentration and physiological reactivity/ intensity during competition:

High positive affect (trait predominant over the long term, but state specifically dormant)

High negative affect (state predominant, probably often during competition)

Medium-low neuroticism (may hinder optimum intensity at the beginning of matches and overall consistency of intensity)

Medium absorption (coupled with high negative affect, this indicates that you have a tendency to catastrophize and experience negative thoughts in high-stress situations)

Low repressive coping (you do not benefit from this potential protective factor, making you susceptible to negative intrusive thoughts especially in light of your high level of state-specific negative affect)

Intervention Approach: Mental Training

Cognitive Therapy

You can immediately engage in cognitive restructuring whereby both before and during competition you practice positive self-talk, especially whenever a negative thought arises. The goal of this intervention is to overwrite "faulty" and "destructive" neural schema or templates. However, keep in mind that this is a long-term thought-altering strategy, so you will really have to work at it.

---

[1]PANAS measures state and trait affect. Positive and negative affect have been found to be orthogonal; therefore it is possible, as with the above athlete, to be concurrently high or low in positive and negative affect.

Brain Laterality Training

This kind of training will be used to shift relative brain hemisphere activation from the right to the left brain in an attempt to induce your trait propensity toward high positive affect during competition.

RSA/HRV Training

This training will be used to help you reduce anxiety that is acute and unexpected. With this technique, you can stop a "panic attack" during competition. It can also be implemented independent of acute competitive stress before action when serving or returning to help facilitate heart rate deceleration.

RSA/HRV training is a form of biofeedback that can easily be transferred to the real world. It involves learning to regulate breathing rate and rhythm to induce greater parasympathetic nervous system activity or more of an immediate relaxation response. It can also be used to facilitate heart rate deceleration.

General Heart Activity Monitoring

Your heart activity will be monitored for confirmatory and diagnostic purposes and to determine the efficacy of the above interventions.

Final Comments

In a sport like tennis, where you can be at the mercy of numerous factors you cannot control, including your opponent's play and ability, your psychological performance must be evaluated in the context of what you do or how you respond physiologically. That is why scores, rankings, and victories are only part of the appraisal criteria and why we need to measure HRV and other factors over time to determine the extent to which you are improving psychologically. Mental improvement may not even be evident in a 6–0, 6–2 victory, yet it could be apparent in a 3–6, 4–6 loss.

Outcome

This highly ranked senior player had lofty goals, wanting to become the number 1 player in his age group in his region. He put enormous pressure on himself to win and spared no expense to achieve his goal, seeking the advice of numerous coaches and sport psychology practitioners. The goal of my intervention was to help this player enjoy tennis more. I hypothesized that this could be achieved by inducing greater positive affect during competition. To accomplish this, I had the player engage in laterality manipulation, using the line bisecting tests on the court in conjunction with the state version of the PANAS to monitor momentary affect. During each change over (time-out), the player was instructed to take the PANAS, score it, immediately generate positive thoughts whenever his PANAS scores indicated a state of high negative affect, and then retake the test. If the PANAS revealed high positive affect, he was told to immediately complete the Line-Bisecting Test. He was also instructed to do the Line-Bisecting Test after generating positive thoughts following a high negative affect score. The player was blind to the meaning of direction of error on the Line-Bisecting Test and was unaware of its relationship to cerebral laterality.

Postmatch analysis of PANAS and line-bisecting scores revealed that rightward error on the Line-Bisecting Test was significantly correlated with positive affect. This is an important finding in that this player exhibited off-the-court trait relative right-brain hemispheric predominance and high negative affect, indicating that he was able to manipulate relative cerebral activation on the basis of self-induced changes in moment-to-moment affect. Here, by generating positive emotions or thoughts after an initial PANAS score revealed high negative affect, the athlete was able to induce a state of relative left-brain hemispheric activation. Because left-brain hemispheric activation is associated with the Athlete's Profile, reduced neuroticism, and increased repressive coping and positive affect, attaining such a cortical state is considered beneficial to performance.

Although this player still experienced bouts of negative affect during competition, he reported that overall, since monitoring his affect on the court, he has been able to enjoy competition much more.

In this case, a negatively predisposed athlete was able to manipulate relative cerebral hemispheric activation and affect momentarily. As the player improves physically and technically, it can be expected that he will also perform better as long as he continues to monitor and, if necessary, manipulate his affective state. When this occurs, he will not only enjoy competition more but will come closer to reaching his goal of becoming a top-ranked athlete.

Although this player appeared to manipulate cerebral laterality cognitively, it is also expected that inducing a right- to left-brain hemispheric shift in negatively predisposed athletes, independent of conscious cognitive attempts to do so, will lead to heightened positive affect, repressive coping, and subsequent enhanced psychological performance. As previously mentioned, this can be achieved using a number of visual or auditory techniques (Carlstedt 2004).

In the case of athletes who are high in hypnotic ability/absorption, active-alert hypnosis may be preferable to cerebral laterality manipulation because it may allow such athletes to bypass the preaction preparation left-hemisphere phase and to directly enter a visuo-perceptual (right-hemisphere) mode associated with decreasing heart rate and zone or flow states, in which intense focus free from intrusive thoughts is immediately directed toward the task at hand (see the case study discussed in Chapter 14; Carlstedt 2004).

14

Active-Alert Hypnosis: Description and Case Study

Athletes who are high in hypnotic ability/absorption, high in neuroticism, and low in repressive coping are thought to be most vulnerable to negative psychological influences during critical moments of competition. However, if they are capable of accessing their inherent ability to intensely focus on the task at hand, these athletes can reach "zone" or "flow" states more easily than athletes who are low in hypnotic ability/absorption. They can be helped using active-alert hypnosis, an intervention designed to enhance task-specific focus and motor performance.

The goal of active-alert hypnosis is to increase absorption in a task at hand to such an extent that negative intrusive thoughts associated with high neuroticism are not manifested, regardless of an athlete's level of repressive coping. Active-alert hypnosis appears to foster a repressive coping-like response by activating task-specific ensembles of neuronal networks while suppressing neuronal networks associated with high neuroticism. Similar to the repressive coping dynamic, during active-alert hypnosis (and hypnosis) a functional disconnection or dissociation of the right from the left-brain hemisphere is hypothesized to occur, thereby helping to prevent intrusive thoughts from disrupting performance.

Although the neurophysiological dynamics of hypnosis have yet to be unequivocally delineated, high hypnotic ability has been associated with greater vagal tone or high-frequency heart rate variability (Harris et al. 1993). Because HRD is under vagal (parasympathetic) control, a response associated with greater relative activation of the right-brain hemisphere, it is possible that active-alert hypnosis helps facilitate the cognitive preparation phase before action that has been observed to occur in the left hemisphere, leading to a "just do it" state free from the cognitive disruptions associated with high neuroticism. Active-alert hypnosis appears to assist efficient cognitive planning by priming visuo-perceptual and motor components of sport-specific tasks while neutralizing negative intrusive thoughts. This intervention is thought to help keep potential manifestations of neuroticism dormant during critical preparation phases of competition, helping to generate greater focus or zonelike states.

Active-alert hypnosis operates under the assumption that hypnosis and motor performance share common neuronal pathways. The process of active-alert hypnosis is thought to enhance kinesthetic awareness, imagery, focusing, dissociation, automaticity, and control of thoughts (Banyai 1976). Similar to traditional hypnosis, active-alert hypnosis attempts to generate intense focused attention and a reduction of both reality orientation and cognitive planning. However, rather than promote relaxation and reduced physiological reactivity as in conventional hypnosis, active-alert hypnosis attempts to increase levels of physiological reactivity or intensity to enhance motor control (Banyai 1993; Robazza and Bortoli 1994).

A state of active-alert hypnosis is achieved by administering suggestions while persons are active. For example, in Banyai and Hilgard's (1976) initial studies, suggestions for focus and heightened intensity were given while persons pedaled on a stationary bicycle. Athletes can engage in active-alert hypnosis during training or competition while performing actual tasks associated with a particular sport. For example, tennis players might be instructed to carry out a shadow stroke routine while suggestions for improving technique or intensity are administered in an attempt to prime them for an impending match.

Suggestions are given before or during competition either by a practitioner or through self-hypnosis, with the application of this technique varying as a function of a sport. For example, if a sport is self-paced (e.g., when an athlete decides to initiate action), active-alert hypnosis can precede competition. In externally paced sports (like most team sports) in which athletes respond to the actions of an opponent, active-alert hypnosis is usually engaged in during time-outs.

Ideally, active-alert induction procedures and suggestions are tailored to the technical and strategic task requirements of specific sports and the individual strengths and weaknesses of a particular athlete. An active-alert hypnosis protocol should be structured to reinforce or enhance technical and motor skills associated with a sport. For example, in golf, inductions may stress a smooth backswing when putting, whereas suggestions in basketball might emphasize focusing on the basket.

First Phase: During Practice

Active-alert hypnosis is induced through specific induction scripts that direct athletes to increase their awareness of certain muscle sensations, images, and thoughts using kinesthetic, visual, auditory, and tactile sensory modalities. The process of active-alert hypnosis includes the following components. First, bodily awareness, which involves having athletes notice bodily sensations that are associated with movement and technical performance (e.g., muscle tension in the arm or legs), feedback relating to handling equipment (e.g., the feel of the tennis racket before serving) and the control of respiration and heart activity to regulate states of arousal. Second, mental imagery involves visualizing sequences of a sport-specific movement, technique, or tactics. Intense absorption in technical and strategic action sequences associated with a sport has been shown to facilitate and deepen the alert-hypnosis experience (Robazza and Bortoli, 1994). Third, focusing requires athletes to attend to important performance cues or feedback while learning to ignore disruptive external stimuli and internal intrusive cognitions. The goal of focusing is to raise awareness of attentional demands during various phases of performance, especially critical moments of competition, in addition to enhancing positive aspects of an athlete's cognitive style. For example, before the serve in tennis, athletes might turn their attention to their fingers to prevent excessive tightening of their grip. Thereafter, focus might be directed toward breathing and heart rate to reduce one's level of physiological reactivity, especially before a critical moment. Fourth, automatic execution involves focusing on the kinesthetic, visual, auditory, and tactile aspects of performance during learning phases to better consolidate motor skills and sport-specific movement patterns in implicit memory. Although, initially, conscious awareness of the technical aspects of a sport-specific motion is necessary for the achievement of memory consolidation, an eventual goal of active-alert hypnosis is to increase automatic responding during competition (Robazza and Bortoli 1994).

Second Phase: After Practice

After training/practice, conventional hypnosis can be used to strengthen connections between the active-alert phase of mental training and posttraining memory consolidation (Robazza and Bortoli 1994). It is hypothesized that mental skills that are important both for sport performance and the hypnotic experience will be strengthened in this manner. Interactive links between active-alert and traditional hypnosis are maintained to help facilitate mind–body interaction (Robazza and Bortoli 1994). For example, if attention during training is focused on somatic perceptions or feedback to develop bodily awareness and to induce alert hypnosis, then hypnosis following training should also involve somatic suggestions and techniques. Similarly, if the training phase stresses imagery, then the same images should be used in hypnosis after practice. If focusing was a priority during practice, then it should also be the goal of postpractice hypnosis and could, for example, entail the use of eye-fixation or cerebral laterality manipulation techniques. Similarly, if tactile methods were emphasized in practice to get a better feel for technical movements, then such methods should also be used in hypnosis after practice (Robazza and Bortoli 1994).

Another goal of conventional hypnosis when combined with active-alert hypnosis is to raise awareness of muscular tension associated with relaxation or stress, along with the perception of weight, heat, and pain or analgesia. Traditional hypnosis after practice is also used to create other hypnotic phenomena including amnesia, space-time distortion, and automatic ideomotor movements (Robazza and Bortoli 1994). These phenomena are thought to be important for recovering feelings associated with experiences of peak performance (Ravizza 1977; Robazza and Bortoli 1994).

Because anecdotal accounts of peak performance describe experiences similar to hypnosis, including total absorption, narrowed attention, effortlessness, dissociation, involuntariness, absence of intrusive thoughts, and amnesia, it is believed that feelings associated with flow-like performances can be reactivated or programmed before competition (Robazza and Bortoli, 1994).

Summary

Active-alert hypnosis can enhance performance in certain athletes, especially those who are high in hypnotic ability/absorption, by helping them remain engaged in movements associated with sport-specific tasks while under hypnosis. This may lead to levels of intensity and priming of motor skills conducive to responding to the demands of upcoming practice or competition. Combining suggestions of alertness, readiness, and attention with motor activity is thought to boost cognitive and perceptual-motor skills when performing. The active-alert hypnotic state is also believed to be helpful for eliminating or reducing intrusive internal and external stimuli through focusing, imagery, and the promotion of dissociation. Active-alert hypnosis is thought to facilitate more efficient motor learning in less-skilled athletes as well (Carlstedt 1995).

It should be noted that hypnosis or active-alert hypnosis may not benefit all athletes. Similar to when contemplating the use of mental imagery, an athlete's level of hypnotic ability or absorption should be considered before implementing active-alert hypnosis. Evidence indicates that persons who are high in absorption or hypnotic ability are most likely to benefit from this intervention, something of which many practitioners are not aware (Wickramasekera 1988). The failure to consider hypnotic ability as a moderator variable that can influence the ability to enter hypnosis may in part account for the mostly negative findings regarding the efficacy of hypnosis as a mental training method (Morgan 2002). As a consequence, hypnosis and active-alert hypnosis should be applied discerningly.

Active-Alert Hypnosis: Case Study

The following script was designed to help improve the psychological performance of a skilled tennis player who was high in hypnotic ability/absorption and neuroticism and low in repressive coping. The player lacked self-confidence and feared "going for his shots" when it counted the most during competition. Even though he had a good technical game, it frequently broke down under pressure. It was decided to implement active-alert hypnosis emphasizing the consolidation of technical skills in implicit memory before competition. The goal was to facilitate intense focus on technical and tactical action sequences that frequently occur during competitive tennis and that this player had failed to master—weaknesses that surfaced especially during critical moments. The following active-alert script was created to allow for frequent repetitions of the technical and tactical sequences he would have to master and involved a scenario that simulated actual competition.

One of the problems with simulated competition, especially as it pertains to elite athletes, is lack of realism. Because most elite athletes tend to perform better during actual competition, training scenarios rarely adequately replicate the pressures of real competition and, thus, often fail to motivate elite athletes to perform to the best of their ability during simulations. As a consequence, this script attempted to create a scenario that an elite athlete would accept as real, something that is easier to achieve when applying hypnosis and imagery to athletes who are high in hypnotic ability/absorption (one of the reasons hypnosis and imagery are not that amenable to athletes who are low in hypnotic ability/absorption).

If realism can be achieved, elite athletes who are hypnotized will believe they are actually playing a real match and exhibit a level of intensity usually observed when competing. This is thought to be beneficial for reducing stress and increasing performance during actual competition. The following hypnotic script also attempts to induce dissociation and suppression of negative intrusive thoughts from surfacing in an athlete who is high in neuroticism. Because negative intrusive thoughts in this player usually centered on his technical weaknesses, the script focused on technical details and parameters associated with optimum tennis strokes or technique. Thus, although it is widely held that athletes should not think about their technique and "just do it," faulty technique must be corrected and reprogrammed, something active-alert hypnosis can facilitate. Because, in this particular player, the way to achieve psychological improvement was through technical mastery, it was vital to correct flawed technique to boost his self-confidence and eventually eliminate negative intrusive thoughts centering on technical problems. The intense repetition of correct technical parameters that active-alert hypnosis affords is designed to help consolidate improved motor skills in implicit memory more efficiently. Faulty technique can lead to poor results and outcome, which in turn can cause a vulnerable athlete to obsess on negative intrusive thoughts such as, "Why can't I hit a winning shot when I have to?" or, "Why did I miss that backhand?"

Active-alert hypnosis scripts and action routines should also be designed to positively reinforce "proper" technique when indicated. Once an improvement threshold is achieved, one can expect negative intrusive thoughts about technique to attenuate, a first step in experiencing play free from internal distractions. As such, because of this player's technically and neuroticism-mediated poor performance, this script addresses and attempts to correct technical flaws in an active manner as opposed to just telling him "to do it." The priority was to eradicate technical miscues and replace them with proper technique since it was expected that once this was accomplished, negative intrusive thoughts about these flaws would recede or be entirely eliminated.

Induction and Hypnotic Suggestions: A Scripted Match Scenario for an Elite Tennis Player

Envision yourself beginning to prepare for your first-round tennis match. Start by going through all of your strokes in a slow and deliberate manner and visualize the different parts of each stroke you have been working on, including the backswing, swing to contact, contact point, and follow through. Try to feel the length of your backswing as well as your swing. After each completed stroke, get back into the ready position. Think about a tactical sequence you are going to carry out in the upcoming match, and then carry it out in a slow and deliberate manner until you have completed all the strokes involved in this sequence. Pay attention to keeping your feet moving and going forward toward the ball. Imagine yourself attacking the ball. As you go through the stroke sequences, practice improving the weakness you were recently made aware of, remembering to stay sideways with your shoulders parallel to the sideline until you have completed the entire backhand stroke.

As you continue warming up, pick up the pace a little bit. Imagine that you are on the court in front of thousands of spectators, and feel yourself become eager to show what you can do. You are gaining confidence, your muscles are loosening up, your breathing is steady and indicative of someone who is in control, and you're absolutely calm and certain that you will play to the best of your ability. As we continue through the warm-up sequence, you are playing points out in your mind. When playing these points you imagine the tactics you are going to carry out to beat today's opponent. You are aware that this player will charge the net after most serves, so you are ready to hit your best passing shots. You know that you'll have to keep your head down when hitting the ball, and if you're trying to pass him with the backhand, your shoulders will remain parallel to the sideline. Things are going well, you are falling deeper and deeper into a state of absolute concentration. When you go out onto the court you will notice nothing but the court—the crowd will not be there, you will be totally focused on playing your best tennis. When you start to warm up against your opponent, your motor system will feel like a finely tuned machine; the prematch routine will have worked wonders. You will feel as though you can beat anyone because you are confident that your technical skills have been optimally prepared and that you have the ideal game plan to beat this player.

Once you are on the court you must rely on yourself, but you will continue to hear me remind you to do certain things, although I will do so only before action when you are returning serve or serving. Once action starts you will react, and everything for which you trained will flow in a natural and effortless manner; you can't beat yourself because you are ready.

When the match starts, try to detach yourself from everything that may disturb you. Don't let anything intrude on your thoughts and interfere with your concentration. Don't pay attention to anything but what has been called to your attention. Concentrate on your positioning and balance and on the feel of your racket in your hands. Your level of concentration and confidence are increasing in preparation for action. As you anticipate the start of the match and the returning serve you feel primed and ready to play. You are looking forward to the opportunity of playing in front of many tennis fans. You can feel a mild positive tension building in your feet and legs as you anticipate the first point. On each point, before your opponent's racket starts to accelerate toward the ball, you are already in motion and preparing to return it. When returning serve you have a neutral grip, but you are preparing your free hand to change to the proper grip depending on where the ball is hit. All systems are go. Continue to concentrate, time your breathing to your opponent's serving motion, and just before you start your split-step, take a deep breath and make your heart decelerate for a few beats, feel it happen, and your reactions will be very quick in response to the serve. When you say "NOW" to yourself, you will explode out of the ready position and react to the serve. Remember to use your free hand to get the proper grip, take a short backswing and step toward the ball. As you swing you notice a free-flowing acceleration of the racket, and just before you make impact with the ball your grip becomes more forceful, allowing you to transfer all of your power through the ball as you hit and follow through. Accelerate through the ball, hit it with confidence, then get back to the neutral position and prepare for the next shot. NOW!

After a point ends listen to the chair umpire call out the score. Whenever he does this, you will know that you have maximum of 20 to 25 seconds until the next point starts. Hearing the score will help you concentrate and prepare for the next point. During this period you will prime your mind and body for the next point. You will think about an appropriate strategy that you have learned and practiced and will be getting ready during this 20- to 25-second interval. Just before action your mind will be blank, you will be totally focused on the ball, and you will carry out the tactic you thought about. Just as you or your opponent commences action, say "NOW."

Commentary

The above script was designed for an elite tennis player. It assumes a high level of technical competence and the ability to carry out numerous tactical strategies. The player's weaknesses were addressed in the two warm-up phases. The first phase occurred 30 minutes before the player was called out to the court. This practice session involved the induction phase of active-alert hypnosis. During this period, the player went through a so-called shadow stroke routine in which he practiced entire stroke sequences without actually hitting the ball. This phase is marked by the constant repetition of key messages that are designed to increase hypnotic depth while simultaneously priming implicit motor memory for impending action. In addition, suggestions for creating the impression that the practice session is a real match are administered. This is intended to raise levels of activation while reducing the mental stress associated with competition. It is hoped that a realistic scenario will reduce precompetition anxiety by desensitizing the player to common distractions including crowd noise, the opponent's presence, and internal intrusive thoughts. Once the active-alert hypnosis session has been completed and a player is sufficiently activated and primed (both mentally and physically), posthypnotic suggestions are administered. These suggestions are intended to induce autosuggestion or self-hypnosis when the player is on the court and can no longer be coached or prompted exogenously.

In the above script, whenever the chair umpire announced the score, the player self-prompted himself to go through a mental preparation routine before the upcoming point. In this period the player was hypnotized to consider implementing an appropriate strategy (similar to what was rehearsed in the active-alert, match simulation phase of the earlier practice session) and to attempt to induce heart rate deceleration before action, using cognitive strategies and breathing techniques. Thereafter, another autosuggestion, saying "NOW," functioned as a cue to ready the athlete for immediate action.

The initial active-alert hypnosis practice session can also be adapted to beginners or less-skilled tennis players whose primary concerns are learning and improving tennis specific motor skills. In such cases, emphasis is placed on the technical components of specific tennis strokes or combinations thereof. The goal here is to facilitate consolidation of tennis-specific motor skills in implicit memory by preventing internal and external distractions from interfering with the attentional demands of learning a motor skill. This is achieved once a student starts to dissociate and focus entirely on the verbal suggestions of the hypnotist. These suggestions pertain to the technical or biomechanical aspects of a tennis stroke. They are not concerned with tactical or other issues (e.g., creating a realistic scenario).

Improvement is evaluated as follows: During active-alert hypnosis in which technical instructions are continually administered, a coach or rater assesses the quality of the student's stroke, or more objectively, how near to a target a student can hit a ball (the better the technique, the higher the rating or score). Ratings for technique or scores on the target test during hypnosis are compared to baseline performance to determine the effect hypnosis may have had on motor skills or technical improvement.

It would be especially interesting to see whether beginners who have problems exhibiting "proper technique" outside of hypnosis do so while under hypnosis. Demonstrating this would go a long way toward confirming the hypothesis that intrusive thoughts can prevent consolidation of motor skills in implicit memory. In these studies, it must also be determined whether a player is really hypnotized or not and whether the same effects can be achieved outside hypnosis, using the same training techniques. Hence, A-B-A designs must be used to establish whether improvement is attributable to hypnotic procedures or to nonspecific factors (see Chapter 15).

Active-alert hypnosis offers promise (especially for athletes who are high in hypnotic ability/absorption) in that it is an imagery-based intervention that departs from conventional paradigms, induction procedures, and suggestions that have not been successful in establishing that hypnosis can improve motor skills (Morgan 1996).

Carlstedt protocol induction scripts and suggestions are based on principles of motor learning and emphasize repetition. It should be relatively easy to test whether "x" amount of repetition of motor skill or tennis stroke "y," under hypnosis, will lead to score "z" on any number of objective measures in accord with the Power-Law of Learning, especially in beginners (Anderson, 1995).

Sport-specific active-alert scripts and protocols can be ordered by contacting Dr. Roland A. Carlstedt via email: DrRCarlstedt@aol.com or RCarlstedt@americanboardofsportpsychology.org.

15

A Design for Implementing and Testing the Efficacy of a Biofeedback Protocol Created for a Former Wimbledon Champion

Sport psychology practitioners are constantly challenged to help their clients reach an optimal level of performance. To ensure that peak performance is achieved, practitioners must use intervention strategies that work. Athletes and teams who do not benefit from performance enhancement methods are soon lost clients. More disturbing is the damage the field of sport psychology can incur when methods are used haphazardly or en masse, without due consideration of what a particular intervention actually does or does not accomplish. As a consequence, practitioners must know whether an intervention works, and both coaches and athletes entrusting themselves to mental trainers need to be shown that assessments are accurate and that the performance enhancement techniques they are told to use are effective.

Unfortunately, evaluating the efficacy of mental training methods is rarely undertaken despite equivocal evidence regarding the effects of many interventions, especially when they are evaluated in the context of objective outcome measures (technical, physiological, or statistical) and ecologically valid situations (e.g., critical moments) and not just on the basis of self-report or subjective appraisals.

My protocol attempts to counter this trend by incorporating an intervention efficacy testing process based on the single case experiment method.

Single-Case Experiment Method

The single-case experiment method is well suited for the study of the efficacy of an intervention. It involves an intense examination of one individual and is also referred to as a single-subject or time-series experiment (Gall et al. 1996). Kratochwill and Levin (1992) refers to single-case experiment as "the intense analysis of behavior in single organisms." Single-case studies use quantitative procedures to achieve experimental control including reliability testing of experimental observations, frequent observations of behaviors of interest, description of an intervention in sufficient detail to permit replication, and replication of intervention effects within the experiment. A major strength of the single-case study is that a person serves as his or her own control.

The Case

AB (initials altered to protect the player's identity) is a former Wimbledon champion considered to be one of the most talented tennis players of all time. A frequent top 10-ranked player, AB was experiencing a long trend of subpeak performance. His managers described AB as a player who could make history if only he could apply himself more intensely. Unfortunately, despite having won the most cherished title in tennis (Wimbledon), AB was an underachiever compared with many of his contemporaries.

In addition to being one of the most talented players in the game, AB was also considered one of the more intellectual. Although he appeared to be happy with his life and career, after his Wimbledon victory, he had not fulfilled his early promise as a tennis player. This was a cause for concern for his management group and sponsors who had invested millions of dollars in him. At one Wimbledon several years ago, his manager approached and asked me for an appraisal of his client. I attributed AB's fluctuating performance and infrequent show of determination to lack of motivation stemming from having obtained too much fame and fortune early in his career and felt that his talent made the game too easy for him. He appeared to lack passion for the game, something I attributed to chronic hypoactivation associated with trait and state low neuroticism. I agreed to meet AB's manager again at the U.S. Open in New York later that year to discuss a possible course of action to help his client play up to his potential.

Over the course of AB's career, I had the opportunity to attend numerous press conferences in which he revealed much about his psyche and approach to the game. He mentioned a lack of motivation along with an inability to generate enough emotion and willpower to win "ordinary" tournaments after having won the most prestigious event in the game. He also once commented that the way he felt in the morning would determine whether he played well that day or not. I sized him up to be low in absorption (because of his realistic orientation and cognitive style), low in neuroticism (because of his self-report of lack of motivation and low energy), and high in repressive coping (based on his self-protective cognitive style and know-it-all attitude [he also did not think much of sport psychology]).

Although the primary higher-order (PHO) constellation I attributed to AB was actually one of the two best possible constellations, recall that PHO factors outside the context of critical moments can exert both positive or negative influences on performance and behavior. Although we could expect AB to perform well during critical moments, if an athlete who is predisposed psychologically to perform well under pressure fails to encounter critical moments for any particular reason (e.g., dominating or poor technical play), his potential psychological prowess will rarely be tested or displayed. As in the case of AB, lately his matches were of such poor quality that he rarely was challenged psychologically, often losing quickly before critical moments could even arise. Therefore, the main issue was not how to make AB play better during critical moments but, rather, how to increase his physiological reactivity to the point that he again would want to play hard and win matches. Once this issue was resolved, one would expect him to master critical moments on the basis of his constellation of PHO factors and superior talent.

One might ask why an athlete who is high in repressive coping, as I suspected was true of AB, would be underactivated, as high repressive coping is associated with tonic physiological hyperreactivity at baseline. Although individuals who are high in repressive coping tend to have a higher level of physiological reactivity than people who are lows, elevated reactivity in a clinical context could still be considered underactivated when viewed in relationship to sport competition.

Moreover, ultimately, an individual's ideal level of reactivity is determined on the basis of differences between his or her physiological responses at baseline and task-specific activity (see individual response specificity and activation in Andreassi 1995). As a consequence, although AB's level of activation at baseline might have been elevated, it may not have been sufficiently high for him to want to get up and compete.

Proposal, Assessment, Intervention, and Efficacy Study

The following proposal was made to AB's manager: I would accompany AB to tennis tournaments and training sessions commencing in the fall. During this time, AB would be intensely observed and evaluated using my protocol. This would involve first assessing AB for Theory of Critical Moments–PHO factors and cerebral laterality, heart rate variability (HRV), muscle tension, and electrodermal activity (skin conductance) and then following up on a daily basis.

On match days he would be assessed psychophysiologically in the morning, before practice, and before a scheduled match. On nonmatch days, measurements would be taken in the morning and before practice and fitness-conditioning sessions. Two weeks would be allotted for data collection to determine baseline values for physiological measures. The PANAS would be used to determine self-report of affective states and their relationship to physiological responding during baseline and when playing. This would be done to determine whether self-report (PANAS scores) could be used to predict physiological reactivity. If this were the case, eventually it would be possible to forgo physiological assessment and to proceed directly to biofeedback, assuming that activation levels fell outside AB's Zone of Optimum Functioning.

Because AB had activation problems that were attributed to his constellation of PHO factors (low hypnotic ability/absorption, low neuroticism [but high state negative affect at times], and low repressive coping), I decided to focus on EMG (muscle tension) to assess his daily level of motivation. Bartoshuk (1955) and Surwillo (1956) have demonstrated that EMG can be a good indicator of motivation and physiological reactivity. HRV and EDA would also be measured in case muscle tension was not revealing.

Prepractice and match measurements would be correlated with various performance measures. During the initial 2-week data-accumulation period, interventions would not be applied. This phase instead was primarily concerned with investigating relationships between prematch baseline states of physiological reactivity, self-report of motivation and emotions, and performance. Practice sessions and matches would be statistically analyzed using the Carlstedt Critical Moment Psychological Performance Index system to assess various performance parameters including physical/technical as well as tactical and outcome measures (performance statistics and success [wins and losses]).

Predictions

It was expected that AB's level of EMG (frontalis muscle tension) would correspond with his self-report of low motivation and emotional reactivity, as well as predict his subsequent performance. Conceivably, other measures including HRV and EDA would covary with EMG or a specific physiological measure might emerge as AB's window of vulnerability. It was expected that the level of physiological reactivity at baseline would be about the same before practice and competition, which would indicate that impending play for him did not give rise to the kind of activation that athletes frequently experience as competition draws near. However, if it was determined that prepractice or match baselines exceeded morning baselines, biofeedback in the morning or before play would attempt to elevate his physiological reactivity above the higher of the two baseline conditions, as even the higher of two baseline measures might not be sufficiently elevated to sustain motivation and focus during competition, especially when an athlete reports being unmotivated.

The Experiment: Baseline and Treatment Conditions

Baseline EMG, EDA, and HRV were to be measured in the morning and before each practice session and match. The length of each measurement session was to be 15 minutes.

A-B-A Design

An A-B-A design was planned whereby treatment would be introduced whenever physiological reactivity for any specific measure was below a threshold that had been established on the basis of correlations between morning and preplay state of activation and subsequent performance in practice or actual matches. For example, if the baseline testing period reveals that a morning frontalis muscle tension level of 5 uV or HRV LF/HF ratio of 1:3 is associated with poor psychological performance or match outcome and statistics, biofeedback would be used before practice or competition to raise physiological reactivity to levels associated with good psychological performance or outcome. If biofeedback-induced elevations in physiological reactivity, for example, an increase to 20 uV frontalis muscle tension or HRV shift in the LF/HF ratio to 3:1 (sympathetic nervous system dominance), are found to be associated with good performance, it is possible that these levels of activation could help mediate proficient performance, especially if withdrawal of biofeedback results in a regression to previous low levels of activation and poor performance. Subsequently, one would then reintroduce biofeedback (A-B-A-B design) and, if levels of activation are again increased and result in improved performance a second time, a strong case could be made that the intervention (biofeedback) contributed to better performance.

Unfortunately, despite AB's manager's desire to implement my plan, AB was not willing to participate. Consistent with a person who is high in repressive coping, AB essentially felt that he had no real psychological issues, just momentary lapses in motivation that he could overcome whenever he wanted to. His reaction was like that of many top tennis professionals I have encountered who are high in repressive coping, skeptical of mental training, and difficult to convince that they should give it a try. Wickramasekera (1988) recognized the difficulty of reaching skeptical patients, leading him to develop the so-called "Trojan horse" induction method to circumvent barriers that individuals who are high in repressive coping and low in absorption typically use to avoid recognizing and confronting their psychological and physical health problems.

Although I was unable to implement my plan with this former Wimbledon champion, an athlete who at the time could have benefited from an objective reality-based intervention such as biofeedback, the "Champion's" plan that I developed for him eventually led to my protocol, an intervention strategy that I have used with scores of athletes. An important aspect to this protocol is efficacy testing using the single-case experiment approach combined with repeated baseline and in-the-field measurements.

16

An Internet-Based Athlete Assessment, Analysis, Intervention, and Database Center: Your Personal Sport Psychology Consultant

After having two near-40–40 seasons (40 home runs and 40 stolen bases), the talented New York Yankee second baseman Alfonso Soriano experienced a debilitating slump in the 2003 playoffs and World Series. To most pundits, his performance was inexplicable, leading the team's General Manager Brian Cashman to suggest offhandedly in a postgame interview that if anyone had the secret to Soriano's—and his team's—collapse, he would be interested in hearing from him or her.

Team-wide slumps like the one the Yankees experienced in the 2003 World Series or individual ones such as Soriano's lead to much speculation as to their origin, but rarely are analysts and sport psychologists able to offer an explanation beyond conjecture regarding the etiology of sudden major decrements in performance. Some said that Soriano was not an intelligent hitter, whereas others called his style of play undisciplined, and some more extreme analysts even called for his head, stating that trading him to another team would be the best thing to do. This latter solution would be quite radical, considering that Soriano produced two of the best back-to-back seasons a young player had generated in the history of baseball. The supertalent who was predicted to go on to a Hall of Fame career suddenly had been reduced to trade-bait,[1] with many so-called experts contending that now was the time to get rid of him before his value plummeted even more.

What was wrong with Soriano? Surely he had not lost all of the skills that had talent scouts drooling when they first sighted him on sandlots in the Dominican Republic? As Cashman wanted to know, what was the secret to his demise, and would it be irreversible or permanent?

What about the Yankees crosstown rivals, the Mets? They had a miserable season. Throughout the year the press had a field day analyzing what was wrong with them. Their general manager was fired, the team's manager was taken to task, and top players including Roberto Alomar were traded in the quest for a winning season. The Mets even called a sport psychologist to "talk" to the team, hoping somehow that he would deliver the Mets out of their season-long funk. In the end, the Mets finished in last place, the Yankees were disgusted with their World Series collapse, and Soriano's future remained uncertain.

In the middle of such turmoil and poor performance, psychobabble often prevails. There is talk about mental toughness, motivation, focus, zone, mental training, and "just do it" notions, as though these and other nebulous psychological constructs and platitudes held the key to understanding the dynamics of terrible performance. Columnists would talk about how unfocused the Mets were, how certain players on the Yankees could not "just do it" when it counted, how some players on both teams were unmotivated despite being overpaid, how Soriano, "just did it," but in "just doing it," was unselective when it came to picking out a pitch to hit, leading to a record number of strike-outs. It was suggested that Jeff Weaver, a highly touted Yankee pitching prospect, see a sport psychologist so that he would finally be

---

[1]Soriano was indeed traded to the Texas Rangers in the off-season and is currently playing very well.

able to harness his enormous potential. According to the New York media, these players and teams just could not find the zone.

Unfortunately, the above speculative comments, analyses, and advice regarding the mental side of the game are just as common among sport psychologists as they are among the laity. Although the above constructs and notions may indeed form the basis of certain aspects of sport performance when used in the context of pop psychological analyses, they are wanting as to their meaning. After all, what does "not focusing" or "just do it," or being "in the zone" really mean? Essentially, the field of sport psychology has fed these meaningless slogans, platitudes, and notions to the masses, such that coaches, athletes and analysts have bought into many ideas advanced by the field. However, without systematically delineating the mental components of the performance equation and operationalizing the pet slogans of sport psychology, coaches, athletes, teams, and analysts have little of empirical value to draw on and use when it comes to making decisions about athletes, such as whether Soriano should stay or go.

In contrast to the physical and technical game, about which there is an abundance of scientific information and data along with huge volumes of actual objective performance statistics (especially in the sports of baseball, football, and basketball), when it comes to the mental side of the game, there is a paucity of valid and reliable information about its dynamics. As a consequence, potentially revealing measures such as "zone," "focus," and "mental toughness" have devolved instead of evolving into potent constructs and sensitive measures of psychological performance. They have become misused and even abused terms that are thrown about with impunity. At face value they mean nothing. In essence, the assessment of psychological performance, mental training, and ultimately, decision making regarding an athlete's mental game and predictions of future performance are often based on anecdotal speculation instead of good science.

The field of applied sport psychology to a large extent can be blamed for this dismal state. It remains mired in a paradigm that is based in part on weak data, nonvalidated interventions, and faulty assessment methods. It is thus no wonder that professional sport teams that spend millions of dollars on the technical and physical development of athletes allow unqualified persons to do "mental training" (usually stereotypical visualization or relaxation) exercises or, at best, employ trained sport psychologists who are well intentioned but woefully unexposed to sophisticated methods and advanced knowledge regarding peak performance, relegating sport psychology to the bottom of a team's priority list.

Although it is widely accepted that the mental game is the most important aspect of peak performance, especially during critical moments of competition (which this book demonstrated), sport psychology still has stepchild status when it comes to player development funding by professional sport teams. Could that be because the field of applied sport psychology and its practitioners have very little to offer in terms of valid methods and hard data? Moreover, although teams recognize the importance of the mental side of the game, decision makers have received only minimal, if any, guidance regarding scientific approaches to mental peak performance from the field of sport psychology. Instead, general managers are sold outdated approaches that largely rely on visualization and relaxation techniques that are applied en masse or, worse yet, they are seduced by charlatans peddling all sorts of mental snake oil as science (e.g., brain typing).

If the field of sport psychology is to make inroads into professional sports and provide all athletes the best possible service and methods, a paradigm shift pertaining to the assessment and mental training needs to occur. It must be based on rigorous scientific approaches and methods, similar to those seen in the clinical realm, where major advances have been made pertaining to patient diagnosis and treatment. New approaches to athlete evaluation must produce meaningful and useful information regarding an athlete's psychological performance that has a high degree of validity and reliability. Just as a professional scout or coach knows an athlete's vertical jumping ability, foot speed, performance average, technical propensities, body-fat index, and oxygen uptake, the time has come to develop individualized normative databases on psychological and neuropsychophysiological functioning in athletes for assessment, comparative, and intervention purposes. Practitioners should know an athlete's "attention threshold," "brain processing speed and reaction time," "emotional reactivity," "critical moment psychological proficiency," "heart rate variability and deceleration response parameters," and "movement related brain-macro potential readings" among other important performance components if they are to effectively advise athletes, coaches and teams.

The era of merely telling athletes "to relax," "just imagine," or "shut out all negative thoughts" is passé. A new era needs to emerge in which slogans like "just relax" are operationalized in terms of "generating more high frequency heart rate variability" before critical moments, or increasing "focus" would involve engaging in neurofeedback to achieve a higher attention threshold. Rather than tell an athlete to "shut out negative thoughts," athletes would be taught to manipulate relative brain hemispheric activation to suppress intrusive thoughts.

The current cliché-laden "just do it" approach needs to be replaced with methods that define many of the nebulous constructs that pervade sport psychology today. It is time to delineate Hanin's (1980) theory and postulates using instruments and methodologies that allow us to measure the states of intensity or physiological reactivity to which his theory refers.

It is no longer tenable for any practitioner delving in the arena of sport psychology to speak in nebulous terms such as, "he doesn't concentrate," or "she's a choker," or "he's not mentally tough" or to recommend interventions just because they are the thing to do. Using "you've got to visualize" or "get your intensity up," as slogans to somehow involve a person in mental training is insufficient. Athletes and coaches need to be provided with standardized measures and parameters of sport-relevant psychological and neuropsychophysiological functioning. The time has come for practitioners to use new language that is based on empirically derived data and on operationalizations of psychological processes and their effects on performance. Advanced technology and methodologies are available to lift applied sport psychology to a new level of sophistication and credibility—they just have to be used.

This brings me to the Athlete Neuropsychophysiological Performance Database project and the Internet Athlete Psychological Assessment and Performance Center. Although I recognize that most practitioners do not have specialized training in psychophysiology, neuropsychology, and ambulatory assessment, the advent of chip technology has given rise to numerous products that can be used by practitioners, coaches, and athletes. These devices can be used to gather data, analyze it, and even entrain ideal neuropsychophysiological states at home and, more recently, on the field. As consequence, I am advocating that all sport psychology practitioners participate in an international, controlled, and standardized protocol designed to create a normative database of neuropsychophysiological functioning in athletes for off-the-field baseline conditions and tasks, for on-the-field real training and competition, and for during critical moments of competition. The project is multifaceted and will be easily accessible to practitioners and athletes.

Central to the ANPD project is the Brain Resource Company (BRC) neuropsychological test battery and quantitative electroencephalography (qEEG) brain functioning analysis protocol. In the clinical world, the BRC approach to the establishment of normative brain databases is emerging as one of the most valid and reliable indices of cortical functioning, primarily because of the rigorously controlled and administered protocol to which the BRC adheres. Not all brain function databases can claim strict levels of control required for accurate interpretations of the data. As a consequence, brain function databases are only as valid and reliable as their protocols.

The BRC protocols allow for highly valid and reliable analyses of the brain functioning that is relevant to sport performance. The BRC brain analysis battery includes measures of executive functioning; subliminal cognitive and emotional processing, responding, and reaction time tasks measured at the level of the brain; comprehensive EEG activity (qEEG); and central nervous system reactivity to select stimuli. As the athlete-specific database evolves, it is expected that clear tendencies in brain functioning will emerge that will distinguish athletes in terms of psychological performance and that some of the findings and hypotheses on cortical functioning in athletes that I presented in this book will be concurrently validated on the basis of multiple neurophysiological measures and markers that the BRC protocol captures.

The BRC approach is also intended to be flexible and dynamic and will evolve to include new measures of athlete-relevant cortical functioning on the basis of the initial database findings. An in-the-field neuropsychological protocol will also be developed in phase II of the BRC project.

The Athlete Psychological Assessment and Performance Center project is an applied field study approach to the assessment and evaluation of athletes. It is independent of the BRC database project, yet is complementary and is predicated on the ecological validity of monitoring procedures and data generation.

Participating practitioners or individual athletes will have access to a new and sophisticated ambulatory monitoring device that was jointly developed by Brainquiry, BioCom Technologies, and myself. The device is capable of monitoring various measures including heart rate variability (HRV), EEG, galvanic skin response, and EMG-muscle tension. The Athlete Psychological Assessment and Performance Center project will primarily focus on HRV, using an adapted version of the Brainquiry Personal Efficiency Trainer containing BioCom Technologies' advanced HRV analysis software, called the Heart-Minder. This device is capable of acquiring continuous data for up to 18 hours and can be used during training and competition to assess and enhance psychological performance. The Heart-Minder is linked to an Internet-based data analysis center. Participants in this project will upload data to the Internet data center for analysis and for report generation. Acquired data will also be used to extend on my own and BioCom Technologies' existing HRV and heart rate deceleration databases for athletes, normal and clinical samples. Practitioners and athletes will receive a customized report along with recommendations for mental training and comparative norms. Practitioners who are specially trained in this protocol will also have access to personal computer-based analysis software for in-office evaluation and mental training purposes.

The advent of the Heart-Minder, Personal Efficiency Trainer, and Internet data analysis center go a long way toward removing barriers associated with ambulatory monitoring and high-tech assessment of athletes (see Carlstedt 2003). The device is quite small, is powerful in its data acquirement and analysis capabilities, and is linked to a professional support team and center. Moreover, the device has biofeedback capabilities that allows for in-the-field mental training and self-regulation interventions.

Revisiting the Soriano and Yankees situation, using the above methods, one could have generated a comprehensive neuropsychophysiological profile on Soriano extending back to when he was first scouted and signed. These data would provide information on numerous measures including brain functioning and HRV during baseline conditions (devoid of tasks and stress), during practice and actual competition. Other tests and measures including assessment of PHO factors and critical moment analyses would have rounded out the evaluation battery. This battery could have been administered to all Yankee players extending down into their minor league organization. Using this approach and protocol, the Yankees would have an internal database of psychological and psychophysiological performance as well as access to a league-wide database.

The data would have revealed Soriano's mental and physiological response tendencies and actual functioning during peak performance and could have been used for comparative purposes whenever performance problems arose, such as during the 2003 playoffs. Having such data would quickly allow one to identify deviations from his personal norms and best functioning parameters. Rather than speculating about why he could not get hits and was striking out so much, this approach gets right to the heart of the problem (no pun intended). The data might have revealed that Soriano's brain processing speed and reaction time were significantly slower during the World Series than during periods of peak performance. Further analysis might have revealed that his responses to subliminal emotion evoking stimuli, coupled with his level of neuroticism and absorption, neutralized his ability to shut out distractions, making him vulnerable to negative intrusive thoughts, thereby hampering his ability to attend toward external stimuli (the pitcher), causing him to strike out excessively.

Having such information could have led to a customized mental training plan designed to restore his baseline parameters for neuropsychophysiological functioning. Such knowledge could also guide other players and coaches as to how they should interact with Soriano during a slump. Rather than put additional pressure on Soriano by benching him or moving him from lead-off hitter to the eighth batting slot, a strategically focused mental training plan could have been implemented to restore his strengths rather than try to hide him in the line-up and hope he didn't hurt the team.

Using the above advanced and revealing methods, one would have been able to tell Brian Cashman or Joe Torre why Soriano slumped so badly during the World Series and could intervene to get him back on track. Instead of just opining about his level of focus or poor mental choices, one would have been able to tell team leaders that Soriano's level of attention as reflected in HRV or qEEG activity was, say, 25% below his norm for these neuropsychophysiological measures associated with attention or focus.

Although such a high-tech approach to athlete assessment and intervention may seem complex and inaccessible to the average practitioner, it need not be and, thus, should be sought by any professional sport organization, coach, athlete, or practitioner who is serious about the psychological side of the game. It is inexcusable and perhaps even unethical for practitioners to continue to advocate and use a paradigm that does not test its methods for efficacy or to not use the most advanced and sophisticated approaches available. One can think of issues of practice and competency using the following analogy: If a psychologist or psychiatrist in the course of routine therapy, on hearing that a patient had chronic headaches, merely dismissed the complaint and failed to refer the patient for further assessment from a neurologist, he or she would be considered negligent and liable were the patient to die of a brain tumor. Just because a practitioner does not have access to a magnetic resonance imaging machine, let alone know how to use it or to evaluate a brain scan, doesn't mean he or she should not seek out experts who use this advanced technology.

Similarly, just because a practitioner does not have high-tech equipment to assess brain functioning or HRV in athletes or do efficacy studies on applied interventions does not mean he or she should not seek out specialists who can. The argument that it is not necessary to validate the effects of interventions or basic assessments in athletes is becoming increasingly tenuous as more research comes to light attesting to the utility and benefits of advanced and technologically sophisticated assessment, monitoring, and mental training methods.

The above multifaceted and high-tech approach to applied sport psychology offers athletes, coaches, and teams access to cutting-edge scientific methods and technology that will illuminate psychological performance as never before.

Interested practitioners and athletes are invited to participate in this Internet database and analysis project. Doing so will help the field of sport psychology generate normative data on the psychological performance of athletes as well assist practitioners in providing coaches and athletes with the most advanced approach to assessment and mental training intervention available.

For more information on this project please visit the American Board of Sport Psychology Web site at http://www.americanboardofsportpsychology.org. A portal or link to the project Web site can be found there. You can also e-mail Dr. Roland A. Carlstedt at DrRCarlstedt@aol.com or call 212-860-8500 (ext. 25) or 917-680-3994 to learn how to participate in this groundbreaking project.

References

Akselrod, S., Gordon, D., Ubel, F. A., Shannon, D. C., Barger, A. C., and Cohen, R. J. (1981). Power spectrum analysis of heart rate fluctuation: A quantitative probe of beat-to-beat cardiovascular control. *Science*, 213, 220–222.

Anastasi, A. (1988). *Psychological testing* (6th ed.). Upper Saddle River, NJ: Prentice-Hall.

Anderson, J. R. (1995). *Cognitive psychology and its implications* (4th ed.). New York: W.H. Freeman.

Andreassi, J. L. (1995). *Psychophysiology: Human behavior and physiological response* (3rd ed.). Hillsdale, NJ: Erlbaum.

Armour, J. A. (1994). *Neurocardiology*. New York: Oxford University Press.

Banyai, E. I. (1976). A new way to increase suggestibility: Active-alert hypnotic induction. *International Journal of Clinical and Experimental Hypnosis*, 24, 358.

Banyai, E. I. and Hilgard, E. R. (1976). Comparison of active-alert hypnotic induction with traditional relaxation induction. *Journal of Abnormal Psychology*, 85, 218–224.

Barabasz, A. (1983). Restricted environmental stimulation and the enhancement of hypnotizability: Pain, EEG alpha, skin conductance and temperature responses. *International Journal of Clinical and Experimental Hypnosis*, 31, 235–238.

Barber, T. X. (1984). Changing "unchangeable" bodily processes by (hypnotic) suggestion. A new look at hypnosis, cognitions, imagining, and the mind-body problem. *Advances*, 1(2), 6–40

Bartoshuk, A. K. (1955). Electromyographic gradients as indicants of motivation. *Canadian Journal of Psychology*, 9, 215–230.

Becker, M. B. (1986). An investigation into the cognitive and personality dimensions of basketball athletes. Unpublished dissertation. Dissertation Abstracts International, 42-02B, 739.

Blix, A. S., Stromme, S. B., and Ursinn, H. (1974). Additional heart rate: An indicator of psychological activation. *Aerospace Medicine*, 14, 1219–1222.

Bonanno, G. A. and Singer, J. L. (1990). Repressive personality style. In J. L. Singer (Ed.), *Repression and dissociation*. Chicago: University of Chicago Press.

Bonanno, G. A., Davis, P. J., Singer, J. L., and Schwartz, G. E. (1991). The repressor personality and avoidant information processing: A dichotic listening study. *Journal of Research in Personality*, 25, 386–401.

Boutcher, S. H. and Zinsser, N. W. (1990). Cardiac deceleration of elite and beginning golfers during putting. *Journal of Sport and Exercise Psychology*, 12, 37–47.

Bradshaw, J. L., Nettleton, N. C., Nathan, G., and Wilson, L. E., (1985). Bisecting rods and lines: Effects of horizontal and vertical posture on left-side underestimation by normal subjects. *Neuropsychologia*, 23, 421–425.

Bradshaw, J. L., Nettleton, N. C., Wilson, L. E., and Bradshaw, C. S. (1987). Line bisection by left-handed preschoolers: A phenomenon of symmetrical neglect. *Brain and Cognition*, 6, 377–385.

Brain, W. R. (1941). Visual disorientation with special reference to lesions of the right cerebral hemisphere. *Brain*, 64, 224–272.

Brewer, B. W. and Petrie, T. A. (1996). Psychopathology in sport and exercise. In J. L. Van Raalte and B. W. Brewer (Eds.), *Exploring sport and exercise psychology* (pp. 257–274). Washington, DC: American Psychological Association.

Brodie, E. E. and Pettigrew, L. E. L. (1996). Is left always right? Directional deviations in visual line-bisecting as a function of hand and initial screening direction. *Neuropsychologia*, 34, 476–470.

Cacioppo, J. T. and Tassinary, L. G. (1990). Inferring psychological significance from physiological signals. *American Psychologist*, 45(1), 16–28.

Cannon, W. B. (1932). *The wisdom of the body*. New York: Appelton-Century Crofts.

Caplan, G. (1974). *Support systems and community mental health*. New York: Behavioral Publications.

Carlstedt, R. A. (1995). *Mentales tennis*. Munich: Sportinform.

Carlstedt, R. A. (1998). Psychologically mediated heart rate variability: A single case study of heart rate deceleration and a spectrum analysis of autonomic function during tournament tennis. Master's thesis, Saybrook Graduate School, San Francisco, CA.

Carlstedt, R. A. (2001). Line Bisecting Test reveals relative left brain hemispheric predominance in highly skilled athletes: Relationships among cerebral laterality, personality, and sport performance. Doctoral dissertation. Saybrook Graduate School, San Francisco, CA.

Carlstedt, R. A. (2002). Ambulatory psychophysiology and ecological validity in studies of sport performance: Issues and implications for intervention protocols in biofeedback. *Biofeedback*, 29(4), 18–22.

Carlstedt, R. A. (2004). Line-bisecting performance in highly skilled athletes: Does preponderance of rightword error indicate unique corticol organization and functioning. *Brain and Cognitions*, 54, 52–57.

Carriero, N. J. and Fite, J. (1977). Cardiac deceleration as an indicator of correct performance. *Perceptual and Motor Skills*, 44, 275–282.

Charman, D. K. (1979). Do different personalities have different hemispheric asymmetries? A brief communique of an initial experiment. *Cortex*, 15, 655–657.

Chaves, J. F. and Brown, J. M. (1978). Self-generated strategies for the control of pain and stress. Presented at the Annual Meeting of the American Psychological Association, Toronto, Canada, August, 1978.

Chaves, J. F. and Brown, J. M. (1987). Spontaneous cognitive strategies for the control of clinical pain and stress. *Journal of Behavioral Medicine*, 10(3), 263–276.

Cohen, W. S. (1985). Health promotion in the work place: A prescription for good health. *American Psychologist*, 40, 213–216.

Cohen, J. (1988). *Statistical power analysis for the behavioral sciences* (2nd ed.). Hillsdale, NJ: Erlbaum.

Cohen, J. (1994). The earth is round (p <.05). *American Psychologist*, 49, 997–1003.

Costa, P. T. and McRae, R. R. (1980). Influence of extraversion and neuroticism on subjective well-being: Happy and unhappy people. *Journal of Personality and Social Psychology*, 38, 668–678.

Costa, P. T. and McRae, R. R. (1997). Longitudinal stability of adult personality. In R. Hogan, J. Johnson, and S. Briggs (Eds.), *Handbook of personality psychology* (pp. 269–292). San Diego, CA: Academic Press.

Cowie, R. and Hamill, G. (1998). Variation among nonclinical subjects on a line-bisection task. *Perceptual and Motor Skills*, 86, 834.

Crawford, H., personal communication, 1999.

Crawford, H.J. and Gruzelier, J. H. (1992). A midstream view of the neurophysiology of hypnosis: Recent research and future directions. In E. Fromm and M. R. Mash (Eds.), *Contemporary hypnosis research*, (pp. 227–266). New York: Guilford.

Crews, D. and Landers, D. (1993). Electroencephalographic measures of attentional patterns prior to the golf putt. *Medicine and Science in Sport and Exercise*, 25, 116–126.

Crocker, P. R., Graham, E., and Thomas, R. (1995). Coping by competitive athletes with performance stress: Gender differences and relationships with affect. *Sport Psychologist*, 9(3), 325–338.

Crossman, D. L. and Polich, J. H. (1989). Hemispheric and personality differences between left- and right-brain individuals for tachistoscopic verbal and spatial tasks. *Personality and Individual Differences*, 10, 747–755.

Crowne, D. P. and Marlowe, D. (1960). A new scale of social desirability independent of psychopathology. *Journal of Consulting Psychology*, 24, 349–354.

Csikszentmihalyi, M. (1990). Flow: The psychology of optimal experience. New York: Harper Perennial.

Curry, L. A., Snyder, C. R, Cook, D. L., Ruby, B. C., and Rehm, M. (1997). Role of hope in academic and sport achievement. *Journal of Personality and Social-Psychology.* 73(6), 1257–1267.

Daino, A. (1984). Personality traits of adolescent tennis players. *International Journal of Sport Psychology*, 16, 120–125.

Davidson, R. J. (1984). Affect, cognition, and hemipsheric specialization. In C. E. Izard, J. Kagan, and R. Zajonc (Eds.), *Emotions, cognition, and behavior* (pp. 320–365). New York: Cambridge University Press.

Davidson, R. J. (1992a). Anterior cerebral asymmetry and the nature of emotion. *Brain and Cognition*, 20, 125–151.

Davidson, R. J. (1992b). Emotion and affective style: Hemispheric substrates. *Psychological Science*, 3, 39–43.

Davidson, R. J., Schwarz, G. E., Pugash, E. and Bromfield, E. (1976). Sex differences in patterns of EEG asymmetry. *Biological Psychology*, 4, 119–138.

Davidson, R. J., Schwartz, G. E., and Rothman, L. P. (1976). Attentional style and the self-regulation of mood-specific attention: An electroencephalographic study. *Journal of Abnormal Psychology*, 85(6), 611–621.

Davis, R. C. (1940). *Set and muscular tension* (Indiana University Publications, Science Series, No. 10). Bloomington: Indiana University Press.

de Geus, E. J. C. and van Doornen, L. J. P. (1996). Ambulatory assessment of parasympathetic/sympathetic balance by impedence cardiography. In J. Fahrenberg and M. Myrtek (Eds.), *Ambulatory assessment: Computer assisted psychological and psychophysiological methods in monitoring and field studies* (pp. 141–164). Goettingen: Hogrefe and Huber.

de Geus E. J. C., van Doornen L. J. P., Vissar A. C., and Orlebeke, J. F. (1990). Existing and training induced differences in aerobic fitness: Their relationship to physiological response patterns during different types of stress. *Psychophysiology*, 27(4), 454–478.

Derogatis, L. R., Abeloff, M. D., and Melisaratos, N. (1979). Psychological coping mechanisms and survival time in metastatic breast cancer. *JAMA*, 242(14), 1504–1508.

Denzin, N. K. and Lincoln, Y. S. (1994). *Handbook of qualitative research*. Thousand Oaks, CA: Sage.

DePascalis, V. (1999). Psychophysiological correlates of hypnosis and hypnotic susceptibility. *International Journal of Clinical and Experimental Hypnosis*, 47(2), 117–143.

Dimon, S. J., Farrington, L., and Johnson, P. (1976). Differing emotional response from right and left hemisphere. *Nature*, 261, 690–692.

Dixon, N. F. (1981). *Preconscious processing*. Chichester: Wiley

Drake, R. A. (1987). Effects of gaze manipulation on aesthetic judgments: Hemisphere priming of affect. *Acta Psychologica*, 65, 91–99.

Drake, R. A., personal communication, April, 2000a.

Drake, R. A., personal communication, June, 2000b.

Drake, R. A. and Myers, L. R. (2004). *Visual perception and emotion: Relative rightward attention predicts positive arousal*. Gunnison, CO: Western State College of Colorado, submitted.

Drake, R. A. and Ulrich, G. (1992). Line bisecting as a predictor of personal optimism and desirability of risky behaviors. *Acta Psychologica*, 79, 219–226.

Duffy, E. (1972). Activation. In N. S. Greenfield and R. A. Sternbach (Eds.). *Handbook of psychophysiology* (pp. 572–622). New York: Holt, Rinehart and Winston.

Edwards, S. W. (1995). Edwards Inventory of Emotions: Assessing emotions in athletes and nonathletes. *Perceptual and Motor Skills,* 80, 444–446.

Edwards, D. C. and Alsip, J. E. (1969). Stimulus detection during periods of high and low heart rate. *Psychophysiology*, 19, 431–434.

Egloff, B. and Gruhn, A. J., (1996). Personality and endurance sports. *Personality and Individual Differences*, 21, 223–229.

Elliott, R. (1974). The motivational significance of heart rate. In P. A. Obrist, A. H. Black, J. Brener, and L. V. DiCara (Eds.), *Cardiovascular psychophysiology* (pp. 505–537). Chicago: Aldine.

Elliott, R., Bankart, B. and Light, T. (1970). Differences in the motivational significance of heart rate and palmer conductance: Two tests of a hypothesis. *Journal of Personality and Social Psychology*, 14, 166–172.

Etnier, J., Witwer, S., Landers, D., Petruzzello, S., and Salazar, W. (1996). Changes in electroencephalographic activity associated with learning a novel motor task. *Research Quarterly for Exercise and Sport*, 67, 272–279.

Evans, F. J. (1977). Hypnosis and sleep: The control of altered states of consciousness. *Annals of the New York Academy of Sciences*, 296, 162–174.

Eysenck, H. J. (1960). *The structure of human personality* (2nd ed.). London: Methuen.

Eysenck, H. J. (1983). Psychophysiology and personality. In A. Galse and J. A. Edwards (Eds.), *Physiological correlates of human behavior*. London: Academic Press.

Eysenck, H. J. and Eysenck, S. (1968). *Eysenck personality inventory: Manual*. San Diego, CA: Educational and Industrial Testing Service.

Eysenck, H. J. and Eysenck, S. (1975). *Manual of the Eysenck Personality Questionnaire*. San Diego, CA: Educational and Industrial Testing Services.

Eysenck, H. J., Nias, D. K., and Cox, D. N. (1982). Sport and personality. *Advances in Behaviour Research and Therapy*, 4, 1–56.

Fahrenberg, J. (1996). Concurrent assessment of blood pressure, heart rate, physical activity and emotional state in natural settings. In J. Fahrenberg and M. Myrtek (Eds.), *Ambulatory psychophysiology: Computer assisted psychological and psychophysiological methods in monitoring and field studies* (pp. 165–188). Goettingen: Hogrefe and Huber.

Fahrenberg, J. and Foerster, F. (1991). A multiparameter study in noninvasive cardiovascular assessment. *Journal of Psychophysiology*, 5, 145–158.

Fahrenberg J. and Myrtek, M. (1996). *Ambulatory psychophysiology: Computer assisted psychological and psychophysiological methods in monitoring and field studies*. Seattle, WA: Hogrefe and Huber.

Fattapposta, F., Amabile, G., Cordischi, M. V., di Venanzio, D., Foti, A., Pierelli, F., D'Alessio, C., Pigozzi, F., Parisi, A., and Morrocutti, C. (1996). Long-term practice effects on a new skilled motor learning: An electrophysiological study. *Electroencephalography and Clinical Neurophysiology*, 99, 495–507.

Flor, H., Turk, D. C., and Birbaumer, N. (1985). Assessment of stress-related psychophysiological reactions in chronic back pain patients. *Journal of Consulting and Clinical Psychology*, 53, 354–364.

Fortino, D., personal communication, November, 2000.

Fortino, D. (2002). Affect regulation, emotional intelligence and addiction: A five-factor personality model and neuropsychological study to predict treatment outcome, and efficacy in heroin abusers. *Doctoral dissertation*. Saybrook Graduate School, San Francisco, CA.

Fox, N. A. and Davidson, R. J. (1984). Hemispheric substrates of affect: A developmental model. In N. A. Fox and R. J. Davidson (Eds.), *The psychobiology of affective development* (pp. 353–381). Hillsdale, NJ: Erlbaum.

Frankel, F. H., Apfel-Savitz, R., Nemiah, J. C., and Sifneos, P. E. (1977). Hypnotizability and recovery from cardiac surgery. *American Journal of Clinical Hypnosis*, 35(2), 119–128.

Fromm, E. and Mash, M. R. (1992). *Contemporary hypnosis research* (pp. 227–266). New York: Guilford.

Fuji, T., Fukatsu, R., Yamadori, A., and Kimura, I. (1995). Effect of age on the line bisection test. *Journal of Clinical and Experimental Neuropsychology*, 17, 941–944.

Galin, D. (1974). Implications for psychiatry of left and right cerebral specialization. *Archives of General Psychiatry*, 31, 572–581.

Gall, M. D., Borg, W. R., and Gall, J. P. (1996). *Educational research: An introduction*. White Plains, NY: Longman.

Gallwey, T. (1974). *The inner game of tennis*. New York: Random House.

Gannon, T., Landers, D., Salazar, W., and Petruzzello, S. (1992). An analysis of temporal EEG patterning prior to initiation of the arm curl. *Journal of Sport and Exercise Psychology*, 14, 87–100.

Geen, R. G. (1996). Psychophysiological approaches to personality. In R. Hogan, J. Johnson, and S. Briggs (Eds.), *Handbook of personality psychology* (pp. 387–416). San Diego, CA: Academic Press.

Geron, D., Furst, P., and Rotstein, P. (1986). Personality of athletes participating in various sports. *International Journal of Sport Psychology*, 17, 98–116.

Gill, D. L. (1988). Gender differences in competitive orientation and sport participation. *International Journal of Sport Psychology*, 19, 145–159.

Goldstein, I. B. (1972). Electromyography: A measure of skeletal muscle response. In N. S. Greenfield and R. A. Sternbach (Eds.), *Handbook of psychophysiology* (pp. 329–365). New York: Holt, Rinehart & Winston.

Gould, D. and Damarjian, N. (1996). Imagery training for peak performance. In J. L. Van Raalte and B. W. Brewer (Eds.). *Exploring sport and exercise psychology* (pp. 25–50). Washington, DC: American Psychological Association.

Graffin, N. F., Ray, W. J., and Lundy, R. (1995). EEG concomitants of hypnosis and hypnotic susceptibility. *Journal of Abnormal Psychology*, 104(1), 123–131.

Grove, J. R. and Heard, N. P. (1997). Optimism and sport confidence as correlates of slump-related coping among athletes. *The Sport Psychologist*, 11, 400–410.

Hahn, W. W. (1973). Attention and heart rate: A critical appraisal of the hypothesis of Lacey and Lacey. *Psychological Bulletin*, 79(1), 59–70.

Hanin, Y. L. (1980). *A study of anxiety in sports*. In W. F. Straub (Ed.), *Sport psychology: An analysis of athletic behavior* (pp. 81–106). Chichester: Wiley.

Hardy, L. and Fazey, J. (1987). *The inverted-U hypothesis: A catastrophe for sport psychology*. Paper presented at the annual meetings of the North American Society of Sport and Physical Activity, Vancouver, British Columbia, Canada.

Harris, R. M., Porges, S. W., Carpenter, M. E., and Vincenz, L. M. (1993). Hypnotic susceptibility, mood state, and vascular reactivity. *American Journal of Clinical Hypnosis*, 36(1), 15–25.

Hassmen, P. and Koivula, N (2001). Cardiac deceleration in elite golfers as modified by noise and anxiety during putting. *Perceptual and Motor Skills*, 92, 947–957.

Hatfield, B. D. (2000). Expertise differences in cortical activation and gaze behavior during rifle shooting. *Journal of Sport and Exercise-Psychology*, 22, 167–182.

Hatfield, B. D., Landers, D. L., and Ray, W. J. (1984). Cognitive processes during self-paced motor performance: An electroencephalographic profile of skilled marksman. *Journal of Sport Psychology*, 6, 42–59.

Hatfield, B. D., Landers, D. L., and Ray, W. J. (1987). Cardiovascular-CNS interactions during a self-paced, intentional attentive state: Elite marksmanship performance. *Psychophysiology*, 24, 542–549.

Heil, J. and Henschen, K. (1996). Assessment in sport and exercise psychology. In J. L. Van Raalte and B. W. Brewer (Eds.), *Exploring sport and exercise psychology* (pp. 229–256). Washington, DC: American Psychological Association.

Helgeson. V. S. (1995). Masculinity, men's roles, and coronary heart disease. In D. F. Sabo and D. F. Gordon (Eds.), *Men's health and illness: Gender, power, and the body: Research on men and masculinity series*, 8 (pp. 68–104). Thousand Oaks, CA: Sage Publications.

Heslegrave, R. J., Olgilvie, J. C., and Furedy, J. J. (1979). Measuring baseline treatment-differences in heart rate variability: Variance versus successive differences mean square and beats per minute versus interbeat interval. *Psychophysiology*, 16, 151–157.

Hilgard, E. R. (1965). *Hypnotic susceptibility*. New York: Harcourt, Brace, and World.

Hilgard, J. R. (1968). Personality and hypnotizability: Inferences from case studies. In E. R. Hilgard (Ed.), *The experience of hypnosis* (pp. 269–300). New York: Harcourt, Brace, and Jovanovich.

Hogan, R. T. (1983). A socioanalytic theory of personality. In M. Page (Ed.), *1982 Nebraska Symposium on Motivation* (pp. 55–89). Lincoln: University of Nebraska Press.

Holmes, T. H. and Rahe, R. H. (1967). The social readjustment rating scale. *Journal of Psychometric Research*, 11, 213–218.

Holyroyd, J. H. (1992). Hypnosis as a methodology in psychological research. In E. Fromm and M. R. Nash (Eds.), *Contemporary hypnosis research* (pp. 227–266). New York: Guilford.

House, J. S., Landis, K. R., and Umberson, D. (1988). Social relationships and health. *Science*, 241, 540–545.

Howell, D. C. (1997). *Statistical methods for psychology* (4th ed.). Belmont, CA: Wadsworth.

Huck, S. W. and Cormier, W. H. (1996). *Reading statistics and research*. New York: Harper Collins.

Ingram, R. E., Saccuzzo, D. P., McNeil, B. W., and McDonald, R. (1979). Speed of information processing in high and low susceptible subjects: A preliminary study. *International Journal of Clinical and Experimental Hypnosis*, 27(1), 42–47.

Jammer, L. D., Schwarz, G. E., and Leigh, H. (1988). The relationship between repressive and defensive coping styles and monocyte, eosinophile, and serum glucose levels: Support for the opiode peptide hypothesis of repression. *Psychosomatic Medicine*, 50, 567–575.

Janelle, C. M., Hillman, M., Charles, H., Apparies, R., Murray, N. Meili, L., Fallon, E., and Hatfield, B. D. (2000). Expertise differences in cortical activation and gaze behavior during rifle shooting. *Journal of Sport and Exercise Psychology*, 22, 167–182.

Jennings, J. R., Stringfellow, J. C., and Graham, M. (1974). A comparison of the statistical distributions of beat-to-beat heart rate and heart period. *Psychophysiology*, 11(2), 207–210.

Jennings, J. R. and Wood, C. C. (1977). Cardiac cycle time effects on performance, phasic cardiac responses, and their intercorrelation in cardiac reaction time. *Psychophysiology*, 14(3), 297–307.

Jewell, G. and McCourt, M. E. (2000). Pseudoneglect: A review and meta-analysis of performance factors in line bisection tasks. *Neuropsychologia*, 38, 93–110.

John, R., Hollander, B., and Perry, C. (1983). Hypnotizability and phobic behavior: Further supporting data. *Journal of Abnormal Psychology*, 92(3), 390–392.

Johnston, D. W. (1996). Improving control and psychological event detection during ambulatory cardiovascular recording. In J. Fahrenberg and M. Myrtek (Eds.), *Ambulatory assessment: Computer assisted psychological and psycho-physiological methods in monitoring and field studies* (pp. 129–140). Goettingen: Hogrefe and Huber.

Jones, J. G. and Cale, A. (1989). Precompetition temporal pattering of anxiety and self-confidence in males and females. *Journal of Sport Behavior*, 12, 183–195.

Jones, J. G., Swain, A., and Cale, A. (1991). Gender differences in pre-competition temporal patterning and antecedents of anxiety and self-confidence. *Journal of Sport and Exercise Psychology*, 13, 1–15.

Jones, G., Swain, A, Harwood, C. (1996). Positive and negative affect as predictors of competitive anxiety. *Personality and Individual Differences*, 20, 109–114.

Jorna, P. G. A. M. (1992). Spectral analysis of heart rate and psychological state: A review of its validity as a work load index. *Biological Psychology*, 34, 237–257.

Kilhstrom, J. F. (1985). Hypnosis. *Annual Review of Psychology*, 36, 385–418.

Kihlstrom, J. F., Register, P. A., Hoyt, I. P., Albright, J. S., Grigorian, E. M., Heindel, W. C., and Morrison, C. R. (1989). Dispositional correlates of hypnosis: A phenomenological approach. *Journal of Clinical and Experimental Hypnosis*, 27, 249–263.

Kinne, G. and Droste, C. (1996). Psychophysiological monitoring of transient ischemic states in patients with coronary heart disease. In J. Fahrenberg and M. Myrtek (Eds.), *Ambulatory assessment: Computer assisted psychological and psychophysiological methods in monitoring and field studies* (pp. 347–364). Goettingen: Hogrefe and Huber.

Kirkcaldy, B. D., (1980). An analysis of the relationship between psychophysiological variables connected to human performance and the personality variables extraversion and neuroticism. *International Journal of Sport Psychology*, 11, 276–289.

Kirsch, I. K. and Council, J. R. (1992). Situational and personality correlates of hypnotic responsiveness. In E. Fromm and M. Nash (Eds.), *Contemporary hypnosis research* (pp. 267–291). New York: Guilford Press.

Klemm, W. R. (1996). *Understanding neuroscience*. St. Louis, MO: Mosby.

Kline, J. P., Allen, J. J. B., and Schwartz, G. E. (1998). Is left frontal brain activation in defensiveness gender specific? *Journal of Abnormal Psychology*, 107, 149–153.

Kolb, B. and Whishaw, I. Q. (1996). *Fundamentals of human neuropsychology* (4th ed.). New York: W. H. Freeman.

Kraemer, H. C. (1981). Coping strategies in psychiatric clinical research. *Journal of Consulting and Clinical Psychology*, 49, 309–319.

Krantz, D. S. and Manuck, S. B. (1984). Acute psychophysiologic reactivity and risk of cardiovascular disease: A review and methodologic critique. *Psychological Bulletin*, 96(3), 435–464.

Krantz, D. S., Gabbay, F. H., Hedges, S. M., Leach, S. G., Gottdiener, J. S., and Rozanski, A. (1993). Mental and physical triggers of silent myocardial ischemia: Ambulatory studies using self-monitoring diary methodology. *Annals of Behavioral Medicine*, 15(1), 33–40.

Kratochwill, T.R. and Levin, J. R. (Eds.), (1992). *Single-case research design and analysis*. Hillsdale, NJ: Erlbaum Associates.

Lacey, J. I., (1967). Somatic response patterning and stress: Some revisions of activation theory. In M. H. Appley and R. Trumbell (Eds.), *Psychological stress: Issues in research* (pp. 14–42). New York: Appleton-Century-Crofts.

Lacey, J. I. and Lacey, B. C. (1964). Cardiac deceleration and simple visual reaction in a fixed foreperiod experiment. Paper presented at the meeting of the Society for Psychophysiological Research, Washington, DC.

Lacey, J. I. and Lacey, B. C. (1966). Changes in cardiac response and reaction time as a function of motivation. Paper presented at the meeting of the Society for *Psychophysiological Research*, Denver, Colorado.

Lacey, J. I. and Lacey, B. C. (1970). Some autonomic-central nervous system interrelationships. In P. Black (Ed.), *Physiological correlates of emotions* (pp. 205–227). New York: Academic Press.

Lacey, J. I. and Lacey, B. C. (1974). On heart rate response and behavior: A reply to Elliott. *Journal of Personality and Social Psychology*, 30(1), 1–18.

Lacey, J. I. and Lacey, B. C. (1978). Two-way communication between the heart and the brain: Significance of time within the cardiac cycle. *American Psychologist*, 33(2), 99–113.

Landers, D., Han, M., Salazar, W., Petruzzello, S., Kubitz, K., and Gannon, T. (1994). Effects of learning on electroencephalographic and electrocardiographic patterns in novice archers. *International Journal of Sport Psychology*, 25, 56–70.

Lane, R. D., Merikangas, K. R., Schwarz, G. E., Huang, S. S., and Pushoff, B. A. (1990). Inverse relationship between defensiveness and lifetime prevalence of psychiatric disorder. *American Journal of Psychiatry*, 147, 573–578.

Lang, P. J., Levin, D. N., Miller, G. A., and Kozak, J. J. (1983). Fear behavior, fear imagery, and the psychophysiology of emotion: The problem of affective response integration. *Journal of Abnormal Psychology*, 92, 276–306.

Langer, E. and Imber, L. G. (1979). When practice makes imperfect: Debilitating effects of overlearning. *Journal of Personality and Social Psychology*, 37, 2014–2024.

Leiderman, P. H. and Shapiro, D. (1962). Application of a time series statistic to physiology and psychology. *Science*, 138(6), 141–142.

Lepore, S. J., Mata, K. A., and Evans, G. W. (1993). Social support lowers cardiovascular reactivity to an acute stressor. *Psychosomatic Medicine*, 55, 518–524.

Lerner, B. H. (1996). Can stress cause disease? Revisiting the tuberculosis research of Thomas Holmes, 1949–1961. *Annals of Internal Medicine*, 124, 673–680.

Lezak, M. D. (1995). *Neuropsychological assessment* (3rd ed.). New York: Oxford University Press.

Lindsley, D. (1969). Average evoked potentials: Achievements, failures and prospects. In E. Donchin and D. Lindsley (Eds.) (NASA Sp-191), *Average evoked potentials: Methods, results and evaluation*. Washington, DC: NASA.

Ludwick-Rosenthal, R., and Neufeld, R. W. J. (1985). Heart rate interoception: A study of individual differences. *International Journal of Psychophysiology*, 3, 57–65.

Lufen, K. (1995). *Psychoregulation im profitennis*. Masters thesis. Deutschesporthochschule Koeln, Cologne, Germany.

Malatesta, C. Z. and Wilson, A. (1988). Emotion, cognition interaction in personality development: A discrete emotions functionalist analysis. *British Journal of Social Psychology*, 27, 91–112.

Malik, M. and Camm, A.J. (Eds.) (1995). *Heart rate variability*. Armonk, NY: Futura.

Mann, S. J. and Delon, M. (1995). Improved hypertension control after disclosure of decades old trauma. *Psychosomatic Medicine*, 57, 501–505.

Mason, J. W. (1971). A re-evaluation of the concept "non-specificity" in stress theory. *Journal of Psychiatric Research*, 8, 323–333.

Martens, R., Vealey, R. S., and Burton, D. (1990). *Competitive anxiety in sports*. Champaign, IL: Human Kinetics.

Martin, R. and Landers, D. M. (1970). Motor performance under stress: A test of the inverted U-hypothesis. *Journal of Personality and Social Psychology*, 16, 29–37.

McCraty, R., Atkinson, M., Tiller, W. A., Rein, G., and Watkins, A. D. (1995). The effects of emotions on short-term power spectrum analysis of heart rate variability. *The American Journal of Cardiology*, 76(14), 1089–1093.

McCraty, R., Tiller, W. A., and Atkinson, M. (1996). *Head heart entrainment: A preliminary survey* (Technical Report from the Institute of HeartMath). Boulder Creek, CA: Institute of Heart-Math.

McCraty, R. and Watkins, A. D. (1996). *Autonomic assessment report: A comprehensive heart rate variability analysis*. Boulder Creek, CA: Institute of HeartMath.

McCanne, T. R., and Sandman, C. A. (1976). Human operant heart rate conditioning: The importance of individual differences. *Psychological Bulletin*, 83, 587–601.

McMaster, N. (1993). Behavior modification with hypnotic visualization, the mental side of golf: A case history. *The Australian Journal of Clinical Hypnotherapy and Hypnosis*, 14(3), 17–22.

McNair, D. N., Lorr, M., and Droppelman, L. F. (1971). *Profile of mood states*. San Diego, CA: Educational and Industrial Testing Services.

Merckelbach, H., and van Oppen, P. (1989). Effects of gaze manipulation on subjective evaluation of neutral and phobia-relevant stimuli. *Acta Psychologica*, 70, 147–151.

Montgomery, G. H., DuHamel, K. N., and Redd, W. H. (2000). A meta-analysis of hypnotically induced analgesia: How effective is hypnosis? *International Journal of Clinical and Experimental Hypnosis*, 48(2), 138–153.

Moran, A. P. (1996). *The psychology of concentration in sport performers: A cognitive analysis*. East Sussex: Psychology Press.

Morgan, W. P. (1996). Hypnosis in sport and exercise psychology. In J. L. van Raalte and B. W. Brewer (Eds.), *Exploring sport and exercise psychology* (pp. 107–132). Washington, DC: American Psychological Association.

Morgan, W. P. (1997). Mind games: The psychology of sport. Perspectives in exercise science. In D. R. Lamb and R. Murray (Eds.), *Recent Advances in the Science and Medicine of Sports* (pp. 3–63), Carmel, IN: Benchmark Press.

Myrtek, M., Bruegner, G., and Mueller, W. (1996). Interactive monitoring and contingency analysis of emotionally induced ECG changes: Methodology and applications. In J. Fahrenberg and

M. Myrtek (Eds.), *Ambulatory assessment: Computer assisted psychological and psychophysiological methods in monitoring and field studies* (pp. 115–128). Goettingen: Hogrefe and Huber.

Myrtek, M. and Spital, S. (1986). Psychophyiological response patterns to single, double, and triple stressors. *Psychophysiology*, 23(6), 663–671.

Newcombe, P. A., Boyle, Gregory, J. (1995). High school students' sports personalities: Variations across participation level, gender, type of sport, and success. *International Journal of Sport Psychology*, 26, 277–294.

Nideffer, R. M. (1993). Concentration and attentional control training. In J. M. Williams (Ed.), *Applied sport psychology: Personal growth to peak performance* (2nd ed., pp. 257–269). Palo Alto, CA: Mayfield.

Nowlin, B., Eisdorfer, C., Whalen, R., and Troyer, W. G. (1970). The effect of exogenous changes in heart rate and rhythm upon reaction time performance. *Psychophysiology*, 7, 186–193.

Obrist, P. A. (1981). *Cardiovascular psychophysiology: A perspective.* New York: Plenum.

Obrist, P. A., Howard, J. L., Sutterer, J. R., Hennis, R. S., and Murrell, D. J. (1973). Cardiac-somatic changes during a simple reaction time task: A developmental study. *Journal of Experimental Child Psychology*, I6, 346–362.

Obrist, P. A., Webb, R. A., and Sutterer, J. R. (1969). Heart rate and somatic changes during aversive conditioning and a simple reaction time task. *Psychophysiology*, 5, 696–723.

Oldfield, R. L. (1971). The assessment and analysis of handedness: The Edinburgh Inventory. *Neuropsychologia*, 9, 97–113.

O'Leary, A. (1990). Stress, emotion, and human immune function. *Psychological Bulletin*, 108(3), 363-382.

Ornish, D., Brown, S. E., Scherwitz, L. W., Billings, J. H., Armstrong, W. T., Ports, L. A., McLanahan, S. M., Kirkeeide, R. L., Brand, R. J., and Gould, K. L. (1990). Can lifestyle changes reverse coronary heart disease? *Lancet*, 336, 129–133.

O'Sullivan, D. M., Zuckerman, M., and Kraft, M. (1998). Personality characteristics of male and female participants in team sports. *Personality and Individual Differences*, 25(1), 119–128.

Patton, G. W. R. (1970). Combined autonomic effects of concurrently applied stressors. *Society for Psychophysiological Research*, 6(6), 707–715.

Pauli, P., Wiedemann, G., and Nickola, M. (1999). Pain sensitivity, cerebral laterality, and negative affect. *Pain*, 80, 359–364.

Pedersen, D. M.(1997). Perceived traits of male and female athletes. *Perceptual and Motor Skills*, 85, 547–550.

Pennebaker, J. W. (1985). Traumatic experience and psychosomatic disease. Exploring the roles of behavioral inhibition, obsession, and confiding. *Canadian Psychology*, 26, 82–95.

Phillips, C. (1977). A psychological analysis of tension headache. In S. Rachman (Ed.), *Contributions to medical psychology*. Oxford: Pergamon.

Piedmont, R. L., Hill, D. C., and Blanco, S. (1999). Predicting athletic performance using the five factor model. *Personality and Individual Differences*, 27, 769–777.

Pilic, N., personal communication, 1989.

Polar Corporation (1996). Polar-vantage heart rate monitoring systems. Users manual. Kempele, Finland.

Porges, S. W. and Byrne, E. A. (1992). Research methods for measurement of heart rate and respiration. *Biological Psychology*, 34, 93–130.

Pribam, K. H. and McGuinness, D. (1975). Arousal, activation, and effort in the control of attention. *Psychological Review*, 82, 116–149.

Qualls, P. J. and Sheehan, P. W. (1979). Capacity for absorption and relaxation during electromyograph biofeedback and no-feedback conditions. *Journal of Abnormal Psychology*, 6, 652–662.

Qualls, P. J. and Sheenan, P. W. (1981). Trait-treatment interactions: Reply to Tellegen. *Journal of Experimental Psychology: General*, 110, 227–231.

Ravizza, K. (1977). Peak experiences in sports. *Journal of Humanistic Psychology*, 4, 35–40.

Reuter-Lorenz, P. and Davidson, R. J. (1981). Differential contributions of the two cerebral hemispheres to the perception of sad and happy faces. *Neuropsychologia*, 19, 609–613.

Robazza, C. and Bortoli, L. (1994). Hypnosis in sport: An Isomorphic model. *Perceptual and Motor Skills*, 79, 963–973.

Roche, S. M. and McConkey, K. M. (1990). Absorption: nature, assessment, and correlates. *Journal of Personality and Social Psychology*, 59, 91–101.

Ross, J. S., Tkach, J., Ruggieri, P. M., Lieber, M., and Lapresto, E. (2003). The mind's eye: Functional magnetic resonance imaging evaluation of golf motor imagery. *American Journal of Neuroradiology*, 24(6), 1036–1044.

Rossi, B. and Zani, A. (1986). Differences in hemispheric functional asymmetry between athletes and nonathletes: Evidence from a unilateral tactile matching task. *Perceptual and Motor Skills*, 62, 29–300.

Rosenbaum, M. A. (1980). A schedule of assessing self-control behaviors: Preliminary findings. *Behavior Therapy*, 11, 109–121.

Roth, D. L., Bachtler, S. D., and Fillingim, R. B. (1990). Acute emotional and cardiovascular effects of stressful mental work during aerobic exercise. *Psychophysiology*, 27(6), 694–701.

Rowan, A. B. (1996). Religious beliefs and health psychology: Empirical foundations. *Health Psychologist*, 18(1), 1117–1131.

Saccuzzo, D. P., Safnan, D., Anderson, V., and McNeil, B. (1982). Visual information processing in high and low susceptible subjects. *International Journal of Clinical and Experimental Hypnosis*, 30, 32–44.

Schwartz, G. E. (1990). Psychobiology of repression and health: A systems approach. In J. L. Singer (Ed.), *Repression and dissociation: Implications for personality theory, psychopathology, and health* (pp. 405–434). Chicago: University of Chicago Press.

Salazar, W., Landers, D. M., Petruzzello, S. J., Han, M., Crews, D. J., and Kubitz, K. A. (1990). Hemisheric asymmetry, cardiac response, and performance in elite archers. *Research Quarterly for Exercise and Sport*, 61(4), 351–359.

Sandman, C. A., Walker, B. B., and Berka, C. (1982). Influence of afferent cardiovascular feedback on behavior and the cortical evoked potential. In J. T. Cacioppo and R. E. Petty (Eds.), *Perspectives in cardiovascular psychophysiology* (pp. 189–222). New York: Guilford.

Sarter, M., Bernston, G. G., and Cacioppo, J. T. (1996). Brain imaging and cognitive neuroscience: Towards strong influence in attributing function to structure. *American Psychologist*, 51, 13–21.

Schell, A. M. and Catania, J. (1975). The relationship between cardiac activity and sensory acuity. *Psychophysiology*, 12, 147–151.

Schiffer, F. (1997). Affect changes observed with right versus left lateral visual field stimulation in psychotherapy patients: Possible physiological, psychological and therapeutic implications. *Comprehensive Psychiatry*, 38, 289–295.

Schmidt, T. and Jain, A. (1996). Continuous assessment of finger blood pressure and other hemodynamic and behavioral variables in everyday life. In J. Fahrenberg and M. Myrtek (Eds.), *Ambulatory assessment: Computer assisted psychological and psychophysiological methods in monitoring and field studies* (pp. 189–214). Goettingen: Hogrefe and Huber.

Schwartz, G. E. (1990). Psychobiology of repression and health: A systems approach. In J. L. Singer (Ed.), *Repression and dissociation: Implications for personality theory, psychopathology, and health* (pp. 405–434). Chicago: University of Chicago Press.

Schwarz, S. and Kirsner, K. (1984). Can group differences in hemispheric asymmetry be inferred from behavioral laterality indices? *Brain and Cognition*, 3, 57–70.

Seyle, H. (1956). *Stress and disease*. New York: McGraw-Hill.

Shames, V. A. and Bowers, P. G. (1992). Hypnosis and creativity. In E. Fromm and M. Nash (Eds.), *Contemporary hypnosis research* (pp. 334–363). New York: Guilford Press.

Shea, J. B. (1985). Effects of absorption and instructions on heart rate control. *Journal of Mental Imagery*, 9, 87–100.

Shields, J. (1962). *Monozygotic twins brought up apart and brought together*. New York: Oxford University Press.

Smokler, I. A. and Shevrin, H. (1979). Cerebral lateralization and personality style. *Archives of General Psychiatry*, 36, 949–954.

Spiegel, D. and Fink, R. (1979). Hysterical psychosis and hypnotizability. *American Journal of Psychiatry*, 136(6), 777–781.

Spiegel, D., Bloom, J. R., Kraemer, H. C., and Gottheil, E. (1989). Effect of psychosocial treatment on survival of patients with metastatic breast cancer. *Lancet*, 2, 888–891.

Steele, W. G. and Lewis, M. (1968). A longitudal study of the cardiac response during a problem solving task and its relationship to general cognitive function. *Psychonomic Science*, 11, 275–276.

Stemmler, G. (1996). Strategies and designs in ambulatory assessment. In J. Fahrenberg and M. Myrtek (Eds.) *Ambulatory assessment: Computer assisted psychological and psychophysiological methods in monitoring and field studies* (pp. 257–270). Goettingen: Hogrefe and Huber.

Sternbach, R. A., Janowsky, D. S., Huey, L. Y., and Segal, D. S. Effects of altering brain serotonin activity on human chronic pain (1976). In J. J. Bomca and D. Albe-Fessard (Eds.), *Proceedings on the First World Congress on Pain: Vol.1. Advances in pain research and therapy*. New York: Raven Press.

Strube, M. J. (1990). Psychometric principles: From physiological data to psychological constructs. In J. T. Cacioppo and L. G. Tassinary (Eds), *Principles of psychophysiology: Physical, social, and inferential elements* (pp. 34–57). New York: Cambridge University Press.

Sullivan, M. J. L. and D'Eon, J. L. (1990). Post-traumatic stress disorder, hypnotizability, and imagery. *American Journal of Psychiatry*, 99(3), 260–263.

Surwillo, W. W. (1956). Psychological factors in muscle action potentials: EMG gradients. *Journal of Experimental Psychology*, 52, 263–272.

Surwillo, W. W. (1971). Human reaction time and endogenous heart rate changes in normal subjects. *Psychophysiology*, 8, 680–682.

Taylor, J. (1996). Intensity regulation and athletic performance. In J. L. Van Raalte and B. W. Brewer (Eds.), *Exploring sport and exercise psychology* (pp. 75–106). Washington, DC: American Psychological Association.

Taylor, G. J., Parker, J. D. A., and Bagby, R. M. (1997). *Disorders of affect regulation. Alexithymia in medical and psychiatric illness.* Cambridge: Cambridge University Press.

Tellegen, A. (1981). Practicing the two disciplines for relaxation and enlightenment: Comment on Qualls and Sheenan. *Journal of Experimental Psychology: General*, 110, 217–226.

Tellegen, A. (1985). Structures of mood and personality and their relevance to assessing anxiety, with an emphasis on self-report. In A. H. Tuma and J. D. Maser (Eds.), *Anxiety and the anxiety disorders* (pp. 681–706). Hillsdale, NJ: Erlbaum.

Tellegen, A. (1992). Note on structure and meaning of the MPQ Absorption Scale. Unpublished manuscript, Department of Psychology, University of Minnesota, Minneapolis.

Tellegen, A. and Atkinson, G. (1974). Openness to absorbing and self-altering experiences ("absorption"), a trait related to hypnotic susceptibility. *Journal of Abnormal Psychology*, 83, 268–277.

Tiller, W. A., McCraty, R., and Atkinson, M. (1996). Cardiac coherence: A new noninvasive measure of autonomic nervous system order. *Alternative Therapies*, 2(1), 52–65.

Tomarken, A. J., Davidson, R. J., Wheeler, R. E., and Doss, R. C. (1992a). Individual differences in anterior brain asymmetry and fundamental dimensions of emotion. *Journal of Personality and Social Psychology*, 62, 676–687.

Tomarken, A. J., Davidson, R. J., Wheeler, R. E., and Kinney, L. (1992b). Psychometric properties of resting anterior EEG asymmetry: Temporal stability and internal consistency. *Psychophysiology*, 29, 576–592.

Tomarken, A. J. and Davidson, R. J. (1994). Frontal brain activation in repressors and nonrepressors. *Journal of Abnormal Psychology*, 103, 339–349.

Turner, J. R., Carroll, D., Hanson, J., and Sims, J. (1988). A comparison of additional heart rates during active psychological challenge calculated from upper body and lower body dynamic exercise. *Psychophysiology*, 25(2), 209–216.

van Doornen, L. J. P., Knol, D. L., Willemsen, G., and de Geus, E. J. C. (1994). The relationship between stress reactivity in the laboratory and in real-life: Is reliability the limiting factor? *Journal of Psychophysiology*, 8, 297–304.

Van Raalte, J. L. and Brewer, B. W. (1996). *Exploring sport and exercise psychology.* Washington, DC: American Psychological Association.

Varni, J. G., Clark, E., and Giddon, D. B. (1971). Analysis of cyclic heart rate variability. *Psychophysiology*, 8(3), 406–413.

Waller, S. (1988). Alterations of consciousness in peak sports performance. Doctoral dissertation. Saybrook Graduate School, San Francisco, CA.

Walter, G. F. and Porges, S. W. (1976). Heart rate and respiratory responses as a function of task difficulty: The use of discrimination analysis in the selcetion of psychologically sensitive physiological responses. *Psychophysiology*, 13, 563–571.

Watson, D. and Clark, L. A. (1984). Negative affectivity: The disposition to experience aversive emotional states. *Psychological Bulletin*, 96, 465–490.

Watson, D. and Clark, L. A. (1997). Extraversion and its positive emotional core. In R. Hogan, J. Johnson, and S. Briggs (Eds.), *Handbook of personality psychology* (pp. 767–794). San Diego, CA: Academic Press.

Watson, D., Clark, L. A., and Tellegen, A. (1988). Development and validation of brief measures of positive and negative affect: The PANAS scales. *Journal of Personality and Social Psychology*, 54, 1063–1070.

Webb, R. A. and Obrist, P. A. (1970). The physiological concomitants of reaction time performance as a function of prepatory interval and prepatory interval series. *Psychophysiology*, 22, 342–352.

Weinberg, R. S., Gould, D., and Jackson, A. (1980). Cognition and motor performance effect of psyching-up strategies on three motor tasks. *Cognitive Therapy and Research*, 4, 239–245.

Weinberger, D. A. (1990). The construct validity of the repressive coping style. In J. L. Singer (Ed.), *Repression and dissociation: Implications for personality theory, psychopathology, and health* (pp. 337–386). Chicago: University of Chicago Press.

Weinberger, D. A., Schwartz, G. E., and Davidson, R. J. (1979). Low-anxious, high anxious, and repressive coping styles: Psychometric patterns and behavioral and physiological responses to stress. *Journal of Abnormal Psychology*, 88, 369–380.

Weiss, T. and Engel, B. T. (1971). Operant conditioning of heart rate in patients with pre-mature ventricular contractions. *Psychosomatic Medicine*, 33, 301–322.

West, S. G. and Finch, J. F. (1996). Personality measurement: Reliability and validity issues. In R. Hogan, J. Johnson, and S. Briggs (Eds.), *Handbook of personality psychology* (pp. 143–164). San Diego, CA: Academic Press.

Wickramasekera, I. E. (1988). *Clinical behavioral medicine*. New York: Plenum.

Wickramasekera, I. E. (1993). Assessment and treatment of somatization disorders: The high risk model of threat perception. In J. W. Rhue, S. J. Lynn, and I. Kirsch (Eds.), *Handbook of clinical hypnosis* (pp. 3–22). Washington, DC: American Psychological Association.

Wickramasekera, I. E. (1994). Somatic psychological symptoms and information transfer from implicit to explicit memory: A controlled case study with predictions from the high risk model of threat perception. *Dissociation*, 7(3), 153–166.

Wickramasekera, I. E. (1998). Secrets kept from the mind but not the body and behavior: The unsolved problems of identifying and treating somatization of trauma. *Advances in Mind-Body Medicine*, 14, 1–18.

Wickramasekera, I. E. (2003). The high risk model of threat perception and the Trojan horse role induction: Somatization and psychophysiological disease. In D. Moss, A. McGrady, T. C. Davies and I. E. Wickramasekera (Eds.), *Handbook of mind-body medicine for primary care*. Thousands Oaks, CA: Sage.

Wickramasekera, I. E., Davies, T., and Davies, M. (1996a). Applied psychophysiology: A bridge between the biomedical model and the biopsychosocial model in family medicine. *Professional Psychology: Research and Practice*, 27(3), 221–233.

Wickramasekera, I. E., Pope, A. T., and Kolm, P. (1996b). On the interaction of hypnotizability and negative affect in chronic pain: Implications for the somatization of trauma. *Journal of Nervous and Mental Disease*, 184(10), 628–635.

Wickramasekera, I. E. and Price, D. C. (1997). Morbid obesity, absorption, neuroticism, and the High Risk Model of Threat Perception. *American Journal of Clinical Hypnosis*, 39, 291–301.

Wilcox, R. R. (1998). How many discoveries have been lost by ignoring modern statistical methods? *American-Psychologist*, 53(3), 300–314.

Williams, J. M. and Leffingwell, T. R. (1996). Cognitive strategies in sport and exercise psychology. In J. L. Van Raalte and B. W. Brewer (Eds.), *Exploring sport and exercise psychology* (pp. 75–106). Washington, DC: American Psychological Association.

Wilson, S. C. and Barber, T. X. (1982). The fantasy prone personality: Implications for understanding imagery, hypnosis, and parapsychological phenomena. In A. A. Sheikh (Ed.), *Imagery: current theory, research, and application* (p. 340–387). New York: Wiley.

Wolk, C. and Velden, M. (1987). Detection variability within the cardiac cycle: Toward a revision of the "baroreceptor hypothesis." *Journal of Psychophysiology*, 1, 61–65.

Yerkes, R. M. and Dodson, J. D. (1908). The relation of strength of stimulus to rapidity of habit formation. *Journal of Comparative Neurology and Psychology*, 18, 459–482.

Zillmer, E. A. and Wickramasekera, I. E. (1987). Biofeedback and hypnotizability: Initial treatment considerations. *Clinical Biofeedback and Health*, 10(1), 51–57.

Index

A

Absorption
  batting average and, 91
  bilateral processing and, 28
  definition of, 27
  disruptive side of, 106
  episodes of intense, 24
  females high in, 93
  high–low differences, 109
  hypnotic ability and, 53
  imaginative capabilities and, 181–182
  interaction of neuroticism and, 73
  line bisecting errors and, 93
  nonreality type of, 42
  –performance relationships, paradox of,
    106
Achievement, requirement of, 40
Acting out, reducing, 35
Action moments
  definition of, 171
  HRD during, 173
Activation theory, 117
Active-alert hypnosis, 192, 205, 207–216
  after practice, 210
  case study, 211–216
    commentary, 215–216
    induction and hypnotic suggestions,
      213–214
  during practice, 209
Aggressive behavior, visualizing, 56
Alexithymia, 27
Alpha power, 87
Ambulatory psychophysiology, 115–138
  athlete monitoring and analysis, 116–117
  background and review of literature,
    118–126
    blood pressure, baro-receptors, and
      HRV, 120–121
    frequency domain measures, 122
    heart activity, 118–120
    heart rate deceleration research, 123
    HRV research, 122–123
    measures of HRV, 121
    mechanistic studies of HRD,
      123–124
    performance studies of HRD,
      124–126
    time domain measures, 121–122
  case study, 126–128

HRD and successful performance,
  126
instrumentation, 127
participant, 126
procedure, 127
research design, 126–127
spectrum analysis of HRV, 126
statistics, 128
total HRD, 126
treatment and analysis of data, 128
video analysis, 127
directions for future research, 137–138
discussion, 133–137
results, 128–133
  HRD and HRA phases, 130–131
  hypotheses, 131–133
  match outcome, 128
  match statistics, 130
  qualitative observations, 129–130
  self-report of psychological state
    during matches, 128–129
  spectrum analysis of HRV, 133
Anger, 50
Anxiety
  HRV spectrum analysis and, 118
  performance-relevant measures, 9–10
  postcompetition, 11
  precompetition, 215
  self-deception and, 58
  stimuli and, 96
Applied sport psychology
  blame of, 225
  psychological influences, 11–12
Archers
  HRD in, 125
  study of elite, 87
Athlete(s)
  assessment, approach to, 230
  body language of, 20–21
  cortical organization in, 86
  elite, 38, 59
  faulty conclusions regarding mental
    toughness of, 143
  female, 90
  high-hypnotic ability/absorption, 65
  lacking other interests, 40
  laterality-based interventions, 96
  most negatively predisposed, 190

personality–performance relationships in, 112
preparation of for competition, 190
psychological proficiency, critical moment and, 15
unexpected blunders in, 107
vs. age-matched nonathletes, 81
well-prepared, 191
Athlete's (Behavioral) Profile of Cerebral Laterality, 100
Athlete Neuropsychophysiological Performance Database project, 227
Athlete's Profile
athletes not favorably predisposed to, 189
conceptualization of, 71
emerging, 4
golfers, 99
ideal, 17, 60
interactions among relative cerebral hemispheric activation, 3
left-brain hemispheric activation and, 204
neuropsychophysiological assessment model for measuring, 5
state and trait issues, 88
weightlifters, 99
women's, 88
Attention
controlled, 41
focus, control of, 37
heightened, 170
hypnotic ability and focused, 60
important marker of, 60
manipulation of attention, 96
performance-relevant measures, 9–10
reality-oriented, 105
TCM and, 43
threshold, 226
Autonomic nervous system activity, 138

B

Baro-receptors, 120, 171–172
Baseball players, 80, 81
Basketball
free-throw shooting percentage, 101
players, 80
Batting average, 91, 111, 141
Behavior
attempts to manipulate, 21
goal-directed, 28
intense analysis of, 218
visualizing aggressive, 56
BioCom Technologies, 167, 228
Biofeedback protocol, 22, 111, 191, 203, 217–222
case, 218–220
proposal, assessment, intervention, and efficacy study, 220–222
A-B-A design, 221–222
experiment, 221

predictions, 221
single-case experiment method, 218
Blood pressure
excessive activation of, 54
HRV and, 120
PST and, 180
regulation of, by baro-receptors, 121
Bodily awareness, 208
Body language
poor, 20–21
response, 21
Body in space, 40
Brain
hemispheric activation, 86
hypothesized relative, 66
measure of relative, 76
laterality training, 203
processing speed, 226, 229
Brainquiry, 228
Brain Resource Company (BRC), 227
BRC, see Brain Resource Company

C

Cancer, patients considered vulnerable to, 34
Cardiac activity, relationships between reaction time and, 118
Cardiac hyperreactivity, PPT and, 33
Cardiac output
disruption of, 176
maintenance of, 174
Cardiovascular psychophysiology, 186
Carlstedt Critical Moment Psychological Performance Index (CCMPP-I), 13, 143, 144, 196
advanced applications of, 151
analysis of psychological performance using, 155
customized, 144
performance parameters assessed using, 221
PST and, 180
Psychological Performance Proficiency Quotient, 145, 148, 152
Carlstedt Protocol (CP), 5, 189–197
basis of, 195
constellation of PHO factors and ideal mental training intervention, 191–192
rationale for applying specific interventions, 192–195
step-by-step overview, 197
Carlstedt Protocol, assessment and intervention using, 199–205
assessment results, 199–202
absorption, 201
neuroticism, 201
positive affect–negative affect schedule scores, 201–202
relative brain hemispheric predominance, 200
repressive coping, 200

intervention approach, 202–203
 brain laterality training, 203
 cognitive therapy, 202
 general heart activity monitoring, 203
 RSA/HRV training, 203
 outcome, 203–205
Catastrophe theories, 64, 117
Catastrophizing
 definition of, 30, 55
 NA and, 29
CCMPP-I, *see* Carlstedt Critical Moment
 Psychological Performance
 Index
Cerebral activation, 94, 108
Cerebral laterality, 81
 Line-Bisecting Test and, 97
 manipulation, 200
Chronic pain disorder, 25
Clutch players, 46
Coaching, 54
Cognition, important marker of, 60
Cognitive activity, 138
Cognitive chaos, 50
Cognitive planning, 208, 210
Cognitive strategies, 109–110
Cognitive style, self-enhancing, 59
Cognitive therapy, 19, 202
 esoteric, 191
 realistic, 191, 192
 somatic symptoms and, 34–35
Competition
 anger during noncritical moments of, 50
 hypnotic ability during, 45
 most stressful times of, 14
 negative self-talk during, 55
 neurophysiological dynamics during, 66
 physiological stress in, 201
 preparation of athlete for, 190
 psychological stress and, 188
 reducing mental stress associated with,
  215
 requirement of, 40
Competitive anxiety, 96
Competitive moments, level of criticality of,
 14, 165
Concentration
 interference with, 214
 loss of, 175
Confidence, 102, 214
Connors, Jimmy, 55
Consciousness, altered states of, 26
Controlled attention, 41
Coping skills, cognitive and behavioral
 adaptive, 35
Cortical dynamics, hypothesized, 68
Cortical functioning, Athlete's Profile of, 64,
 71
Cortical organization, developmental factors
 related to, 89
Cortical quieting, 177
CP, *see* Carlstedt Protocol

Criticality
 points, 146, 147
 total level of, 145, 151
Critical moments
 definition of, 13
 heightened fear of, 49
 ideal Athlete's Profile during, 60
 technical mistakes apparent during, 187
Critical moments, assessing, 141–168
 assessing technical performance,
  158–165
  games, 159–163
  total match statistics, 163–165
 assessment of critical moments using
  physiological measures,
  166–168
 assessment of psychological performance
  using technical outcome
  measures, 157–158
 Carlstedt Critical Moment Psychological
  Performance Index, 144–157
  match summary, 154–155
  match totals, 155
  percentage of criticality weight level
   won, 155–157
  sets, 145–154
 operationalizations of critical moments,
  141–144
 using CCMPP-I in other sports, 157
Cross-modal experiences, 75, 105
Crowd
 excess awareness of, 48
 noise of, 47, 48, 52

D

Decision, 28
Depression, self-deception and, 58
Distracting influence, 107, 111
Drake paradigm, 76, 97

E

Edinburgh Handedness Inventory, 76, 81
EEG
 activity
  right-hemispheric, 125
  trait levels of cortical functioning
   associated with, 195
 alpha activity, 117
 left-to-right shift in, 65
 profile(s)
  left-biased, 99
  TCM prediction, 44
 PST and, 180
 slower-wave, 119
Elite athlete(s)
 developmental processes associated with
  becoming, 38
 frailties of, 59
Emerging evidence, 71–82
 criterion variables, 76–78
 hypotheses, 72–73

participants and sampling, 74
predictor variable measures, 74–76
    Edinburgh Handedness Inventory, 76
    Eysenck Personality Inventory, 75
    Line-Bisecting Test, 76
    Marlowe-Crowne Scale, 74–75
    Tellegen Absorption Scale, 75
predictor variables, 81–82
results, 78–81
EMG, *see also* Muscle tension
activity, flexor, 184
baseline, 221
biofeedback, 185
data, integrated, 185
Emotion(s)
facilitating of positive, 97
manipulation of, 95
unacknowledged, 22
Emotional reactivity, 226
Empirical implications, *see* Statistical and
    empirical implications
Endocrine activation, heightened, 31
Energy expenditure, sympathetic activity
    and, 135
EPI, *see* Eysenck Personality Inventory
Esoteric cognitive therapy, 191
Experiential set, 28
Explicit defensiveness, 34
Eysenck Personality Inventory (EPI), 75, 199

F

Facial expressions, 95, 96
Fantasy proneness, 42
Faulty cognitions, 17
Females, repressive coping in, 110
Final victory, 41
Flow
experiences, 24, 25, 39, 54
states, 168, 175, *see also* Zone or flow
    states, assessing
    hypnotic ability and, 207
    task-specific focus during, 192
Focus
ability, 49
-orientation, 105
Forced errors, 130
Free-throw-shooting performance, 84, 85,
    101, 143
Frontalis EMG, 186
Functional disconnection syndrome, RC as,
    31

G

Game
mental side of, 226
pivotal, 150
return, 147, 153
service, 147, 153
winner as loser, 162
Global psychological performance, method
    for assessing, 169

Global statistics, 142
Goal
-directed behavior, 28
orientation, 54
setting, 193
Golfers
Athlete's Profile, 99
magnetic resonance imaging study of,
    177
Grand Slam winner, 145
Great moderator of thought processes,
    repressive coping as, 58

H

Hall of Fame career, 224
Hallucination, 25
Heart
activity
    competitive moments and, 177
    monitoring, 203
    –performance timeline, 128
    PSD and, 122
disease, patients considered vulnerable
    to, 34
–muscle interactions, 174
parasympathetic stimulation of, 122
vagus nerve stimulation and, 120
Heart-Minder, 228, 229
Heart rate acceleration (HRA), 119, 172, 174
Heart rate deceleration (HRD), 60, 122–123
control, 208
data analysis, 128
expected, 167
heightened attention and, 170
-HRA, 176
interbeat intervals, 132
mechanistic studies of, 123
performance studies of, 124
PHO-SLO and, 137
psychologically mediated, 63
quantification of zone or flow states
    using, 174
research, 123
responses, measurement of, 196
successful performance and, 126
tennis matches and, 144
total, 126
trends, 126, 171, 173
Heart rate variability (HRV), 10, 116, 201,
    220, 228
analysis software, 228
blood pressure and, 120
frequency domain measures, 122
low-frequency, 166
measures of, 121
PHO factors and, 120
profile, 63
PST and, 180
research, 122
shifts in, 62
spectrum analysis of, 118, 126, 133, 137

time domain measures, 121
High hypnotizables, 61
High-Risk Model of Threat Perception
(HRMTP), 18, 19–35, 191, 193
absorption and, 53
catastrophizing and, 29
individualized interventions, 33–35
high hypnotizability/absorption, high
neuroticism, and high repressive
coping, 34–35
high hypnotizability/absorption, low
neuroticism, and high repressive
coping, 33–34
low hypnotizability/absorption, low
neuroticism, and high repressive
coping, 34
predictions from HRMTP, 31–33
primary higher order mind–body
predictor variables, 23–31
absorption, 27–29
hypnotic ability, 23–27
neuroticism or negative affect, 29–30
repressive coping, 30–31
studies, absorption used in, 27
Trojan horse approach, 32
HRA, *see* Heart rate acceleration
HRD, *see* Heart rate deceleration
HRMTP, *see* High-Risk Model of Threat
Perception
HRV, *see* Heart rate variability
Hyperreactivity, 62
Hypnosis, 19, 108, *see also* Active-alert
hypnosis
active-alert, 192, 205, 207
conventional, 208, 210
efficacy of, as mental training method,
211
goal of, 210
heart rate and, 28
-imagery, 191
losing control during, 41
Hypnotic ability, 24
athletes low in, 44
characteristics associated with, 46, 47
focused attention and, 60
high, double-edged sword of, 39
hypothesis of, 39
maintenance of, by TCM, 101
somatic symptoms and, 26, 32
Hypnotic experience, characteristics of, 40
Hypnotic insusceptibility, 40
Hypochondriacs, 20
Hypothalmic-pituitary-adrenal feedback
systems, 27

I

IBIs, *see* Interbeat intervals
Imagery, 108, 191
Imaginative capabilities, absorption and,
181–182
Inattention, selective, 42, 43, 49

Incidental learning, 26
Intake-rejection hypothesis, 135
Intensity, 117
Interbeat intervals (IBIs), 131, 132, 170
HRD trend of, 175
sequences, 171
Internal consistency, 75
Internal negative thoughts, 130
Internet Athlete Psychological Assessment
and Performance Center, 227
Internet-based athlete assessment analysis,
intervention, and database
center, 223–231
Intrusive thoughts
negative, 171
neuroticism and, 104
PHO factors and, 164
suppression of, 193, 226
Inverted-U Theory, 116
"In the zone" experience, 39

J

"Just do it" attitude, 51, 103, 175, 208, 212,
227

L

Laboratory stressors, 90, 181
Laterality interventions, goal of, 96
Learning, incidental, 26
Left-based personality measures, 92
Left-brain hemisphere
activity, 62, 204
changes in, 87
dissociation of the right from, 207
Left-brain to right-brain hemispheric shift,
64
Left hemisphere-based personality measures,
91
Lendl, Ivan, 45
Likert-like scale, 128
Line bisecting
correlations between certain PHO factors,
89
error, 95, 97–98
Line-Bisecting Test, 73, 76, 100, 199, 202
cerebral laterality and, 97
direction of error on, 204
Edinburgh Handedness Inventory and, 76
errors on, 87, 88
experiments with, 194
first psychometric information on, 98
internal consistency of, 76
less-rightward errors on, 110
need to validate, 98
self-report of affective states and, 95
test–retest reliability, 98
Long-distance running, 107
Loser, winner as, 162
Loss of concentration, 175

M

Magnetic resonance imaging study, 177
Marlowe-Crowne Scale (MC), 30, 74, 108,
    199
MC, *see* Marlowe-Crowne Scale
McEnroe, John, 45
Meaningless slogans, 225
Mecir, Miroslav, 55
Memory(ies)
    ability to focus away from aversive, 58
    functions, altered, 26
    transfer from short- to long-term, 52
Mental health settings, avoiding referral to,
    32
Mental imagery, 20
Mental states, altering of, 50
Mental toughness, 143, 224, 225
Mental training, 105
    brain laterality training, 203
    cognitive therapy, 202
    goal, 22–23
    heart activity monitoring and, 203
    in-the-field, 229
    intervention, 191
    method, efficacy of hypnosis as, 211
    recommendations for, 199, 229
    RSA/HRV training, 203
    widely taught method of, 109
Metabolic demands, 174, 186, 187
Microlevel critical moment, 14, 15
Micropsychophysiological moment, 174
Mind–body incongruence, 20, 22
Mind–body interaction(s)
    facilitated, 210
    feedback about, 192
    physiological measure best illuminating,
        169
    psychophysiological psychotherapy and,
        33
Mind–body mechanisms, similar, 37
Mind–body model, sports performance, 63
Mind–body motor control, 163
Mind–body–performance interactions, denial
    of, 51
Mind–body processes, PHO predictor
    variables and, 10
Mind-power, 189–190
Model(s)
    mind–body, 115
    multiple regression, 85
    peak performance, 64
Motivation, 135, 167, 224
Motor ability, 10
Motor complaints, 38
Motor control, optimum, 174
Motor performance propensities, 45
Motor skills, learning, 87, 215
Multiple objective performance outcome
    measures, 12
Multiple regression
    analyses, baseball and softball players, 81

models, 85
Muscle(s)
    activity, 180
    nontask essential, 60
    task-irrelevant, 183, 186, 188
    task-specific, 183
    tension, 10, 117, 208, 220
        activity, influence of TCM-PHO
            factors on, 186
        control profile, 63
        measurement of, 182
        TCM and, 183

N

NA, *see* Negative affect
National Collegiate Athletic Association, 74
Negative affect (NA), 29, *see also*
        Neuroticism
    catastrophizing and, 29
    self-report of, 29
Negative images, 180
Negative intrusive thoughts
    absence of, 55
    PHO-mediated, 171
    suppression of, 16, 193
Negative stimuli, 112
Negative thoughts, 129, 130
Negative trait manifestations, potential, 104
Negatively predisposed athlete, 190
Nervousness, 128
Neurofeedback protocols, 194, 195
Neuronal networks, task-specific ensembles
        of, 207
Neurophysiological measures, instability of,
        101
Neuropsychophysiological assessment
        model, 5
Neuropsychophysiological processes,
        hyperactivated, 38
Neuroticism, 29
    –absorption interaction, 73
    batting average and, 91
    components of, 56
    correlation of with free-throw shooting,
        101, 103
    data on, 4
    great moderator of, 193
    hypnotic ability and, 24, 61
    interaction of repressive coping and, 72
    intrusive thoughts associated with, 104
    location of, in brain, 57
    -mediated poor performance, 212
    negative health consequences associated
        with, 37
    performance and, 57, 83
    potential manifestation of, 129
    potential negative consequences of high,
        65
    role of, in mediating thought processes,
        54
    score, 201

ZOF and, 103
New York Yankees, 223
Nonhypnotizable people, 40
Norepinephrine metabolism, 30, 56

O

Opponent distractions, 48, 107, 111
Optimism, repressive coping and, 102
Outcome
    diametrically opposed performance and,
        134
    measures, conventional, 165

P

Pain tolerance, 49, 52
PANAS, *see* Positive Affect–Negative Affect
        Schedule
Panic
    attacks, precipitation of, 55
    disorders, 118
Perceptions, self-serving, 59
Performance
    assessment of, in tennis, 158
    diametrically opposed outcome and, 134
    -enhancement modalities, 32–33
    equation, critical psychological factor in,
        3–4
    -facilitative cognitions, 194
    important cognitive element of, 165
    influences of TCM PHO-identified
        factors on, 84
    kinesthetic aspects of, 209
    measure, 101
    models, 64
    neuroticism and, 57, 83
    outcome
        measures, multiple objective, 12
        relationships between PHO factors
            and, 78, 79
    panic attack, 55
    personality and, 111
    PHO factors and, 108
    psychological influences on, 85
    relationships between psychological
        factors and, 8
    repressive coping and, 83
    role of attention in successful, 42
    statistics, 114, 142
    strongest finding between PHO factors
        and, 101
    trait marker of, 91
    undermined, 43
Peripheral feedback systems, dysfunctional,
        26
Personal Efficiency Trainer, 229
Personality
    –laterality relationships, 106
    –performance relationships, 112
    risk factors, PHO, 19
Personal optimism, 91

Personal sport psychology consultant, *see*
        Internet-based athlete
        assessment analysis,
        intervention, and database
        center
PHO, *see* Primary higher order
Phobias, precipitation of, 55
Physical space travelers, 42
Physiological measures, assessment of
        critical moments using, 166
Platitudes, 225
Point Progression Protocol, 145
Polar Vantage Heart Rate Monitoring
        System, 127, 170
Pop psychology, 225
Positive Affect–Negative Affect Schedule
        (PANAS), 95, 201, 202, 204,
        220
Positive emotions, facilitating of, 97
Positive–Negative Affect Schedule, 199
Posthypnotic suggestion, 193
Power spectral density analysis (PSD), 118
PPPQ, *see* Psychological Performance
        Proficiency Quotient
PPT, *see* Psychophysiological psychotherapy
Precompetition anxiety, 215
Predictor–criterion relationships, 12, 113
Primary higher order (PHO), 63, 71
    behavioral and personality risk factors,
        19
    -cerebral laterality relationships, 100
    constellation, worst possible, 60
    measures, important finding on, 105
    mind–body predictor variables, 23
    personality traits, 38
    psychological measures, 9, 13
    variables, 8
Primary higher order factor(s), 4
    Athlete's Profile of, 194
    cerebral activation and, 108
    constellations of, 59
    criticality levels, 83
    frequent constellation of, 86
    gender and, 92, 104
    HRV and, 120
    hypothesized cortical dynamics of ideal
        athlete's profile of, 68
    ideal constellations of, 16
    influence of on performance, 219
    intrusive thoughts and, 164
    neuropsychophysiological concomitants
        of, 63–68
        cortical organization and functioning,
            64–65
        relative brain hemispheric activation,
            64
    performance and, 108
    predicted, 136
    relative brain hemispheric activation and,
        93

strongest finding between performance
and, 101
task-specific sport performance and, 86
TCM and, 44, 142
theoretical conceptualizations of, 137
Primary higher order predictor variables,
37–62
absorption in athletes, 53–54
hypnotic ability in athletes, 39–53
case study, 45–46
high hypnotic ability, 46–50
low hypnotic ability, 50–53
neuroticism in athletes, 54–57
predictions, 59–60
rationale, 60–62
repressive coping in athletes, 58–59
Profile of Mood States, 95
PSD, *see* Power spectral density analysis
PST, *see* Psychophysiological stress testing
Psychological distress, failure to report
symptoms of, 20
Psychological immunity, boosting of, 35
Psychological performance
analysis of using CCMPP-I, 155
drawback to assessing, 143
poor, 155
Psychological Performance Proficiency
Quotient (PPPQ), 145, 148,
152, 154
mean, 156
Psychophysiological Index/HRD, 173
technical, 157, 158, 160, 164
Psychological pressure, abated, 150
Psychological state, self-report of, 128
Psychological statistics, tennis, 156
Psychological stress, phases of competition
associated with, 188
Psychophysiological monitoring devices, 196
Psychophysiological psychotherapy (PPT),
19, 33
Psychophysiological stress testing (PST),
179–188
background, 182–183
definition of PST, 180–181
discussion, 184–188
muscle tension and Theory of Critical
Moments, 183
player's window of maximum
vulnerability, 181–182
prestress test measurement, 184
procedure, 183
Psychosomatic disorders, alexithymia and,
27
Psychosomatic symptoms, physiological
hyperreactivity associated with,
200
Psychotherapy
gradual approach to, 34
physiological profile of person monitored
during, 22

Q
qEEG, *see* Quantitative
electroencephalography
Quantitative electroencephalography
(qEEG), 227, 228

R
RC, *see* Repressive coping
Reaction time
paradigm, 122–123
relationships between cardiac activity
and, 118
Reactivity, determination of level of, 220
Reality
-based cognitive therapy, 191, 192
-oriented focus, 52, 208
Real world stressors, 88
Regression model, predictive capability of,
12
Relaxation response, 28
Repression, 34
Repressive coping (RC), 19, 30, 170, 193
assessment of, 110
description of, 200
effects of, 99
functions, left-brain hemisphere-based,
64
high, 33–34
hypothesis, 109
interaction of neuroticism and, 72
measure of, 74
negative health consequences associated
with, 37
optimism and, 102
performance and, 3–4, 83
self-confidence and, 58
self-deception associated with, 30
somatic complaints and, 23
Respiration, excessive activation of, 54
Right-brain hemisphere
activity, 58, 93–94, 170
negative cognitions, 193
predominance, 201
Risk-taking, 91
Road racing video game, 113
Routine return game, 147, 153
Routine service game, 147, 153
RSA/HRV training, 203
Running, long-distance, 107

S
Secondary lower order (SLO) psychological
variables, 8, 9
predictor, 10
psychological processes, PHO variables
capable of affecting other, 17
Selective inattention, 42, 43, 49
Self-confidence, 134
facilitator of, 58
lacking of, 211

Self-deception, 58, 74
Self-enhancing cognitive style, 31, 59
Self-esteem, enhanced, 102
Self-paced sports,125
Self-report instruments, 116
Self-serving perceptions, 59
Self-statements, negative, 55
Self-talk, 55, 193
Sensory cues, denial of, 51
Sensory feedback, competing, 135
Sensory flooding, 135
Sensory memory, 49
Sensory stimuli, hypersensitivity to, 45
Serotonin metabolism, 30, 56
Single-case experiment method, 218
Situational underactivation, 56
Skin conductance
    excessive activation of, 54
    measurement of, 182
    PST and, 180
SLO psychological variables, see Secondary
            lower order psychological
            variables
SNS activity, elevated levels of, 41
Softball players, 80, 81, 90
Somatic complaints, catastrophizing and, 30
Somatic symptoms
    development of, 31
    seeking help for, 32
    transducing threat perception into, 33–34
Sony video-editing system, 127
Source amnesia, 26
Split-half reliability, 75
Sport(s)
    absorption, 107
    active-alert scripts, 216
    analysis protocols, 157
    basic performance statistics of, 11
    intense movement associated with, 179
    performance
        mind–body model of, 63, 115
        task-specific, 86
        zone trait, 39
    psychology
        damaging uses of, 217
        faulty assumption in, 20
        practitioners, challenge to, 217
    self-paced, 125
    task, regulation of visuoperceptual
            components associated with, 94
State-dependent learning, 26
Statistical and empirical implications,
            83–114
    athlete's profile, 88–93
    hypotheses, 83–86
    implications, 108–111
        absorption, 108–109
        neuroticism, 110–111
        repressive coping, 109–110
    limitations and issues, 111–113

PHO factors and performance
            relationships, 101–108
    absorption, neuroticism, repressive
            coping, and performance,
            105–108
    gender, 104–105
PHO factors and relative brain
            hemispheric activation, 93–100
    absorption, neuroticism, and
            repressive coping, 93–94
    athlete's profile, 99–100
    implications and future research,
            94–97
    limitations and issues, 97–99
    relative brain hemispheric predominance/
            activation, 86–88
    repressive coping and neuroticism, 108
Stress
    HRMTP and, 21
    negative cognitive intrusions during
            heightened, 187
    psychological, phases of competition
            associated with, 188
    stimuli, EMG values and, 184
Superior concentration, 38
Support systems, persons deficient in, 35
Surplus pattern recognition, 48
Sympathetic response, 29
Symptom induction, learning mechanisms of,
            25

T

Talk therapy, 193
TAS, see Tellegen Absorption Scale
Task-irrelevant muscles, 183, 186, 188
Task-specific focus, 49, 192
Task-specific muscles, 183
Task-specific sport performance, PHO
            factors and, 86
TCM, see Theory of Critical Moments
Team
    coaching staff, 144
    priority list, sport psychology and, 225
Tellegen Absorption Scale (TAS), 75, 199
Tennis
    champions, 45
    heart activity, 124
    match(es)
        errors in, 136
        HRD and, 133, 144
        most critical moments if match, 165
        opponent volley error, 160
        player, elite, 213
        psychological statistics in, 156
        strokes, simulated, 184
        technical performance, 158
        tie breaker, 151, 154
Test–retest reliability, 75, 98
Theory of Critical Moments (TCM), 5, 7–18,
            115, 170
    Athlete's Profile, 195

free-throw shooting and, 85
  proposal of, 64
attention and, 43
central tenet of, 141–142
conceptualization of, 71, 74
criticality tenet, driving force of, 89
definition of critical moments, 13–17
driving hypothesis of, 83
-HRD action theory, 173
maintenance of hypnotic ability by, 101
methodological approaches and tenets,
  8–12
    identification of specific PHO
      psychological predictor, 8–10
    study of psychological factors
      longitudinally, 12
    study of psychological factors and
      performance at microlevel,
      11–12
muscle tension and, 183
PHO factors and, 189
PHO personality measures, 16
PHO predictor and criticality tenets, 72
potent and meaningful objective
      microoperationalizations of
      performance outcome, 12–13
potent and meaningful PHO
      psychological predictor
      variables, 17–18
prediction, 23, 44, 102
Therapeutic relationship, 35
Thinking, lack of, 55
Thought processes, great moderator of, 58
Tie breaker, 151, 154
Trait neuroticism, psychosomatic illness and,
  31
Trojan horse role-induction method, 32–33,
  34, 222

U

Unacknowledged emotion, 22
Underachiever, 218
U.S. Tennis Association tennis tournament,
  126

V

Victory, 154, 164
Videotaping, 180
Visuoperceptual components, regulation of,
  94

W

Wandering mind, 107
Weightlifters, Athlete's Profile, 99
Window of maximum vulnerability, 180–181
Winners-to-unforced errors ratio, 130
Winning
    satisfaction and, 48
    thinking about, 119
Winning ugly, 50
Won–loss percentage, 78
World Series, 223, 224, 230

Z

ZOF, *see* Zone of Optimum Functioning
Zone of Optimum Functioning (ZOF), 9, 64,
  220
    neuroticism and, 103
    time to reach, 56
Zone or flow states, assessing, 24, 169–177
    analysis of data, 170–173
    hypnotic ability and, 207
    participant and procedure, 170
    task-specific focus during, 192
    toward quantification of zone or flow
      states using HRD, 174–177

Date Due